International Organisations and Glo

International organisations (IOs) are considered fundamental in addressing global problems, but how effective are they?

Conflict (war), human rights, global health, financial governance, international trade, regionalisation, development and the environment are all issues that international organisations have been created to address.

In this book, we look at these eight key issue areas and guide you through an analysis of the successes and failures of international organisations in solving issues in global politics.

With an introduction to international relations theory, this book incorporates the best and most up-to-date scholarly research, and applies it to examples from around the world to show you how to answer the question, 'Are IOs a help or a hindrance?'

This textbook is an essential resource for courses on global governance, international organisations and international relations. Including an expanded further reading list for each global issue, as well as a thorough bibliography of the most up-to-date research, this is a resource that will be useful during your studies and on into the future.

Susan Park is an Associate Professor in International Relations at the University of Sydney. She has published in journals including *International Politics*, *Global Governance* and *Global Environmental Politics*. She is also the author of *The World Bank Group and Environmentalists: Changing International Organisation Identities* (2010) and co-editor of *Owning Development: Creating Global Policy Norms in the IMF and the World Bank* (Cambridge, 2010).

International Organisations and Global Problems

THEORIES AND EXPLANATIONS

Susan Park
University of Sydney

CAMBRIDGE
UNIVERSITY PRESS

University Printing House, Cambridge CB2 8BS, United Kingdom

One Liberty Plaza, 20th Floor, New York, NY 10006, USA

477 Williamstown Road, Port Melbourne, VIC 3207, Australia

314–321, 3rd Floor, Plot 3, Splendor Forum, Jasola District Centre, New Delhi – 110025, India

79 Anson Road, #06–04/06, Singapore 079906

Cambridge University Press is part of the University of Cambridge.

It furthers the University's mission by disseminating knowledge in the pursuit of
education, learning, and research at the highest international levels of excellence.

www.cambridge.org
Information on this title: www.cambridge.org/9781107077218
DOI: 10.1017/9781139924788

First published 2018

Printed in the United Kingdom by TJ International Ltd. Padstow Cornwall

A catalogue record for this publication is available from the British Library.

ISBN 978-1-107-07721-8 Hardback
ISBN 978-1-107-43422-6 Paperback

To Matt, my help-meet. I can't thank you enough for quietly and unquestion-ingly taking on an extra load in the final months of writing this book. It simply would not have been possible to complete it otherwise. You are amazing. And for my boys, always.

Brief Contents

Contents

Figure

Boxes

Preface

The purpose of this book is to introduce students to the study of international organisations (IOs) by examining how they address global problems. The idea of the book emerged out of a growing realisation that the study of IOs diverges at the highest and lowest levels of the field. Research on IOs continues to advance at a fast pace, yet textbooks on IOs, where many budding scholars are first introduced to international organisations, have retained a familiar mould: a conceptually oriented historical narrative of the emergence of IOs with a focus on a few key international organisations or issue areas where IOs play prominent roles. What was needed was a book that took the theoretical testing and application, fine-grained empirical analysis and case-study depth found in contemporary research and repackaged it for students beginning their study of international organisations.

With a quick introduction to IO history and structure, this book uses contemporary theories of international relations and international organisation – realist, liberal, rationalist P–A model and constructivist organisational culture – to examine how and why IOs behave the way they do. Applying the relevant theories to the IOs in each chapter gives students tools to investigate the activities of IOs and evaluate the importance of these organisations in solving twenty-first-century problems.

Plan of the Book

Chapter 1 introduces the history and structure of international organisations to provide a base for the theoretical approaches to follow. Chapter 2 traces the emergence of liberal, functionalist and realist approaches to assessing IOs before identifying how contemporary neorealist and neoliberal institutionalist theories have been used to identify the benefits of international cooperation through IOs. More recent IO-specific theories, such as the principal–agent (P–A) model, stemming from domestic politics in the United States, are then counterposed with the constructivist organisational culture approach that seeks to understand how the culture of an IO shapes its actions. Chapter 2 will show that some theories are better at explaining why international cooperation does not proceed, or does so with unexpected consequences.

Where appropriate, other theories, including feminist and critical approaches, are highlighted in text boxes throughout the chapters, and references are provided for budding scholars to take up these alternative approaches to investigate IO action and inaction on critical international issues.

The remaining chapters of the book (Chapters 3–11) are thematic, analysing how IOs operate in addressing various problems at the international level. The chapters address issues that are central to international relations: on minimising and halting conflict, on eliminating and regulating weapons, on protecting human rights, providing global health, upholding financial governance, promoting international trade, creating and maintaining economic and political unions such as the European Union (EU), furthering international development and protecting the environment. In each of these issue areas IOs play an important role in trying to reach agreement and advance solutions to global problems. Each of the chapters will review the main IOs acting in each issue area, identify the key problems IOs are tasked with addressing, provide theoretical analysis of how we can evaluate their activities and compare them with other transnational actors seeking to solve global problems.

Each of these thematic chapters examines the dominant IOs operating in that international issue area, examines the problem they are tasked with addressing, demonstrates how specific theories have been used to explain their behaviour, and examines what constraints limit their actions and the actors they compete with to solve global problems. The final chapter locates IOs within the dominant concept on international cooperation today: global governance. How and where IOs are different from and contribute to global governance is unpacked. This provides students with the conceptual tools needed to further their understanding of international cooperation and the organisation of world politics.

The book is intended for upper undergraduate and graduate students who are interested in understanding how IOs operate in the international system by unpacking what IOs are tasked with doing and what constraints they operate within. The book is suitable for classes on IOs and international institutions.

Chapter Structure

This book introduces students to international relations (IR) and to the workings and theories of IOs, identifies why IOs operate the way they do, what autonomy and authority they have, and whether IOs make a difference in trying to solve global problems. It provides students with the analytical tools to distinguish between the rhetoric and the reality of the role IOs play in international politics, to identify whether they are doing what they are tasked to do, and to consider what alternatives might be used to address these problems.

Following Chapter 1, which introduces students to what IOs are, and Chapter 2, which examines the theories of IOs outlined above, Chapters 3–11 use the following framework to shed light on the effect of IOs in world politics.

1. Identify the key IOs in the international system.
2. Highlight the issues and problems dominant IOs are tasked with addressing.
3. Use theory to examine the constraints and opportunities IOs face in meeting their mandates, including the tools at their disposal.
4. Locate IOs within an increasingly crowded field of international and trans-national actors seeking to govern the globe.

Within each theme the main IOs operating within the issue area are identified. After doing so, the nature of the problem the IO is tasked with addressing is examined, particularly in the light of how problems have developed and changed over time. The theoretical and conceptual tools are then used to interrogate the capacity of IOs for 'solving' international problems by unpacking the structure and function of the IO alongside its power to act and its mission. We can then use these tools to evaluate the efforts of a specific IO on the basis of its ability to act within the confines of its member-state composition and its power to act autonomously. Finally, we situate the IOs within the field of competing international and transnational actors seeking to govern the globe and ask whether alternatives to solving these sorts of problems exist.

Key features of this book include those listed below.

- A dedicated chapter on the four main theories used to examine IOs which provide an overarching guide on how to 'read' IOs.
- Dedicated thematic chapters, each focusing on one of the nine issues central to IR.

- Guiding questions stemming from the main theories at the end of each chapter for students to apply to the IOs mentioned in the chapter.
- Chapter overviews outline the main issues addressed in the chapter, which allows instructors to set whole or part chapters for their students.
- Feature boxes throughout the chapters that provide more detail on a particular historical event, IO or theoretical line of enquiry to illustrate the main points in the chapter.
- A glossary of key theoretical terms and concepts relevant to IOs and IR at the end of the book to give students a ready source of reference.
- A competition section in each chapter that questions what alternative types of organisations exist in the issue area that both compete and cooperate with IOs.
- Further references consisting of the most important research in the field are provided at the end of each chapter.

Acknowledgements

Thank you to everyone who has commented on this book as it has developed: Elizabeth Thurbon, Maria Ivanova, Adam Kamradt-Scott, Megan MacKenzie, Ainsley Elbra, Gorana Grgic and John Brookfield. And to all of my research assistants: Madison Cartwright, Abi Taylor, Sarah Thomas, Janetta McKenzie, Hugh Tuckfield, Haneol Lee and Joseph Gorshe. A big thank you also to everyone on the GEP-Ed list who gave me fantastic sources for the environment chapter – what a great community!

Abbreviations

ADB	Asian Development Bank
AEC	ASEAN Economic Community
AFC	Asian Financial Crisis
AfDB	African Development Bank
AFTA	ASEAN Free Trade Area
AI	Amnesty International
AIIB	Asian Infrastructure Investment Bank
APEC	Asia Pacific Economic Cooperation
APT	ASEAN Plus Three
ARF	ASEAN Regional Forum
ASEAN	Association of Southeast Asian Nations
ASP	Assembly of the Parties of the Rome Statute
AU	African Union
BIS	Bank of International Settlements
BSE	Bovine spongiform encephalopathy
CAT	Convention Against Torture
CBD	Convention on Biological Diversity
CEB	Chief Executives Board for Coordination of the United Nations
CEDAW	Convention on the Elimination of All Forms of Discrimination Against Women
CEPT	Common Effective Preferential Tariff Scheme for the ASEAN Free Trade Area
CERD	Convention on the Elimination of All Forms of Racial Discrimination
CFSP	Common Foreign and Security Policy of the European Union
CHR	Commission on Human Rights of the United Nations
CIDI	Inter-American Council for Integral Development
CITES	Convention on the International Trade of Endangered Species
COMESA	Common Market for Eastern and Southern Africa
COREPER	Committee of Permanent Representatives of the European Union Council of Ministers

CPED	International Convention for the Protection of All Persons from Enforced Displacement
CRC	Convention on the Rights of the Child
CRPD	Convention on the Rights of Persons with Disabilities
CSD	Commission on Sustainable Development of the United Nations
CTC	Counter-Terrorism Committee
DDA	Doha Development Agenda of the World Trade Organization
DEA	Department of Economic Affairs of the United Nations
DFID	Department for International Development of the United Kingdom
DPKO	Department of Peacekeeping Operations of the United Nations
DSB	Dispute Settlement Body of the World Trade Organization
EBRD	European Bank for Reconstruction and Development
EC	European Commission
ECJ	European Court of Justice
ECLA	Economic Commission for Latin America of the United Nations
ECOSOC	United Nations Economic and Social Council
ECOSOCC	Economic, Social and Cultural Council of the African Union
ECOWAS	Economic Community of West African States
ECSC	European Coal and Steel Community
EEC	European Economic Community
EFF	Extended Fund Facility of the IMF
EMU	Economic and Monetary Union
ENGO	Environmental non-governmental organisation
ESAF	Enhanced Structural Adjustment Facility of the International Monetary Fund
EU	European Union
FAO	Food and Agriculture Organization
FSAP	Financial Sector Assessment Program of the International Monetary Fund
FSB	Financial Stability Board (replacing the Financial Stability Forum)
FSF	Financial Stability Forum
FTA	Free trade agreement
FTAA	Free Trade Agreement for the Americas
G5	Group of Five
G7	Group of Seven

G20	Group of Twenty
G30	Group of Thirty
G33	Group of 33
G77	Group of 77
G90	Group of 90
G110	Group of 110
GATS	General Agreement on Trade in Services
GATT	General Agreement on Tariffs and Trade
GAVI	Global Alliance for Vaccines and Immunization
GDP	Gross domestic product
GEF	Global Environment Facility
GFATM	Global Fund to Fight AIDS, Tuberculosis and Malaria
GNI	Gross national income
GNP	Gross national product
GOARN	Global Outbreak Alert and Response Network of the World Health Organization
GRID	Global Resource Information Database
HDI	Human Development Index
HDR	Human Development Reports of the United Nations Development Programme
HIV/AIDS	Human immunodeficiency virus/acquired immune deficiency syndrome
HLP	High-Level Panel on Threats, Challenges and Change
HLPF	High-Level Political Forum on Sustainable Development
HRC	Human Rights Council of the United Nations
HRW	Human Rights Watch
IACD	Inter-American Agency for Cooperation and Development
IADB	Inter-American Development Bank
IAEA	International Atomic Energy Agency
IAIS	International Association of Insurance Supervisors
IBRD	International Bank for Reconstruction and Development (World Bank)
IBWM	International Bureau of Weights and Measures
ICC	International Criminal Court
ICCPR	International Convention on Civil and Political Rights
ICESCR	International Convention on Economic, Social and Cultural Rights

ICISS	International Commission on Intervention and State Sovereignty
ICJ	International Court of Justice
ICMW	International Convention on the Protection of the Rights of All Migrant Workers and Members of Their Families
ICRC	International Committee of the Red Cross
ICTFY	International Criminal Tribunal for the Former Yugoslavia
ICTR	International Criminal Tribunal for Rwanda
IDA	International Development Association (of the World Bank)
IDB	Inter-American Development Bank
IED	Improvised explosive device
IFAD	International Fund for Agricultural Development of the United Nations
IHR	International Health Regulations
IHRR	International Human Rights Regime
ILO	International Labour Organization
IMF	International Monetary Fund
IO	International organization
IOSCO	International Organization of Securities Commissions
IPCC	Intergovernmental Panel on Climate Change
IR	International relations
ISAB	International Standards Accounting Board
ITO	International Trade Organization
ITU	International Telecommunications Union
LoN	League of Nations
MEA	Multilateral Environmental Agreement
MERCOSUR	Mercado Commun del Sur
MDB	Multilateral Development Bank
MDG	Millennium Development Goals
MFN	Most Favoured Nation treatment of the General Agreement on Tariffs and Trade/World Trade Organization
MPI	Multidimensional Poverty Index
MSF	Médecins Sans Frontières
NAFTA	North American Free Trade Agreement
NAM	Non-Aligned Movement
NATO	North Atlantic Treaty Organization
NDB	New Development Bank
NGO	Non-governmental organisation

NHRI	National human rights institution
NIEO	New International Economic Order
NPT	Non-Proliferation Treaty
NTB	Non-tariff barrier
OAS	Organization of American States
OAU	Organisation of African Unity
ODA	Official development assistance
OECD	Organisation for Economic Co-operation and Development
OECD-DAC	Development Assistance Committee of the Organisation for Economic Co-operation and Development
OHCHR	Office of the High Commissioner for Human Rights of the United Nations
OIHP	Office International d'Hygiène Publique
ONUC	United Nations Operation in the Congo, 1960–1964
OPEC	Organization of the Petroleum Exporting Countries
P-5	The five permanent members of the United Nations Security Council
PAHO	Pan American Health Organization
P–A model	Principal–agent model
PCB	Programme Coordination Board of the Joint United Nations Programme on HIV/AIDS
PCIJ	Permanent Court of International Justice of the League of Nations
PGRF	Poverty Reduction Growth Facility of the International Monetary Fund
PIU	Public international union
PMC	Private military company
PRC	People's Republic of China
PSC	Peace and Security Council of the African Union
PTA	Preferential trade agreement
R2P	Responsibility to Protect
RCEP	Regional Comprehensive Economic Partnership
ROSCs	Reports on Observances of Standards and Codes of the Financial Stability Board
RPF	Rwandan Patriotic Front
RTA	Regional trade agreement
SADC	South African Development Community

SAF	Structural Adjustment Facility of the International Monetary Fund
SAP	Structural adjustment programme (of the International Monetary Fund and World Bank)
SARS	Severe acute respiratory syndrome
SBA	Stand-by arrangement, a programme of the International Monetary Fund
SCO	Shanghai Cooperation Organisation
SDG	Sustainable Development Goals
SDRs	Special drawing rights of the International Monetary Fund (unit of account)
SORT	Strategic Offensive Reductions Treaty
TAC	Treaty of Amity and Cooperation of ASEAN
TB	Tuberculosis
TNC	The Nature Conservancy
TPP	Trans-Pacific Partnership
TPRM	Trade Policy Review Mechanism of the World Trade Organization
TRIMs	Agreement on Trade-Related Investment Measures of the World Trade Organization
TRIPs	Agreement on Trade-Related Aspects of Intellectual Property of the World Trade Organization
TTIP	Transatlantic Trade and Investment Partnership
UDHR	Universal Declaration of Human Rights
UK	United Kingdom
UKIP	United Kingdom Independence Party
UN	United Nations
UNAIDS	The Joint United Nations Programme on HIV/AIDS
UNCED	United Nations Conference on Environment and Development
UNCHE	United Nations Conference on the Human Environment
UNCSD	United Nations Conference on Sustainable Development
UNCTAD	United Nations Conference on Trade and Development
UNDP	United Nations Development Programme
UNEF	United Nations Emergency Force, 1956–1967
UNEO	United Nations Environment Organization
UNEP	United Nations Environment Programme
UNESCO	United Nations Educational, Scientific and Cultural Organization
UNFCCC	United Nations Framework Convention on Climate Change

UNFPA	United Nations Population Fund
UNGA	United Nations General Assembly
UNHCR	United Nations High Commissioner for Refugees
UNICEF	United Nations Children's Fund
UNIDO	United Nations Industrial Development Organization
UNOPS	United Nations Office for Project Services
UNSC	United Nations Security Council
UNSG	United Nations Secretary General
UPR	Universal Periodic Review of the Human Rights Council of the United Nations
UPU	Universal Postal Union
US	United States
VDPA	Vienna Declaration and Programme of Action
WEO	World Environment Organisation
WFP	World Food Programme
WHA	World Health Assembly of the World Health Organization
WHO	World Health Organization
WMD	Weapons of Mass Destruction
WSSD	World Summit on Sustainable Development
WTO	World Trade Organization
WWI	World War One
WWII	World War Two

1 Introduction: IOs as Problem Solvers

Chapter Overview

Introduction

Terrorism. War. The Arab Spring. Refugees. Poverty. Financial crisis. Climate change. Pandemics. One or more of these events may affect you or someone you know. **International organisations** (IOs), such as the United Nations (UN), the European Union (EU), the International Monetary Fund (IMF) and the World Health Organization (WHO), are all charged with addressing problems like these that your government, as a **sovereign state**, cannot address by itself. The definition of an IO is a permanent organisation designed to perform continuous tasks for a common purpose with three or more states represented. In the twenty-first century IOs play a large role in solving global problems. Despite the fact that some IOs are household names, with experts from the UN, IMF and

WHO commonly seen informing the public of whatever crisis is unfolding, the role of IOs is not just important but also controversial. International organisations can be viewed both as vital instruments for states to achieve their common goals and as bureaucratic apparatuses that can hinder effective international cooperation.

Two aspects make IOs worthy of investigation: first, IOs have proliferated significantly over time, particularly since the early 1900s, including an increase in the number of IOs created by other IOs through a process called **emanation**. Second, many (if not most) problems in the twenty-first century simply cannot be solved by individual states acting alone, leading states to continue creating them.

The Historical Evolution of Multilateralism

The number of IOs increased from 37 in 1909 to over 1,000 in 1980, with 7,653 IOs operating as of 2017. That the number of IOs has increased rapidly seems to have been inevitable. As the world has become economically integrated, as technology and telecommunications have advanced and become more widespread, as states enabled the flow of goods, services, capital and labour across borders, IOs have been used by states to regulate and improve transboundary interactions.

According to one of the early scholars of international organisations, Inis Claude Junior, four prerequisites are required for the establishment of **multilateralism** among states: that states are independent political units; that substantial contact must exist between states; that states must be aware of problems that arise from their co-existence; and, lastly, that states recognise the need for creating institutions to regulate inter-state relations. Even though there were some historical instances of multilateralism (see Box 1.1), these conditions were met by the middle of the nineteenth century in Europe, leading states to move beyond primarily diplomatic **bilateral** relations between two states to multilateralism.

In the nineteenth century states began to create a range of IOs to facilitate relations across borders in a range of areas that would come to include tariffs; maritime trade and shipping routes; rules for aviation, roads and railways; postal services; telecommunications; patents and copyright; and information technology. Arguably, such regulations have made inter-state relations more

Box 1.1 Historical Multilateral Precursors to Modern IOs

The sovereign state system established in Europe was later extended to the rest of the world as the colonial empires were overthrown, and city states and colonies became independent sovereign states. However, precursors to modern IOs can be found well before the seventeenth century. The Delian League was founded in 478 BC as a **collective defence** alliance amongst Greek city states, and the Hanseatic League existed from the eleventh to the seventeenth century as an economic association among North German towns. Both examples of multilateralism sought to improve the fortunes of the cities through cooperation and were distinct from the usual political practices at the time.

efficient and effective. The emergence of non-political **public international unions** (PIUs) began this trend during the second industrial revolution after 1850: the International Telegraphic Union (1865), which is now the International Telecommunications Union (ITU), and the Universal Postal Union (UPU, 1874) are two of the oldest IOs in existence. These are now part of the UN system. They were created along with the International Bureau of Weights and Measures (IBWM, 1875) to ease **coordination** and commerce across states, and were therefore seen as bodies created to serve a functional purpose.

Here, then, are early examples of IOs solving international problems as they emerged. Political scientist Harold K. Jacobson argued that the rise of technology and the increasing demand for higher living standards in industrialising states propelled the need for IOs with specific functions to operate (Jacobson 1984: 62). PIUs served as a focal point for interactions between states. They enabled the sharing of information and provided a space for discussing the problems states faced. This further propelled agreement for coordinating national policies and the agreement and promotion of common standards. These IOs were tasked with solving technical problems and smoothing relations between states, such as the IBWM upholding internationally uniform standards for weights and measurements. The Bureau determined the means to verify when a kilogram was a kilogram, and a pound a pound. Without such basic minimum standards, commerce across borders and trust amongst traders could not be maintained. IOs therefore became vital for facilitating the increasing volume of international interactions.

The Rise of International Organisations

IOs are a specific form of multilateralism. **International organisations** is shorthand for international governmental organisations, but international organisation is also used as an umbrella term to include both governmental and **non-governmental organisations** (NGOs). IOs have the following features: state membership is voluntary; the scope and purpose of an IO are limited by its mandate and constitution; the primary allegiance of members is vested elsewhere (in states); often competing organisations have overlapping tasks; and such organisations often function as political actors and interact with governments (Farley 1982). IOs are often established by states through an international treaty, they have a constitution or charter, staff, headquarters, a budget and a logo. IOs have a particular structure and function that is unique to the international realm, and they differ from profit-driven corporations and NGOs. IOs are also distinct from domestic public bureaucracies, which exist at the behest of a government as opposed to collective governments. The PIUs were the first IOs to create secretariats with permanent staff to carry out specific functions. Moreover, they introduced the division between the member-state conferences where policy was made and a delegated council or governing body that could enact the wishes of the members in between conferences.

IOs and Restoring International Order

The trend towards multilateralism and the creation of IOs surged during wars, highlighting how important IOs would become for restoring **international order**. Prior to the conclusion of the Napoleonic Wars in 1815, diplomacy in Europe took place between states bilaterally, between two sovereigns or their representatives, rather than multilaterally. Although large conferences among states were established to negotiate the Peace of Westphalia in 1648 and the Treaty of Utrecht in 1713–1714, these were one-off events, and it was not until the **Congress of Vienna** at the end of the Napoleonic Wars that states began to establish a system of high-level multilateral political conferences. This emerged out of the peace amongst the **Great Powers** of Europe: Austria, Britain, France, Prussia and Russia. It resulted in cooperation for maintaining an agreed-upon international order, including a **balance of power** in Europe. States cooperated in defining boundaries, and their cooperation even included establishing some states' constitutions.

The building blocks of modern IOs were constructed slowly. The Congress of Vienna in 1814 and 1815 established the beginning of a new European order by codifying the rules of diplomacy for what became known as the **Concert of Europe**. The Congress lasted 10 months and 216 delegations attended. Throughout the nineteenth century the Concert of Europe system established diplomacy by conference in order to achieve consensus through negotiation. The Great Powers established regular consultations or board meetings in order to manage Europe. The system helped establish a notion of European solidarity while also creating a system of de facto Great Power hegemony. The alliance system for preventing war, that had sustained four conferences, collapsed due to states' competing interests.

Nonetheless, diplomacy by conference became an ad hoc means of diplomacy throughout the nineteenth century, with states meeting 30 times over 100 years to deal with pressing political issues. For example, at the Congress of Berlin in 1878, which was the last conference of the European Powers prior to World War One (WWI), they negotiated a resolution to the 'Scramble for Africa' by carving up the African continent into colonies, without knowledge of the areas inhabited by local populations and irrespective of natural geographical boundaries. The 1878 meeting was also important because it established a conference secretariat. The Concert of Europe system demonstrated how states could use multilateralism to further their interests, while laying the foundation for modern IOs.

The Hague System

At the turn of the century two peace conferences fundamentally different in nature from the Concert of Europe were held in The Hague. These two international peace conferences, called **the Hague System**, were organised by Czar Nicholas II of Russia in 1899 and 1907 for all states, not just the Great Powers. The second conference included European states, Latin American Republics, Japan and China. These conferences have been described as the first 'General Assembly' because they were based on the notion of universality and the legal equality of states, rather than power politics.

The Hague System aimed to reform the rules of the international system rather than rely on the ad hoc 'crisis' meetings that had characterised the Concert of Europe. The Hague meetings instituted techniques such as electing chairs and organising committees and roll calls. The 1899 Hague Conference established a Convention on the Pacific Settlement of Disputes and created the

Permanent Court of Arbitration, which was an attempt to establish permanent procedures for resolving disputes peacefully. The Permanent Court of Arbitration still exists today. Such actions would lay the bureaucratic foundation for modern IOs like the League of Nations (LoN, which existed between 1920 and 1946), including its Permanent Court of International Justice (PCIJ). These were prototypes for the UN and the current International Court of Justice (ICJ, see Chapter 4).

States therefore found IOs useful for establishing a stable international order; they used IOs as a means to stop war, prevent future conflict and aid recovery from war through the use of martial, economic and diplomatic power. This is particularly evident during the two world wars, which saw a surge in the number of IOs created. For example, over 300 IOs were created during WWI and over 400 were created during World War Two (WWII) (Cupitt *et al.* 2001). Overtly political IOs were also formed during these periods, such as the North Atlantic Treaty Organisation (NATO), which was explicitly designed as a **collective defence** organisation to defend a limited number of member states from a common threat.

Furthermore, IOs with membership open to all sovereign states, such as the LoN founded in 1919 and the UN founded in 1945, were explicitly mandated to authorise the use of force through a system of **collective security** to prevent war and replace **balance-of-power** politics. The design of liberal international IOs such as the LoN and the UN, and economic IOs such as the IMF, the World Bank and later the World Trade Organization (WTO; its precursor was the General Agreement on Tariffs and Trade or GATT), exemplify the interests of powerful states in ensuring international cooperation in the aftermath of both of the world wars.

Why IOs Are Important

The proliferation of IOs in the modern period attests to their perceived utility in solving international problems for states. IOs smooth relations among states across a range of issues, from peace negotiations to shipping and postal services. Two factors reveal their importance as an object of study for students of international relations outside their relation to states: first, their low death rate; and second, the ability of IOs to spawn new IOs outside inter-state treaties.

The Longevity of IOs

Once created, IOs tend to hang around. For example, 15 IOs established in 1865, such as the ITU, existed for a century! Generally most IOs survive their first five years of existence. Prior to WWI IOs tended to survive for 30 years; after 1945 they tended to exist for 15–20 years. Of course, organisations do not last forever. Although IOs tend to die off twice as frequently as domestic American government agencies, they tend to exist for twice as long. The UN, IMF and World Bank have existed for over 70 years.

The world of IOs continues to expand, but IOs are more likely to be killed during times of rapid changes in the balance of power and the world order. For example, 25 per cent of PIUs did not survive WWI, and IOs comprised of Soviet Bloc states, such as the Council for Mutual Economic Assistance and the Warsaw Treaty Organization, did not survive the end of the Cold War. While the number of IOs jumped dramatically during both world wars, there has been a slower birth-rate of IOs since the 1970s. In other words, even though states are not creating as many IOs now as in the past, states continue to see IOs as useful and the number of IOs continues to grow (see Box 1.2 on the creation of the new Asian Infrastructure Investment Bank). That IOs continue to be created and

Box 1.2 The Asian Infrastructure Investment Bank: A New IO on the Block

In 2013 China's President Xi Jinping and Premier Li Keqiang outlined the prospect for a new China-led multilateral development bank (MDB) during inter-state visits to Southeast Asia. The idea behind the bank is to provide 'financial support for infrastructure development and regional connectivity in Asia' (AIIB 2015). It is widely recognised that there is a significant gap in meeting the infrastructure needs of the region and that the existing MDBs, namely the World Bank and the Asian Development Bank, are unable to meet such a demand (see Chapter 9). In October 2014, 22 states signed a memorandum of understanding to create the Asian Infrastructure Investment Bank (AIIB), with its headquarters located in Beijing. Fifty-seven members signed up to become its founding members in March 2015. The United States chose not to join it. Some see the AIIB as a direct challenge to US-led institutions such as the World Bank and to a US-led international order.

survive even though the world around them has changed highlights the need to analyse what they do and why.

Emanation IOs

While IOs continue to proliferate, most new ones are not created by states (the AIIB in Box 1.2 is an exception). 'Traditional' IOs created by states through international treaties have been in the minority since the beginning of the twentieth century. Instead, most new IOs are established by pre-existing IOs, a process which is called **emanation**. Like popular television programmes, IOs establish other 'spin-off' IOs, which may include libraries, banks, courts, laboratories and libraries. Indications that an IO may be an emanation of another IO include its having the parent IO's name in its title, or its having been created from a resolution in the parent IO's constitution. An emanation IO may also be comprised as a joint IO with the parent IO (while the latter retains its own mandate, function and structure). An example is the Association of Southeast Asian Nations (ASEAN) Regional Forum (ARF). The ARF is a unit within ASEAN that provides an independent forum for the 10 ASEAN member states to engage with 17 other states on issues of regional politics and security (ASEAN 2012; see Chapter 3).

Establishing an emanation IO requires member states of the parent IO to cast a majority vote for it to exist, compared with devising a new international treaty requiring signatures and ratifications for the establishment of a traditional IO. The emergence of emanation IOs may correspond to the increasingly technical nature of relations between states requiring more cooperation on more specific activities that emerge from the original IO's operations. Although it is harder to create traditional IOs owing to the difficulties inherent in international treaty-making among states, traditional IOs are more tenacious in survival terms than emanation IOs, which are easier both to create and to kill.

We need to look not just at traditional and more enduring IOs created by international agreement among states but also at less robust emanation IOs spawned by other IOs. The increase in emanation IOs has contributed to the tendency to examine cooperation through the concept of **global governance** (see Chapter 11), or how a range of actors will interact to address specific issues internationally. Often traditional IOs, emanation IOs, states and non-state actors work in the same issue area. This book focuses specifically on IOs. IOs need to be examined in terms of helping states solve cooperation and coordination problems at the international level and compared with an increasing number of transnational actors. By doing this, we get a better sense of whether IOs can help solve problems of the twenty-first century or whether we should look to alternatives to IOs to help solve international problems. In other words, do IOs help or hinder?

Examining International Organisations

Decision-making within IOs varies, but they all are comprised of member states, management and staff who field pressure for how they address particular problems from state and non-state actors, including rebels, activists, scientists, corporations, philanthropists and other IOs (see Figure 1.1). While IOs are answerable to their member states for their performance in meeting their mandates, their actions may be viewed differently by these various audiences. IO actions in response to a refugee crisis, for example, would be viewed differently by a refugee, a rebel, the government, neighbouring states, powerful states and by governments and people accepting refugees into their countries. To get at different vantage points for assessing IO behaviour, scholars of IOs use a variety of theoretical lenses that prioritise different **units of analysis**.

Figure 1.1 shows how we can break down the strata of IOs to better understand their decision-making. IOs are constituted by states, but they are often directed by management teams installed to act on the member states' behalf. These management teams may have more or less authority depending on the degree of autonomy and discretion given to them by the IO's member states.

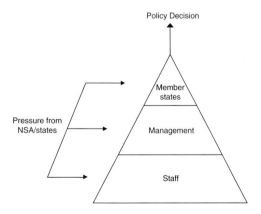

Figure 1.1 Policy change in international organisations

Staff work to enact the mandate of the IO under management. As with all organisations, different factors may affect the interpretation and implementation of the IO's mandate as spelled out in its constitution or charter, which delimits its activities. How IOs decide what their policy will be is influenced by real-world events and actors, the balance of power, international norms or even a shift in the internal bargaining or organisational culture of the IO.

Looking at IOs as problem solvers means grappling with how IOs are affected at the different strata by non-state actors when attempting to do their job. How do member states debate terrorism at the UN compared with the specialised committees they create? How does management, like the Secretary General of the UN, interpret the Charter to improve its responses to new threats and challenges? Thinking through the different strata in terms of how international events and actors exert pressure on an IO provides a more comprehensive analysis of how and why IOs act the way they do. And this can help determine whether this makes them better at addressing global problems.

International relations (IR) and IO-specific theories can provide insight into IOs' efforts to tackle global problems. Prominent **realist** scholars such as John Mearsheimer have argued that IOs do not have much effect in world politics, yet they have been an object of scholarly attention from liberals, functionalists, rationalists and constructivists throughout the history of international relations. While some realists dismiss the claim that IOs can play a separate role from their member states, others debate their efficacy; some shake their heads at the inefficiency, ineffectiveness, bureaucratic malaise and **mission creep** they see at the organisational level, while others see a real possibility for these organisations to make the world a better place through international cooperation and application of their bureaucratic expertise. Chapter 2 delves into how we can examine IOs through different theoretical lenses.

Chapter Summary

This chapter introduced international organisations as actors in international relations. Despite many having household names like the European Union, their role remains contested. Some see them as inefficient, wasteful bureaucracies with little effect on world politics. Others argue that IOs play an important role in helping states cooperate across a range of issue areas. This is why they remain subject to investigation. The foundation for the emergence of modern IOs was built over a long time. Multilateral conferences for inter-state diplomacy evolved from the nineteenth century in Europe. PIUs would help smooth relations between states by allowing a space for international agreement over how to conduct interactions such as trade and commerce. IOs surge in number during war, and the number of IOs continues to expand. States create IOs through international treaties, but more IOs are created now through a process of emanation. Examining how an IO operates, however, requires us to analyse the demands being placed on the member states of the IO as well as its management and staff.

Guiding Questions

1. What are IOs?
2. Why are IOs important?
3. How are they created?
4. How can we examine them?

Further References

The Emergence of IOs

Claude, I., 1971, *Swords into Ploughshares: The Problems and Progress of International Organization*, fourth edition, New York, Random House.

Farley, L. T., 1982, *Change Processes in International Organizations*, Cambridge, MA, Schenkman Publishing.

Haas, E. B., 1990, *When Knowledge Is Power: Three Models of Change in International Organizations*, Berkeley, CA, University of California Press.

Jacobson, H. K., 1984, *Networks of Independence: International Organizations and the Global Political System*, second edition, New York, Alfred A. Knopf.

Murphy, C., 1994, *International Organization and Industrial Change: Global Governance since 1850*, London, Polity Press and Oxford University Press.

The Growth of IOs

Cupitt, R., R. Witlock and L. W. Witlock, 2001, 'The (Im)mortality of International Governmental Organizations', in P. Diehl (ed.), *Politics of Global Governance*, second edition, Boulder, CO, Lynne Rienner: 44–60.

Jacobson, H. K., W. M. Reisinger and T. Mathers, 1986, 'National Entanglements in International Governmental Organizations', *American Political Science Review* 80 (1): 141–159.

Shanks, C., H. Jacobson and J. Kaplan, 1996, 'Inertia and Change in the Constellation of International Governmental Organizations, 1981–1992', *International Organization* 50 (4): 593–627.

Theoretical Approaches to IOs

Barnett, M., and M. Finnemore, 2004, *Rules for the World: International Organizations in Global Politics*, Ithaca, NY and London, Cornell University Press.

Haas, E. B., 1964, *Beyond the Nation-State: Functionalism and International Organization*, Stanford, CA, Stanford University Press.

Kratochwil, F., and J. G. Ruggie, 1986, 'International Organizations: A State of the Art on the Art of the State', *International Organization* 40 (4): 753–776.

Martin, L. L., and B. Simmons, 1998, 'Theories and Empirical Studies of International Institutions', *International Organization* 52 (4): 729–757.

Mearsheimer, J. J., 1994–1995, 'The False Promise of International Institutions', *International Security* 19 (3): 5–49.

Miller, L., 2001, 'The Idea and Reality of Collective Security', in P. Diehl (ed.), *The Politics of Global Governance*, second edition, Boulder, CO, Lynne Rienner: 171–201.

Mitrany, D., 1975, 'A Working Peace System', [1943] in D. Mitrany, *The Functional Theory of Politics*, London, London School of Economics and Political Science: 123–135.

Ruggie, J. G., 1992, 'Multilateralism: The Anatomy of an Institution', *International Organization* 46 (3): 561–598.

2 Using Theory to Evaluate IOs as Problem Solvers

Chapter Overview

Introduction

How can we understand, explain and evaluate the actions of IOs in grappling with major problems? For example, can we point to the failure of the WTO to implement, administer and operate multilateral trade agreements because negotiations among its 164 member states have been deadlocked for over a decade? As indicated in Chapter 1, scholars use a number of different theoretical approaches to examine IOs. In the post-WWII period **liberal** and **functionalist** approaches sought to explain the rise of IOs as a result of increasing **interdependence** among states. Functionalism remains valuable because it was the antecedent to viewing IOs as useful for states and for solving problems. Specific international relations theories such as **neorealism** and **neoliberal institution-alism** build on this platform, and seek to explain how IOs are used as tools for statecraft. While they view the potential outcomes of international **cooperation** differently, they continue to be the main lenses for analysing states' decisions to use IOs to solve problems.

In comparison, IO-specific theories such as the rationalist **principal–agent (P–A) model** and constructivist **organisational culture** investigate IOs by opening the **black-box** of the organisations themselves, to assess the likelihood of the IO being able and willing to respond to specific problems. Although these approaches are wildly different, both of them recognise that IOs can operate independently of their member states, with different interests and preferences (rational P–A model) and identities and cultures (constructivists). This provides us with greater insight into the workings of organisations beyond member-state dictates. In elaborating on each of these theories, their strengths and weaknesses are identified. The final section of the chapter distils questions from the various theories into a single table to provide a starting point for analysing the impact of IOs.

Emergence of Liberal and Functionalist Approaches

In Chapter 1 we noted the rise of IOs from the middle of the nineteenth century. Most of these organisations were single-purpose IOs with limited membership, established to tackle a particular issue. For example, the earliest IO was the Central Commission for the Navigation of the Rhine, which was created in 1815 to facilitate states' riparian relations. The founders of **public international unions** (PIUs) aimed to address issues arising from the industrial revolution, including new scientific knowledge, improving transport and applying technology. Critical IO scholar Craig Murphy argues that these IOs performed important services for extending liberal markets internationally: they created common standards for goods and services, while ensuring that commerce was regulated rather than dependent upon the behaviour of petty officials. These PIUs emerged alongside unions seeking to address nascent international social issues, including public health, labour and humanitarian issues.

The experience of technically oriented IOs in addressing economic, social and humanitarian concerns contributed to a theory of **functionalism**, which was most prominently identified by David Mitrany (1975 [1943]). Functionalism argued that states could increasingly cooperate through non-political IOs. Doing so would bind states together according to their common interests, ultimately contributing to peace between states. This would later lead to a theory of **integration**.

According to this functionalist logic, politics could be stripped from inter-state relations by staffing functional IOs not with diplomats but with professional experts, such as scientists within the United Nations Educational, Scientific and Cultural Organization (UNESCO), health professionals within the WHO and economists at the IMF. In this way, the IO could devise the best means of solving problems between states rather than decisions being made according to national power and prestige. This approach emerged in the dying days of WWII. This apolitical, technical understanding of IOs would be embodied in the constitution or Articles of Agreement of organisations such as the IMF and the World Bank in 1944.

Advocates for peace took up this logic to argue that IOs could help build an international order around low-level bureaucratic interactions, enmeshing states in peaceful relations that would become increasingly difficult to sever, making conflict less likely. This **liberal internationalist** approach viewed IOs as a means towards a 'working peace' between states (Mitrany 1975 [1943]). Some theorists saw it as a first step towards a global federation of peaceful states as envisaged by the political philosopher Immanuel Kant.

The development of IOs in Europe is instructive for liberal internationalist arguments: the European Coal and Steel Community (ECSC) was established in the aftermath of WWII, bringing France and West Germany together, despite France and Germany having fought against each other in both world wars. The aim was to regulate the use of coal and steel, which are vital for war-making, and enmesh the West German economy in Western Europe. This functional body has been credited with aiding the creation of the European Economic Community (EEC), the precursor of the European Union (EU). This provided evidence that cooperation could **spill over** from one functional area to another political realm, thus contributing to peace in Europe. Thus cooperation in the steel and coal economic sectors in these states could lead to further cooperation in other areas of their economies affected by steel and coal (transport, for example). Similar functionalist arguments have been made with regard to ASEAN in Asia. While there is a correlation between the increased number of IOs in the international system and the decline of war over time, being a member of an IO does not make states less war-prone. However, the *more* IOs states join the less likely they are to use force against other member states.

There are four weaknesses in functionalism. First, it overlooks the efforts states made in designing peace plans such as the Treaty of Versailles and the creation of the League of Nations rather than just economic and social IOs. Second, the functionalist view argues that war stemmed from poor economic and social conditions globally rather than from the national aggression from the advanced industrial state of Germany that triggered WWII. Third, the distinction between functional and political bodies is a false one. Decisions made by technical bodies advance some groups' values and interests over others, which is an inherently political process. Four, functionalism promotes non-democratic decision-making: leaving decisions to technical experts acting as international civil servants places them outside the realm of national-level decision-making. This issue resurged in the late 1990s with claims that IOs suffered a **democratic deficit**. This is because it became clear that IOs were making decisions with global repercussions without broad public participation (see Box 2.1).

Box 2.1 The WTO and the Battle of Seattle

Beginning on 30 November 1999, Seattle hosted the WTO ministerial meeting, where states met to agree on a new 'round' for furthering **trade liberalisation**. It led to one of the largest protests ever held against an IO, with several thousand marching against the IO over three days. Protestors opposed the WTO on numerous grounds: labour rights, the environment, human rights, even anti-abortion. While many protestors were peaceful, anarchist groups smashed windows of multinational chains such as McDonald's. The protests intensified, with fires being lit, looting and the throwing of debris at delegates and police. Police used tear gas in response. The Mayor of Seattle declared a civil emergency. Delegates were locked in the convention centre unable to leave. The ministerial meeting was abandoned: not because of the protest, but because delegates could not agree on further liberalisation. The popular view that global rules that affect everyone were being made behind closed doors led to ongoing protests against other meetings of the World Bank, the IMF, the G7 and the corporate World Economic Forum. Pointedly, the resumption of the WTO meetings in 2001 took place in non-democratic Qatar, which protestors were barred from entering.

Neofunctionalism

In the 1950s, prominent political scientist Ernst Haas took up the functionalist idea that cooperation between states could be facilitated through low-level bureaucratic interactions. This **neofunctionalist** approach predicted that increased cooperation would lead to **integration** through **spillover**, where cooperation in one area spills over into another area. Ernst Haas agreed with the broader liberal approach: groups within societies act to advance their own interests. They could benefit from the creation of IOs led by technical experts, but experts had to be aware of the political implications of their tasks. This could lead to integration where states would agree to give decision-making power to a common agency or IO to determine a shared policy approach. However, it was unclear whether Haas was describing a federal United Europe leaving states in charge or the creation of a **supranational** IO where states cede power to the organisation.

Haas argued that functional bodies could impact on high-level politics, like questions of war and peace, but this would not happen automatically. Rather, IOs could affect issues of war and peace only by influencing the political decisions of elites and policy-makers. Jean Monnet, as head of the ECSC and a powerful advocate of neofunctionalism, argued that technical experts could craft policies to precipitate further integration. For example, the ECSC integrated six Western European states' coal and steel markets (France, West Germany, Italy, the Netherlands, Belgium and Luxembourg). Monnet argued that distortions in coal and steel prices could be eliminated if transport and social security were integrated as well. Thus, integration in one sector of an economy or society could be used to justify further integration across other areas.

Despite the creation of the European Community in 1967, which merged the ECSC, the EEC and Euratom, spillover into other areas had not occurred by the 1970s. Nor had it occurred outside Europe. This led neofunctionalists to retrench on the future of regional integration in Europe and its applicability to other regions. Neofunctionalism was then abandoned as a predictive theory of what will happen once IOs have been created. It became clear that the integration of Western Europe was not leading to the creation of a world government. Moreover, further refinements were needed to explain states' behaviour towards IOs, states' behaviour within IOs and the effect of IOs on international relations. Nonetheless, neofunctionalism continues to inform debates between those who argue that to a large extent Western European states pursue their **interests** through IOs, as advocated by the **intergovernmentalist** approach, and those who highlight the role of regional IOs in shaping Europe (see Chapter 8).

International Relations Theories on International Cooperation

From the nineteenth century onwards states increasingly created new IOs across a whole range of issues in areas previously considered outside their domain. For example, the International Labour Office was created as a private association, but states chose to take this idea and create the International Labour Organization (ILO) in 1919. For many new sovereign states, joining IOs is a right once sovereignty has been attained through decolonisation, war or peaceful separation. International relations (IR) theories of **liberalism** and **realism** examined whether international cooperation between states was possible. From the 1980s IR theories aimed to become more scientific, establishing generalisable rules to explain states' behaviour (see Box 2.2 below). According to the theories of **neorealism** and **neoliberal institutionalism**, states used IOs and broader

Box 2.2 The Great Debates in International Relations

In the first great debate, traditional IR theories were divided into liberal, realist and revolutionary theories, such as historical materialism or Marxism. During the third great debate in IR, these theories and their 'neo' variants were labelled 'rationalist' theories, compared with 'reflectivist' social and critical theories. More scientifically 'behaviourist' theories, such as neorealist and neoliberal institutionalist theories, had emerged from the second great debate. These are also rationalist because they seek to objectively identify states' interests under conditions of anarchy. Rationalism is defined as behaviour that can be evaluated as best adapted to a specific situation by an independent observer. Rationalist theories examine whether actors make the most optimal decision to achieve their interests. In comparison, reflectivist approaches such as constructivism aim to understand how the intangible social context, including ideas and states' identities, mediates their interactions with one another according to what is considered appropriate behaviour. Other reflectivist work on IOs includes Foucauldian (Neumann and Sending 2010) and critical feminist (Griffin 2010) scholarship that looks at how power relations are re-created through social interactions within and through IOs.

international **institutions** as part of their foreign policy toolkit to advance their interests. States act rationally in response to the various problems they face.

IOs are designed by states for a specific purpose. Some are created to be open to all states, such as the universal UN. Or they may be limited in their state membership according to region, such as ASEAN and the EU. There may be historical reasons for creating an IO such as the Commonwealth, which is based on the British Empire. Membership for other IOs may be determined by their specific purpose around states' shared interests, such as the Organization of the Petroleum Exporting Countries (OPEC). Snapshots of IOs over time reveal changes in how states design IOs: restrictive criteria for joining IOs were apparent during the 1940s, while geographically oriented IOs declined at the end of the 1980s with the collapse of the Soviet Union. The universal versus particularistic nature of IO purpose and membership shows why states join IOs, but it raises questions as to whether we can make law-like generalisations about all of them.

Instead we can think through the impact of IOs in terms of whether they are **forum** or **service** IOs. Are IOs the realm for state decision-making, or have they been given **autonomy** to serve states and make their own decisions? We can analyse the actions of forum IOs like the WTO, which provides space for consensus among its 164 member states, and of other forum IOs like the United Nations Security Council (UNSC), where members must come to agreement over what constitutes a breach of international peace or an act of aggression. These forum IOs are quite different from service organisations such as the IMF, World Bank, WHO and UNESCO. These IOs have varying degrees of independence from their member states, and may have greater discretion for undertaking actions on their behalf.

The relatively autonomous IOs have a secretariat or management that is able to direct the daily activities of the organisation and must report back to member states on the IO's achievements. We can draw different conclusions about the capacity of forum and service IOs to effect change in the international system. This is dependent on whether IOs are able to further international **cooperation, collaboration** and **coordination** between states as per neorealism and neoliberal institutionalist theories. Are IR theories better for investigating forum IOs? Can we best examine whether service IOs can effect change through acting as bureaucracies with **technical expertise** as per IO-specific theories such as the **principal–agent model** and **constructivist organisational change** approaches? Or can all approaches shed light both on forum IOs and on service IOs?

Classical Liberal and Realist Approaches to IOs

Original views of IOs derived from understandings of the international system itself. **Liberal** conceptions were based on the potential for peace for all individuals. Locating the **unit of analysis** at the individual meant not only that states were to act in the interests of individual freedom and prosperity, but also that IOs should be used to achieve this (see Box 2.3). The liberal approach is backed by the fact that popular participation in national politics and high levels of economic growth are linked to states' decision to join IOs (Jacobson *et al.* 1986; Shanks *et al.* 1996). In contrast, **realists** view the international system as an endless struggle for dominance between **sovereign states**, leading to competition and conflict. IOs were viewed as mere products of political leaders who use whatever changes in technology and communication emerge to achieve their own interests. Thus, IOs may be seen as constructing universal peace as per liberalism or, by realists, as merely providing a better framework for diplomacy by improving the means for negotiation among states.

In the aftermath of WWI and the subsequent failure of the League of Nations, Liberals were labelled **idealists** for their faith in the ability of IOs to bring peace, and realism became ascendant. **Classical realism** focused on states' desire for power and advantage, which undermines inter-state cooperation and leads states into cyclical violence. The focus became the high politics of war and peace, not on how IOs further economic, social and cultural cooperation. Yet even classical realists acknowledged that international **institutions** and law provide the platform for state interactions, especially for negotiation and bargaining. Arguably though, cooperation is fleeting, as states remain distrustful of each other. Short-lived cooperation in the form of **alliances** was frequent. States

Box 2.3 Liberal International Organisations

IOs often have liberal goals such as 'promoting and encouraging respect for human rights and for fundamental freedoms for all' in the UN, the World Bank's declared intention to 'work for a world free of poverty' and the WHO's aim to achieve 'Health for All' by 2000. Each of these aims embodies liberal values that seek to improve the lives of people, not states. It is no accident that powerful states that helped create the post-WWII international order are liberal democratic states.

may cooperate to achieve their interests, namely to ensure their own survival and power. Once the conditions favouring cooperation have changed, each state reverts to acting in its own interests.

Key classical realist Hans Morgenthau went beyond this to advocate that international institutions could provide a means for transforming the **international system**. Yet most realists reject the claim that international organisations can play an independent role in the international system, and maintain that states merely use IOs as instruments of statecraft. As a result, interest in IOs during the Cold War became a niche area that focused on recording states' voting patterns in IOs. Increasingly many wondered whether IOs made any difference whatsoever in international relations. Despite the proliferation of IOs, by the late 1970s the IR debate had moved away from examining IOs' activities.

Neorealism

Kenneth Waltz (1979) reinterpreted realism as a more scientific structural account of the international system. In emphasising the fragility of inter-state cooperation he ignored IOs. This **neorealist** theory posited that the international system was anarchic in the sense that it was not under the control of any single hegemonic power. The structure of the international system over-rides all other influences for explaining state behaviour. States engage in **balance-of-power** politics as they compete for survival.

However, neorealists are more likely to include an examination of states' interests in economic issues or low politics than classical realists. When IOs were recognised by neorealists, they were seen to reflect powerful states' interests. States establish IOs for their own advantage. In terms of the balance of power, **hegemons** could create IOs to further their own interests, but so too could weak states. Weak states could use IOs either to **balance** against the hegemon or to **bandwagon** with it. In this regard, IOs are the handmaidens of states. However, neorealists caution that cooperation takes place only if states perceive that they will gain more from it relative to others.

The distribution of capabilities of states within the international system may determine the extent to which cooperation crystallises in IOs. In a multipolar system, with competing powers including those that wish to alter the status quo (revisionists), there may be temporary forms of international cooperation. However, in a multipolar system with no revisionist states there is greater room for formal centralised cooperation between **Great Powers**, leading to the creation of IOs. In a bipolar system, such as between the two superpowers during the Cold War, the creation of IOs depended on their interactions. Given that the super-powers operated in different spheres of influence, there were not many universal IOs. The main one, the UN, ensured they could veto each other's actions to ensure neither gained.

In a unipolar system the structure of the IO depends on the characteristic of the dominant power. If it is liberal then it does not solely rely on its dominance but creates rules based on the consent of other states to achieve its interests. A dominant state in a unipolar system may also be a **hegemon**. A hegemon may seek not only to maintain its power in the international system but also to ensure the system's overall stability. Hegemonic stability theory argues that the hegemon can ensure a stable international order by providing **public goods** that benefit all states, such as the international monetary system to enable trade, providing a security umbrella over its allies, and covering the costs of creating and maintaining multi-purpose IOs like the UN to promote peace, economic development and the promotion of human rights.

The benefits states receive from international cooperation in IOs vary because powerful states can lock in institutional rules from which they gain most. A prime example of this is the unanimity principle or veto of the five permanent members of the UNSC that was agreed upon in 1945. This effectively allows the United States (USA), United Kingdom (UK), France, Russia (formerly the Soviet Union) and (since 1971) the People's Republic of China (PRC) to determine what constitutes a breach of international peace and security and what response, if any, should be undertaken. Despite the best efforts of states such as Japan, Germany, India and Brazil that have become powerful over the last seven decades, they have been unable to change the rules of the UNSC to reflect the changing balance of power.

Powerful states such as the United States do use IOs like the UN to signal their strategic interests. Why do weak states agree to this? Arguably they still sign up to IOs even when the terms of cooperation are not in their favour because the benefits of joining still outweigh the costs of exclusion. Despite the disadvantages, weak states may bind themselves to IOs in order to achieve a voice within the IO which they would not otherwise have. This is why small and developing states favour the UN General Assembly. While extreme neorealists such as John Mearsheimer argue that IOs are **epiphenomenal** to the structure of the international system, others argue that IOs can be effective arenas for states to achieve their interests.

Neoliberal Institutionalism

Both neorealism and **neoliberal institutionalism** examine state cooperation in the international system, thus shaping our understanding of multilateralism and IOs. They agree on the **anarchic** nature of the international system and that states are self-interested. Yet they differ on whether cooperation is less or more likely, depending on their assessment of whether some states gain more than others (neorealist) or whether all states gain overall (neoliberal). Recognisably both neorealism and neoliberalism are **rationalist** theories of international relations (see Box 2.2). According to Robert Keohane, the principal advocate of neoliberal institutionalism, international **cooperation** requires the policy coordination of separate states. This means that IOs can help manage interdependence and overcome **collective-action** problems among states.

Taking its cue from micro-economics, neoliberal institutionalism views states as self-interested 'utility-maximising' actors who expect to benefit from the creation of IOs. In other words, IOs can be used by rational states to fully realise their interests under anarchy. Neoliberals point to the functional benefits of multilateralism for states: IOs can reduce the costs of transactions between states by enabling cooperation to be undertaken more efficiently. IOs can provide states with information to which they might not otherwise have access. IOs can enable more effective cooperation to achieve one's goals (or maximise utility pay-offs in neoliberal parlance). IOs can also promote linkages amongst states with regard to various issues, leading to greater inter-state cooperation through bargaining and collaboration as means of organising states' activities.

Neoliberals concentrated their research agenda on the problems states face in attempting to create international agreements, establish international institutions, and design IOs. **Collective action** at the international level therefore revolved around states' incentives to cooperate or cheat on multilateral agreements. Using **game theory** such as the Prisoner's Dilemma, neoliberals examined how states solve problems through devising agreements to benefit all players and reduce the risk of states' cheating. Once states have agreed to cooperate, they still may have highly divergent preferences for how collaboration should be undertaken, which can lead to multiple possible scenarios and therefore outcomes, each of which could lead to some states benefiting more than others. Some argue that IOs and institutions should be designed with a small number of members from the beginning, and that one should add further members later. This allows the original member states to cooperate at a deeper level than in the

Box 2.4 Informal Multilateralism

Informal multilateralism can include the annual meetings of the Group of Seven (G7, comprised of Canada, France, Germany, Italy, Japan, the UK and the United States) and the more recently established G20. These 'G-groupings' are informal meetings by Heads of State, originally for financial matters but now extending across a range of issues. The 'Gs' are not IOs because they were not established by an international treaty, they do not have a permanent secretariat to perform ongoing tasks, and they do not have headquarters. They nevertheless provide a forum for states to make decisions, and they have a loose structure, regularised meetings, a logo and a website. In international trade, rules were coordinated through the General Agreement on Tariffs and Trade (GATT) via regularised meetings of the trade ministers in 'negotiation rounds' from 1947 until the creation of the World Trade Organization (WTO) in 1995 (see Chapter 7).

case of establishing universal IOs where some member states desire less cooperation, leading to shallow or lowest-common-denominator agreements.

Why do states choose to establish IOs over other forms of international cooperation, such as informal multilateral arrangements? If we look at issue areas that require multilateral solutions, we don't necessarily need IOs. Indeed, there is no good reason why we should make the world so complex by creating all of these bodies. Instead, states could choose to establish informal multilateralism rather than IOs (see Box 2.4). States might prefer informal agreements for four reasons: (1) to avoid formal pledges; (2) to avoid ratification; (3) because informal agreements enable them to change their position in negotiations quickly; and (4) to come to a speedy agreement (Lipson 1991). Nonetheless, states do establish IOs and, once created, IOs tend to last (see Chapter 1). As a result, neoliberal institutionalists examine the extent to which states benefit from agreeing to cooperate in IOs and how they collaborate within these organisations by identifying the various games states play.

Once states have agreed to cooperate, they then enter a collaboration game over how to do so. Collaboration games are where equilibrium outcome among the players is suboptimal and the threat of states defecting from the agreement is high. IOs are created in order to monitor and to assess compliance with the agreement between states. In contrast, IOs are not seen as necessary for coordination games, where states have different preferences and where multiple outcomes are expected. Once states have negotiated the outcome, there is little reason to expect defection and therefore no need for IOs to undertake monitoring and compliance. IOs may, however, play a role in the suasion game, where there is asymmetry between states such as the **hegemon** and the rest of the world, and the hegemon uses IOs to serve its own interests. It can do so by persuading others to cooperate with it by providing other states with **public goods** such as international security or international financial stability (Martin 1992). Ultimately the dynamics around creating IOs needs to take into account the interests of the hegemon and the changing distribution of power that may alter states' preferences.

IOs are preferred vehicles for international cooperation among states because of their **centralisation** and their **independence** (Abbott and Snidal 1998). These twin factors are important because they enable states to achieve goals that might not be possible through decentralised means (without an IO) or across different fora where impetus for action may be lost. A degree of **autonomy** also allows IOs to undertake a range of activities, including promoting negotiations, implementing agreements, managing disputes, providing technical assistance and outlining international rules and norms.

Such state-centric approaches dominated analysis of IOs throughout the 1980s and 1990s, meaning that IOs were not seen to have any initiative. While states delegate power to IOs to carry out set operations as defined in their Articles of Agreement or Charter, neither neorealist nor neoliberal approaches provided insight into IOs' **interests** or actions, especially when they operated relatively autonomously or deviated from state dictates. Yet even neoliberal institutionalist research would demonstrate that IOs can help change states' **preferences** over the outcomes of international cooperation as a result of cooperation within IOs (Jervis 1999). Increasingly it was recognised that IOs can alter states' beliefs about what is possible and desirable. In other words, IOs were able to shape states interests.

While constructivists agree that IOs do help facilitate inter-state cooperation by shaping states' preferences and interests, the dominant view of IOs was that they were there to ensure that states abide by the rules. Constructivists view the world as socially constructed, examining how intersubjective ideas shape the structure of the international system and inform actors' behaviour. Since their approach is a social theory, constructivists could take a range of actors as their main unit of analysis. To counter neorealists and neoliberals, many examined the role of the state in the international system, with a small sub-set examining IOs specifically. Generally speaking, neoliberalism, just like neorealism, retains the view that IOs serve states rather than act as agents with their own interests.

In sum, neorealists and neoliberals do not look inside the **black box** of organisations and thus overlook IOs' actions that are not determined by inter-state bargaining. It would take IO-specific approaches to do that.

IO-Specific Theories

By the mid 1990s, both neorealists and neoliberals agreed that they had overlooked the role IOs play in international relations. Realists recognised that they did not have a model to explain the emergence and effectiveness of IOs (Schweller and Priess 1997). Neoliberals also acknowledged that they needed a better explanation of institutions. Precisely because of the absence of a discussion of the actions of IOs themselves, the principal–agent (P–A) model and constructivist organisational culture approaches emerged. Both of these approaches take the independent and autonomous nature of IOs as their starting point.

The Principal–Agent (P–A) Model

The P–A model analyses the relationship between principals (states) and the agent (IO). In this relationship, the principal gives authority to the agent to act on its behalf. This is a rationalist approach to examining IOs' behaviour. The model is an extension of neoliberal institutionalism's focus on states gaining efficiency and effectiveness from international cooperation but focuses on when IOs are given decision-making authority (Nielson and Tierney 2003). The formulation accepts the **autonomy** of IOs in undertaking states' designated tasks. States choose to delegate activities to states for seven reasons: (1) this establishes a division of labour that allows states to concentrate on what they can achieve through other means; (2) IOs have greater opportunity to address particular problems owing to their specialisation (as centralised autonomous agencies with set tasks); and states also gain from IOs' abilities to (3) manage policy externalities; (4) facilitate collective decision-making; (5) resolve disputes; (6) enhance credibility; and (7) create a policy bias, such as by locking in particular rules and organisational structures (Hawkins *et al.* 2006). Having established the rational reason for states to create IOs that have some autonomy to conduct operations on states' collective behalf, advocates of the P–A model then seek to test whether agents' (IOs') actions are commensurate with principals' (states') preferences.

In recognising IOs' autonomy, the model is used to examine agent outcomes in the light of principals' expectations and their ability to oversee agents. In other words, rationalist IO scholars adopted the P–A model to explain and assess IOs' performance. Precisely because the IO has been given autonomy to undertake its designated tasks, the principal may be able to view the outcome but not specifically see all of the agent's actions. Without detailed oversight, the IO may engage in other activities. IOs' autonomy allows space for 'agency slack', where the actions of the agent may not be in the interests of the principal. Such slack may also lead to **slippage** when the agent begins to shift its activities towards its own preferences rather than those of the principal. The IO may also engage in **shirking**, where the IO does little to meet the tasks set by the principals (Hawkins *et al.* 2006).

Within the P–A model the focus is on how the principal can control its agent. The principal has the authority to create the agent and to provide incentives for it to meet the principal's interests, but the agent has an informational advantage as an expert and authority in its area of expertise. The IO is constrained by the degree to which the principal establishes the agent's parameters: designing its contract; establishing procedures for staff selection and screening; and imposing demands for monitoring, reporting and institutional checks to prevent agent slack. Member states also choose mechanisms for overseeing IOs' actions, including rewards and punishments, and these are based on the tools available and their cost. Two types of oversight strategy that principals can use to oversee agents have been identified: **police patrols** and **fire alarms** (McCubbins and Schwartz 1984). The P–A model has been applied to the World Bank to assess how member-state principals can alter incentive systems to improve the IO's performance.

Of course, the P–A model is complicated because IOs have more than one member state or **collective principals**. With more principals, there is a greater potential for agency slippage. This is because any one principal has less control over the agent. Additionally there is an increase in cost for individual principals in convincing other principals to follow their **preferences**. Where member states differ over their preferences for agent action, there is greater room for agency slack, and this may affect IO performance.

Different member states also have different degrees of power. This affects which principals' preferences are realised, including their ability to establish and enforce oversight mechanisms and to change incentive structures and procedures in such a way as to favour their interests. Principals' disagreements over preferences for an IO's action (and reform) may give the agent leverage to ignore criticisms or refuse to change its behaviour, thus undermining principals' credibility. Of course, the P–A model is even more complex than this because principals are also made up of a number of groups, such as state executives, parliaments, bureaucracy, political parties and lobby groups, with divergent interests and preferences.

In the P–A model equation, it is assumed that agents pursue their own interests within the confines of the relationship with the principal. It is assumed that IOs aim to protect themselves to survive; that they aim to increase their autonomy; and that they seek to maintain or expand their budget and personnel or their power. Rationalist studies on state delegation to EU agents have analysed how and why European organisations such as the European Court of Justice extend their reach (Alter 1998). Yet, for the most part, agents' interests are not addressed by the P–A model. The P–A model is useful for examining the relationship between states and IOs, but provides little in the way of explaining IO behaviour that is not based on the dependency of the IO on states. Empirical research both by rationalists and by constructivists continues to unpack the interests and ideas of IOs such as the EU, WTO, IMF and World Bank.

The Constructivist Organisational Culture Approach

Constructivists agree with advocates of the P–A model that many relatively autonomous IOs in the international system, such as the IMF and the World Bank, are capable of acting independently. However, they question whether this is based on the self-interest of the IO or based on its organisational culture (Barnett and Finnemore 1999). Constructivists began to document the power of IOs by tracing how the autonomous actions of IOs led to the spread of new international norms such as the World Bank addressing poverty in international development. This power stems from two sources: the fact that IOs are considered legitimate international actors on the basis of their **rational–legal authority** as bureaucracies; and their control over **technical expertise** and information.

That IOs have rational–legal authority is based on their role as independent and impartial bureaucracies comprised of international civil servants whose primary allegiance is not to states' national interest but to the mandate of the IO. This often gives them an independent and valued voice in international debates, compared with states seeking to protect their national interest. IOs also have extensive technical expertise in particular areas, such as climate change through the Intergovernmental Panel on Climate Change (IPCC), to which states often defer.

Rational–legal authority and technical expertise provide IOs with **authority** in addition to the delegated authority provided by states and moral authority derived from taking a normative stand in debates over human rights, for example. Constructivists argue that authority is a social construction that does not exist outside of social interactions. Authority is conferred, meaning that some form of consent from other actors is required in order for it to be recognised. IOs are given authority when they are granted the right to speak and when their statements are deferred to as credible. Other views may be voiced, but they do not receive the same hearing as an authoritative voice. Constructivists argue that authority is important not just because it is a force for getting people to act but also because it tells actors what the right thing to do is.

Indeed, IO authority may shape states' understanding and interests, and IOs may promote certain norms and practices among states that may lead to unanticipated effects. It is important to examine IOs in their own right because they are able to shape the international agenda, and may socialise states into certain ways of thinking and behaving. IOs can do so through forming international regimes, defining discourses, enforcing rules and mediating conflict between states. IOs can also determine which state and non-state actors' interests are legitimate, for example through recognising states as sovereign in the UN as well as accrediting NGOs. This legitimising role, along with their ability to shape international politics, makes IOs purposive actors. The interests of IOs therefore need to be analysed independently of states' interests as a result of their expertise, authority and norm-diffusing and -legitimising roles.

Even as independent autonomous actors, IOs may still be structured to reflect unequal power relations between states. This means that IOs may be hardwired to reflect the interests of powerful states. However, this does not mean that they share the same beliefs. Scholars have begun to probe the extent to which **organisational culture** shapes the interests of an IO and determines how it behaves. Constructivists argue that rationalists do not identify how IOs' preferences are formed, leaving much ground unexamined in analysing change within IOs. Explanations of IOs' behaviour should therefore take ideas into account. This is because the staff of IOs often have deeply internalised the mission of the IO they work for, whether they be prosecutors for the International Criminal Court (ICC), doctors working for the WHO, or development economists working to free the world from poverty at the World Bank. The rationalist P–A model does not take into account the staff's personal belief in the IO's mission and how this may influence the IO's actions.

Constructivists prioritise the role of ideas in shaping an IO's actions and identity. This is not to downplay the role of strategic action in accounting for IO decision-making either in relation to external actors, such as member states and non-state actors, or in relation to internal bargaining among staff and management. Rather, constructivists focus on the identity or culture of the IO, which informs and shapes strategic action both within and outside the IO. Although we should not assume that IOs reflect powerful states' interests even if powerful states created the rules of the organisation in their favour, constructivists have identified cases in which IOs have been staffed mainly by nationals of powerful states. In other words, they have begun documenting instances where most of the staff come from powerful states or were predominantly educated in powerful states, thus sharing the same ideas and therefore interests as powerful states.

The direction of influence between powerful states and staff interests can only be determined through empirical questioning, not by making an assumption. For example, scholars have examined the role of the IMF's organisational culture, which is based on its staff's neoclassical economist training in US universities, in driving its emphasis on capital account liberalisation. That emphasis occurs despite this policy being neither within the IO's mandate nor driven by the demands of its powerful member states such as the United States. This norm flowed up from staff to management and member states rather than being dictated to the organisation by the member states on the IMF's Board (Chwieroth 2008).

Other examples also show when member states' demands and IMF management reform have been stalled in relation to the IMF's conditional lending measures as a result of the Fund's organisational culture (Momani 2005). Some research even points to the influence of the private sector rather than member states in shaping the IMF's conditionality for borrowers (Gould 2003). In sum, we need to examine whether ideas or interests shape IO decision-making and whether these ideas or interests come from inside or outside the organisation – and from whom.

An IO's actions may stem from the organisation's culture or how it thinks it should undertake its mandate. The reasoning for tackling an IO's mandate in a certain way is based on the dominant profession of the organisation. Organisational culture can lead IO staff to promote norms rather than implementing policies determined by management or member states, or it may prevent the organisation from changing and taking up new tasks. Organisational culture may lead to **pathological** or **dysfunctional** behaviour as the IO follows its internal approach to problem solving rather than properly addressing the issue. Organisational culture may also lead to **organised hypocrisy** as the IO attempts to continue its established practices despite pledging to member states that it will change its ways (Weaver 2008).

Some scholars, bridging the rationalist–constructivist divide, examine how principals can seek to change an IO's behaviour if the reforms they demand fit within the existing culture of the IO (Nielson *et al.* 2006). The central aim of constructivist theorising of IOs has been to understand how and why they behave the way they do and whether they are capable of change.

How does the constructivist organisational culture argument square with the idea of IOs as problem solvers? An IO's culture may make it more likely to be able to address issues that align with values held by the organisation. Even more importantly, an IO may propose to its member states that it should be authorised to undertake new work, given its technical expertise in solving the work problem it proposes. IOs may therefore attempt to frame a specific issue as a problem that only they can address.

Weaknesses of the approach include difficulties reconciling the focus on organisational culture when IOs' actions are clearly the result of material power from member states. Moreover, it is unclear whether constructivist research can be proven wrong or 'false', based as it is on determining an IO's action from its culture. For example, had the IO behaved another way in the same circumstance, would this too have been a result of its organisational culture? Falsifiability is a key concern for scholars seeking to build robust theories of IO behaviour and change. The various theories presented in this chapter all seek to identify what motivates IOs' actions and can be applied to the IOs that attempt to solve problems across a range of international issue areas.

Chapter Summary

Thus far we have identified the creation of functional and political IOs emerging in the nineteenth century as states became increasingly aware of the problems of co-existence and the need to regulate their international relations. IOs continued to proliferate throughout the twentieth century, ranging from particularistic to general-function IOs, from regional to universal IOs, and from forum to service-structured organisations.

Various theories seek to explain why and how states choose to create and use IOs rather than other forms of multilateralism: these theories include liberal, functionalist, neorealist and neoliberal institutionalist theories, the rationalist P–A model and constructivist organisational culture. Liberal and realist theories explain IOs through their lens on how the international system operates. Functionalism argued that IOs can contribute to international cooperation through enmeshing states in low-level interactions. Neofunctionalism predicted that this would lead to integration between states.

Both neorealism and neoliberal institutionalism view the international system as anarchic, but they differ over the likelihood of international cooperation. Yet neither focused on the actions and interests of IOs. Later IO-specific theories would unpack the behaviour of IOs through the P–A model and constructivist organisational culture. Each raises important issues for understanding and explaining IOs' behaviour.

Questions for Evaluating the Impact of IOs

We can extract from these theories a series of questions students should ask when examining whether IOs are capable of solving problems in the twenty-first century.

Assessing the Independent Role of IOs in Solving Problems

1. Did the organisation frame the problem to be tackled? (That is, did it define the problem and did this become the dominant understanding of the issue?)

2. Did states agree that there was a problem to be fixed?

3. What role did the IO play in brokering agreement between states in this issue area?

4. Did states agree that the problem was best solved by an IO (or more than one IO)?

5. Was the IO given sufficient resources to address the issue?

6. Was the IO given autonomy to address the problem?

7. What constraints were placed on the IO's discretion in solving the problem?

8. Does the problem fit within the mandate of the IO?

9. How does the IO's technical expertise and organisational culture shape the IO's response to the problem? (Did it help or hinder tackling the issue?)

10. Did states determine metrics for evaluating the IO's performance?

11. Was the timeframe for the activities of the IO sufficient for its operations to work?

12. What other actors are engaged in trying to solve the problem, and how do their efforts in tackling the problem compare?

13. Do competitor IOs or other organisations help or hinder how the IO is attempting to solve the problem?

14. Is there a way to measure the effectiveness of the IO's activities?

These questions provide a guide for students in examining how IOs enact their state-determined mandates and tackle international problems. These questions are practical means of testing international relations and IO-specific theories regarding the actions of IOs.

Guiding Questions

1. What is the classical liberal view of IOs?
2. Does classical realism recognise the role of IOs in international relations?
3. What is the main argument of functionalism?
4. How does neorealism differ from neoliberal institutionalism?
5. What are the benefits of IO-specific theories for explaining IOs' behaviour?

Further References

Liberal Theories on IOs

Abbott, K. W., and D. Snidal, 1998, 'Why States Act through Formal International Organizations', *Journal of Conflict Resolution* 42 (1): 3–33.

Haas, E. B., 1958, *The Uniting of Europe: Political, Social, and Economic Forces, 1950–1957*, Stanford, CA, Stanford University Press.

Haas, E. B., 1964, *Beyond the Nation-State: Functionalism and International Organization*, Stanford, CA, Stanford University Press.

Jervis, R., 1999, 'Realism, Neoliberalism, and Cooperation', *International Security* 24 (1): 42–63.

Kant, I., 1796, *Project for a Perpetual Peace: A Philosophical Essay*, London, Vernor and Hood.

Keohane, R. O., 1984, *After Hegemony: Cooperation and Discord in the World Political Economy*, Princeton, NJ, Princeton University Press.

Keohane, R. O., 1988, 'International Institutions: Two Approaches', *International Studies Quarterly* 32 (4): 379–396.

Lipson, C., 1991, 'Why Are Some International Agreements Informal?', *International Organization* 45 (4): 495–538.

Martin, L. L., 1992, 'Interests, Power, and Multilateralism', *International Organization* 46 (4): 765–792.

Martin, L. L., and B. Simmons, 1998, 'Theories and Empirical Studies of International Institutions', *International Organization* 52 (4): 729–757.

Mitrany, D., 1975, 'A Working Peace System' [1943], in D. Mitrany, *The Functional Theory of Politics*, London, London School of Economics and Political Science: 123–135.

Realist Theories on IOs

Grieco, J., 1990, *Cooperation among Nations: Europe, America and Non-Tariff Barriers to Trade*, Ithaca, NY, Cornell University Press.

Gruber, L., 2000, *Ruling the World: Power Politics and the Rise of Supranational Institutions*, Princeton, NJ, Princeton University Press.

Lebow, R. N., 2007, 'Classical Realism', in T. Dunne, M. Kurki and S. Smith (eds.), *International Relations Theories: Discipline and Diversity*, Oxford, Oxford University Press: 52–70.

Mearsheimer, J. J., 1994–1995, 'The False Promise of International Institutions', *International Security* 19 (3): 5–49.

Morgenthau, H. J., 1940, 'Positivism, Functionalism and International Law', *American Journal of International Law* 34: 260–284.

Morgenthau, H. J., 1966, *Politics among Nations: The Struggle for Power and Peace*, New York, Alfred A. Knopf.

Rosecrance, R., 2001. 'Has Realism Become Cost–Benefit Analysis? A Review Essay', *International Security* 26(2): 132–154.

Schweller, R. L., and D. Priess, 1997, 'A Tale of Two Realisms: Expanding the Institutions Debate', *Mershon International Studies Review* 41 (1): 1–32.

P–A Model Theories

Alter, K., 1998, 'Who Are the "Masters of the Treaty?" European Governments and the European Court of Justice', *International Organization* 59 (1): 121–147.

Elsig, M., 2010, 'Principal–Agent Theory and the World Trade Organization: Complex Agency and "Missing Delegation"', *European Journal of International Relations* 17 (3): 495–517.

Gutner, T., 2005a, 'Explaining the Gaps between Mandate and Performance: Agency Theory and World Bank Environmental Reform', *Global Environmental Politics* 5 (2): 10–37.

Gutner, T., and A. Thompson, 2010, 'The Politics of IO Performance: A Framework', *Review of International Organizations* 5 (3): 227–248.

Hawkins, D. G., D. A. Lake, D. L. Nielson and M. J. Tierney, 2006, *Delegation and Agency in International Organizations*, Cambridge, Cambridge University Press.

McCubbins, M. D., and T. Schwartz, 1984, 'Congressional Oversight Overlooked: Police Patrols versus Fire Alarms', *American Journal of Political Science* 28 (1): 165–179.

Nielson, D., and M. J. Tierney, 2003, 'Delegation to International Organisations: Agency Theory and World Bank Environmental Reform', *International Organization* 57 (2): 241–276.

Nielson, D., M. J. Tierney and C. Weaver, 2006, 'Bridging the Rationalist–Constructivist Divide: Re-engineering the Culture at the World Bank', *Journal of International Relations and Development* 9 (2): 107–139.

Pollack, M. A., 1997, 'Delegation, Agency and Agenda Setting in the European Community', *International Organization* 51 (1): 99–134.

Tallberg, J., 2000, 'The Anatomy of Autonomy: An Institutional Account of Variation in Supranational Influence', *Journal of Common Market Studies* 38 (5): 843–864.

Vaubel, R., A. Dreher and U. Soylu 2007, 'Staff Growth in International Organizations: A Principal–Agent Problem? An Empirical Analysis', *Public Choice* 133 (3–4): 275–295.

Constructivist IO Theories

Barnett, M., and M. Finnemore, 1999, 'The Politics, Power and Pathologies of IOs', *International Organization* 53 (4): 699–732.

Chwieroth, J., 2008, 'Normative Change from Within: The International Monetary Fund's Approach to Capital Account Liberalisation', *International Studies Quarterly* 52 (1): 129–158.

Finnemore, M., 1996, *National Interests in International Society*, Ithaca, NY, and London, Cornell University Press.

Momani, B., 2005, 'Limits on Streamlining Fund Conditionality: The International Monetary Fund's Organizational Culture', *Journal of International Relations and Development* 8 (2): 142–163.

Park, S., 2010, *The World Bank Group and Environmentalists: Changing International Organization Identities*, London, Manchester University Press.

Park, S., and A. Vetterlein, 2010, *Owning Development: Creating Global Policy Norms in the IMF and the World Bank*, Cambridge, Cambridge University Press.

Reinalda, B., and B. Verbeek (eds.), 1998, *Autonomous Policy Making by International Organizations*, London and New York, Routledge.

Weaver, C., 2008, *The Hypocrisy Trap: The World Bank and the Poverty of Reform*, Princeton, NJ, Princeton University Press.

3 Minimising and Halting Conflict

Introduction

IOs are considered both vital for the maintenance of international peace and security and ineffective in achieving it. How can they be both? This chapter examines the mandate, function and structure of the main UN apparatuses that deal with international security and disarmament: the General Assembly, the Security Council (UNSC) and the Secretary General. At the end of the **Cold War** the threat of nuclear war receded, but it became increasingly clear that conflicts were overwhelmingly taking place not between states but within them. The UN became overstretched by the sheer number of **intra-state conflicts** it sought to prevent or ameliorate. Regional organisations such as the African Union (AU, formerly the Organisation of African Unity) and the North Atlantic Treaty Organization (NATO) were increasingly asked to share the burden.

The chapter will assess the following issues.

- The mandate, function and structure of the UN General Assembly and Security Council, with a box on the Secretary General.
- The mandate, function and structure of NATO and the AU.
- The changing nature of weapons and **war** for how IOs recalibrate their actions to address new and emerging conflicts, including countering **terrorism**.
- The role of the International Atomic Energy Agency (IAEA) regarding the safe use of nuclear energy.
- The broadening of UN **peacekeeping** to **peace-enforcement**, post-conflict reconstruction and the **responsibility to protect**.
- The main IR and IO theoretical approaches that explain IOs' behaviour.
- The rise of **non-governmental organisations** (NGOs) and private military companies (PMCs) in promoting peace and mitigating conflict.

The Mandate, Function and Structure of the UN and Regional Security Organisations

The UN's founders envisaged an IO that could prevent another world war between states, yet the rise of nuclear weapons and the threat of **mutually assured destruction** between the superpowers sidelined the UN until the end of the **Cold War**. Since then the IO has had to grapple with the changing nature of conflict.

The United Nations

According to Article 1 of the Charter, the UN is mandated to maintain international peace and security (UN 1948a). It can do so through the following means:

- the peaceful settlement of disputes (Chapter VI of the Charter);
- the use of force (Chapter VII, Article 39);
- authorisation of enforcement by regional security IOs (Chapter VIII, Article 53);
- invocation of the UN's Trusteeship functions (Chapter XII; now defunct).

The UN functions as a **collective-security** IO, which sought to replace **balance-of-power** politics with an apparatus to deter aggression between **sovereign** states. Collective security goes beyond **alliances**. It transcends states' interests to maintain the international system for the greater good. The UN provides a credible threat that the overwhelming power of states acting together through the UN will enforce the peace.

The UN General Assembly

The UN General Assembly (UNGA) is a universal body. Its mandate is four-fold: to maintain international peace and security; to develop friendly relations among people according to equality and self-determination; to promote international cooperation concerning economic, social and cultural rights and promote human rights; and to harmonise relations between states (UN 1948a, Article 1). The UNGA's functions are laid out in Article 11 of the UN Charter. It may consider principles for international peace and security, and make recommendations to the Security Council, including identifying threats to the peace.

Its 193 member states each have one vote. The UNGA makes resolutions by two-thirds majority voting. Changes to the Charter require a two-thirds majority *including* the permanent members of the UNSC (see page **39**). The UNGA has a circumscribed role in addressing peace and conflict (see page **43**), but it controls the budget for security operations.

The United Nations Security Council

Only the UNSC has the power to make binding resolutions to which all UN members must adhere. Collective security differs from pacific settlement because it assigns moral guilt for a breach of the peace. Under Chapter V of the Charter, the UNSC was given the mandate to identify breaches of the peace, determine acts of aggression and identify an appropriate response. The UN's ability to authorise a response to aggressors using Chapter VII is the only legitimate use of force beyond states acting in self-defence (Article 51).

The UNSC functions to pass resolutions that include to

- investigate a situation that may lead to conflict;
- recommend that an agreement be reached between parties;
- dispatch a mission or special envoy to assist the parties;

- mediate between parties;
- establish a system for disarmament;
- delegate to the UN Secretary General to use his good offices to resolve a dispute;
- promote a ceasefire to defuse a conflict;
- send observers or peacekeepers to separate hostile forces;
- use diplomatic boycotts;
- impose economic sanctions;
- initiate arms embargoes;
- institute financial restrictions and travel bans;
- devise blockades;
- instigate the use of collective force;
- authorise regional security IO enforcement.

The UNSC is a forum IO for states to collectively respond to breaches of the peace. Beyond the functions outlined above, the UNSC can recommend the admission of new UN members; use the trusteeship function of the UN in strategic areas; recommend the appointment of the Secretary General to the UNGA; and, with the UNGA, elect judges for the International Court of Justice (see Chapter 4).

The UNSC has the power to back its resolutions. The Charter allows for detachments of national forces under the UNSC's direct command. Article 47 outlined a permanent Military Staff Committee, comprised of the **Great Powers**, to direct such forces. Owing to deep divisions in the UNSC arising from the Cold War, the Military Staff Committee is a minor subsidiary body that has never operated as intended.

Instead the UN has relied upon the voluntary contribution of forces from member states for peacekeeping operations (see pages 41–43). Article 48 provides room for the UNSC to authorise state-led coalitions to use force. Examples of US-led coalitions rather than UN-commanded forces have included actions in Korea (1950), Iraq–Kuwait (1990), Somalia (1992) and Haiti (1994). Other states have led coalitions, such as France in Rwanda (1994), Italy in Albania (1997) and Australia in East Timor (1999) (Roberts 2004). State-led coalitions have also been used with peacekeeping missions, such as that led by France in the Democratic Republic of Congo (2003).

Structurally, the UNSC has 15 members, five of which are permanent. The permanent members (P-5) were Great Powers when the UN was founded: Britain, China, France, the Soviet Union (now Russia) and the United States.

Ten non-permanent members are elected for two-year terms from the UNGA according to a system of regional representation. The UNSC's representation has been amended just once, after pressure from newly independent states in 1965, enlarging it from 11 to 15 member states.

The Council has resisted reform, despite repeated efforts to restructure it since its inception. Momentum for change built in preparation for the 2005 World Summit of UN members. Competing groups proposed to recast Council membership to better reflect the changing **balance of power** among states, such as the increased power of Japan, Germany, Brazil and India. These proposals failed to garner the two-thirds of the UNGA vote (including the P-5) required in order for them to be adopted. An inability to agree on which states should be added to the Council, and their permanent or non-permanent status, left the Council unchanged. However, there have been improvements in transparency, accountability and interactions with non-Council members and non-state actors as a result of World Summit preparations.

The UNSC and the Cold War

The UNSC's decisions are based on the principle of 'Great Power unanimity', otherwise known as the veto of the P-5. A resolution becomes binding only if nine members of the UNSC vote in favour, *including* all of the P-5. One of the results of this design was that the Cold War hamstrung the UNSC. The United States and the Soviet Union would not countenance the other's interference in their respective spheres of influence, invoking a veto whenever this occurred. For example, the Soviets vetoed any UNSC resolution regarding their intervention in Afghanistan in 1979, while the United States' involvement in Vietnam did not even go to the Council for consideration.

Initially, the Soviet Union was by far the most frequent user of the veto. Up until 1970, the Soviet Union had used its veto 105 times, the UK four times, France three times and China twice. The United States used its veto for the first time in March 1970 (Claude 1971). Since 1970 the United States has been the most frequent user of the veto. China primarily relied on abstentions during the Cold War to indicate its opposition to a resolution.

As a result, the UNSC used its Chapter VII powers just twice during the Cold War: first in Korea in 1950 when the Soviet Union boycotted the Council, and second in the Congo in 1961 after a peace operation (see pages 41–42). The UNGA adopted the 'Uniting for Peace' resolution, which articulated the UNGA's ability to recommend a collective response to escalating situations when the Council was deadlocked. It passed resolutions to hold 10 emergency special sessions with regard to peacekeeping under this resolution, regarding the Suez Canal in 1956, Hungary in 1956, the Congo in 1960 and the Middle East at various times.

While the use of force was stymied, the UNSC would authorise a range of activities under Chapter VI provisions, including peacekeeping, arms embargoes and economic sanctions. Yet these too were infrequent. There were only 15 peacekeeping missions in the UN's first 40 years. In comparison, between 1988 and 1998 25 peacekeeping missions were approved. The Council used economic sanctions just twice: against white rule in Southern Rhodesia (Zimbabwe) and against apartheid South Africa.

The UNSC and the Post-Cold-War Period

After the Cold War the Council was reinvigorated. Between 1946 and 1989 the UNSC passed an annual average of 15 resolutions. From 1990 the Council passed an annual average of 60 (Wallensteen and Johansson 2004). The use of the veto also declined significantly: it was used 188 times before 1990 but only 38 times between 1990 and November 2017. Decisions were increasingly passed by consensus. Yet the newly resurgent Council began to respond to a greater number of conflicts that did not fit UN answers to inter-state conflicts or peacekeeping.

The UNSC and Peacekeeping

There is no reference to peacekeeping in the Charter, with its remit falling somewhere between Chapter VI on pacific settlement and Chapter VII on the use of force. In the 1990s peacekeeping was referred to as being authorised under Chapter '6½'. The Secretary General, Dag Hammarskjöld, was asked to respond to the 1956 Suez Canal crisis, which involved the UK, France, Israel and Egypt. The UN Emergency Force (UNEF, 1956–1967) passed by the UNGA had the following provisions that would become guidelines for classical peacekeeping: that the UN force would keep the peace between states; that there would be no P-5 troops committed; that there would be consent of the host state for the force; that the force would be impartial with regard to the conflict; and that it would use force only as a means for self-defence.

During the Cold War most peace operations were to keep the peace between states (Palestine, Cyprus, Kashmir). There were two examples of limited force: UNEF, noted above, and the Congo (ONUC, 1960–1964). ONUC's mandate was expanded to include the use of force to prevent civil war. It was unable to do so, and ONUC remains the peacekeeping mission with the highest number of fatalities from malicious acts (attacks on UN troops).

In the post-Cold War period the UN was increasingly asked to intervene in **intra-state** war: internal conflicts that involved transnational actors and could destabilise regions. Frequently there was no peace to keep. UN 'Blue Helmets' were deployed in conflicts with irregular forces rather than soldiers, where the main victims and targets were women and children. These conflicts often led to humanitarian emergencies.

These 'second-generation' peacekeeping efforts involved imposing ceasefires and controlling buffer zones, as well as humanitarian operations and subsequent efforts regarding national reconciliation and state-building. The UNSC began to use force for humanitarian purposes, beginning in 1991 to protect the Kurdish minority in northern Iraq. This would be followed by operations in Somalia, Rwanda, Bosnia, Haiti and Kosovo.

In the immediate post-Cold War period the UNSC was able to demonstrate positive outcomes: ending conflicts in the Iran–Iraq war, Namibia, Cambodia and Haiti. In 1992 UN Secretary General Boutros Boutros-Ghali presented his *Agenda for Peace* plan, which envisaged that peacekeepers could be given **peace-enforcement** powers under Chapter VII, including the prospect of a standing army under UN command.

Yet peacekeeping efforts soon began to fail. The UN was unable to stop the war in Somalia in 1992, after expanding its mandate to use force for humanitarian purposes. During the mission, UN troops were killed in conflict with the forces of the warlord Mohamed Farrah Aidid, including members of the US armed forces whose bodies were dragged through the streets. The UN was unable to stop the resumption of the Angolan civil war in 1992 that killed 300,000 people. It withdrew troops from Rwanda in 1994, providing no obstruction to **genocide** (see Chapter 4). Peacekeeping forces were given limited capacity, with horrific outcomes when men and boys were exterminated in UN-designated 'safe havens' as part of a campaign of **ethnic cleansing** during the Bosnian war in 1995. By 1997 Boutros-Ghali's *Supplement to the Agenda for Peace* had to recant on peace-enforcement provisions.

In response, the Secretary General created a Panel on United Nations Peace Operations. The 2000 Brahimi report recommended 'robust peacekeeping' provisions that would enable peacekeepers to defend themselves and protect civilians when necessary. In 2004 the report was followed up by the High-Level Panel on Threats, Challenges and Change (HLP). The HLP recommended the current practice of giving both peacekeeping and peace-enforcement operations Chapter VII mandates.

There have been 71 peacekeeping missions between 1948 and October 2017, 15 of which are currently active. The 15 active missions involve over 106,000 personnel from 125 states; 77,203 of these are troops. The UN's annual peace-keeping budget from mid 2017 to mid 2018 is $6.8 billion. The role of the UN Secretary General is pivotal to peacekeeping missions (Box 3.1).

Box 3.1 The UN Secretary General (UNSG) and Conflict

The Secretary General is the chief administrative officer of the UN, who is appointed by the UNGA upon the recommendation of the UNSC for a five-year term. The Secretary General's functions are broad: to uphold the values and principles of the UN, and act as a spokesperson for the peoples of the world. The Secretary General has the power to bring to the UNSC's attention any matter that could threaten international peace and security (Article 99). The Secretary General performs functions the UN organs give them, including the use of their 'good offices' to undertake mediation to prevent a conflict.

Located in New York, the Secretary General oversees the UN Secretariat, which employs over 9,000 people worldwide. The Secretary General chairs the UN System Chief Executives Board for Coordination (CEB), which comprises the Executive Heads of all UN funds, programmes and agencies. They meet biannu-ally to further coordination and cooperation across the UN. The Secretary General reports to the UNGA annually.

Since Dag Hammarskjöld's term, the Secretary General has been given oper-ational control of peacekeeping missions. In 1992 the Department of Peacekeep-ing Operations (DPKO) was created to provide executive direction, which had previously been managed in an ad hoc way. The DPKO maintains relations between the troop-contributing member states, financial contributors, the UNSC and actors involved in the conflict. Its budget is derived from a formula set by the UNGA for member-state contributions. After the Brahimi report (see page 42) the DPKO was expanded to over 500 staff, and, although its capacity was increased to respond to complex situations, it was not enough for the volume of requests. Secretary General Ban Ki-moon increased the staffing of the DPKO further, and separated its activities from the Department of Field Support in 2007. Since then it has developed operational guidelines, and improved peacekeeping training and logistical support.

The UNSC and Ongoing Politicisation

The Security Council remains highly politicised. For example, in 1998 a war broke out when the Serbian government threatened ethnic cleansing against the 90 per cent ethnic Albanian population in its semi-autonomous province of Kosovo. The UNSC members were divided. NATO (see pages 46–47) undertook an illegal, non-UNSC-authorised operation for humanitarian purposes. Although this was illegal, many argued that it was a legitimate measure to protect ethnic Albanians. Later the UN Secretary General would implicitly endorse NATO's actions, and authorised state-building activities to support Kosovo's independence.

Not long after, the United States would demand the invasion of Iraq on the basis of its failure to implement its disarmament requirements from the 1990–1991 Gulf War. In the aftermath of the 11 September 2001 terrorist attacks on the United States, this was widely seen as a means to oust dictator Saddam Hussein for his ties to terrorists and for Iraq's ongoing **weapons-of-mass-destruction** (WMD) programme. The UNSC was again divided. In 2003 the United States and a coalition of the willing invaded without UNSC authorisation. Without accepting the invasion, the UN would later engage in post-conflict rebuilding. As with conflicts in Darfur in Sudan (2003–) and Syria (2011–) (see pages 45–46), the UNSC remains divided over authorising the use of force in cases of concern to the Great Powers.

UNSC Activities

The post-Cold War period witnessed an increase in all UNSC activities. The dramatic increase in the use of sanctions during the 1990s led it to be labelled the sanctions decade (Malone 2004a). The use of sanctions against Iraq for invading Kuwait in 1990 would be criticised for not having its intended effect and for being harmful to local populations. In response the UN created an Oil-for-Food programme to ensure that Iraqis could access humanitarian assistance. However, this would enable the black market to flourish in Iraq and enable corruption within the Iraqi government, by private firms and even within the UN. Later, targeted 'smart' sanctions would be devised.

Beyond pacific settlement and the use of force, the UNSC has authorised investigative commissions, ad hoc criminal tribunals (see Chapter 4), judicial tribunals and sanctions committees. It has created over 25 subsidiary bodies to further reporting, monitoring and standardising of members' responses to resolutions. These include adopting anti-terrorism measures (such as Resolution 1373) and domestic controls on the spread of WMD (Resolution 1540). These overlap with the UNGA's committees.

The UNSC and the Responsibility to Protect

In 2001, the International Commission on Intervention and State Sovereignty, a Canadian initiative, released a report on the **responsibility to protect** (R2P). It argued that states have the responsibility to protect their citizens, but, where they are unable or unwilling to do so, then the principle of non-intervention yields to the international responsibility to protect (ICISS 2001).

R2P includes preventing and reacting to humanitarian crises, and rebuilding states that are no longer functioning. R2P aimed to overcome deadlocks in the UNSC over whether and when to intervene, but also to prevent humanitarian intervention being abused by states for other purposes. It detailed six criteria for the use of force for humanitarian interventions:

1. that it be undertaken by the right authority;
2. that it be undertaken for a just cause (see page 55);
3. that it be undertaken for the right intention;
4. that it should be a last resort;
5. that the means used should be proportional to the situation and the ends;
6. that it should be undertaken with reasonable prospects for success.

At the World Summit in 2005, 150 UN member states endorsed R2P. UN members articulated that the UNSC has the competence to authorise humanitarian intervention but does not have a duty to do so. In other words, member states gave the UNSC the power to enact R2P, without making it mandatory.

During this period mass human rights violations and ethnic cleansing were well under way in Darfur in Sudan. While all recognised the crisis as a case befitting R2P, there was little real effort to act. Repeated resolutions responding to Darfur would be opposed by Russia and China until they allowed the case to be referred to the ICC (see Chapter 4) and agreed to a weak joint mission with the AU.

Where R2P has been invoked is Libya (2011). The UNSC authorised an invasion of Libya to halt Muammar Gadhafi's attacks on his own people. Yet the UNSC did not authorise the use of force in neighbouring Syria, despite the conditions being similar. Since then, Syria has been mired in a civil war, with factions backed by the Great Powers and various regional powers, with evidence of the use of chemical weapons by the Assad regime against people living in areas not under government control. Over 400,000 people have died in the conflict (United Nations 2018). Over 5.5 million have fled, contributing to the largest wave of refugees since the founding of the UNHCR in 1950. Russia, frequently backed by China, has refused to allow UN intervention in the conflict, despite a UNGA 2012 resolution requesting it.

The Mandate, Structure and Function of NATO

In contrast to the UN, NATO is a **collective-defence** organisation. It was created in 1949 to serve the North Atlantic Alliance between the United States and 11 Western European states, and its primary mandate is to defend the peace and security of its members against attack. The North Atlantic Alliance is the most enduring and successful regional alliance, now comprised of 29 states. Under the Washington Treaty, parties agreed to respond individually or collectively to any attack on a member (Washington Treaty, Article 5). Article 5 has only been invoked once: in response to the 2001 terrorist attacks against the United States (see page 51). This was also the first time that NATO was deployed outside the Euro-Atlantic region, in Afghanistan.

The Alliance aimed to serve three purposes: deter aggression by the Soviet Union; contain militarism in Europe; and encourage European integration (NATO 2017). The Alliance is credited with avoiding direct conflict with the Soviet Union. In the post-Cold War period it expanded its core tasks to include crisis management and **cooperative security**. Crisis management refers to non-Article 5 operations that have included interventions in Bosnia, Kosovo, Macedonia, Iraq, Sudan, Somalia and Libya, as well as providing relief after natural disasters in Europe.

NATO functions to enable member states to cooperate and coordinate their political and military actions. There is no voting. All decisions, at every committee level of the organisation, are made by consensus amongst the member states. Given their ongoing interactions, decisions can be made swiftly. Each member is represented at NATO headquarters by an Ambassador. The peak decision-making body is the North Atlantic Council on which the Ambassadors sit. It meets weekly or as needed, with states' ministers attending biannually. The Secretary General chairs the Council. An alternative body, the Nuclear Planning Group, is the primary body for nuclear weapons. The Secretary General helms the IO and facilitates cooperation among the members, implements their decisions, and oversees staff.

NATO's Military Committee provides advice to the North Atlantic Council and the Nuclear Planning Group. The Military Committee is comprised of member states' Chiefs of Defence. The Military Committee works closely with NATO's two Strategic Commanders: the Supreme Allied Commander Europe and the Supreme Allied Commander Transformation. They are responsible for all military conduct.

NATO has been considered a success in being able to respond quickly to crisis situations. Yet it has been heavily criticised for seeking a new mandate when the Cold War ended, although a resurgent Russia has renewed interest in meeting its original purpose. After 1991, NATO began to reach out to Russia in an attempt to decrease tensions, while accepting as new members former Warsaw Pact states that met its values of democracy, liberty and the rule of law.

Although NATO was invigorated by its operations in Bosnia and Kosovo, its efforts in Afghanistan (2003–present) revealed a reluctance among European states with regard to participation in the war, and the uneven military capability of European members compared with the United States. Its operations in Iraq divided Europe, while its intervention in Libya was viewed as a war, not a humanitarian operation. NATO remains a contested IO for providing peace and security beyond Europe, but it is one of the most powerful IOs ready to act in the face of threats to international security.

Mandate, Structure and Function of the African Union

The Organisation of African Unity (OAU) was created in 1963 by newly independent African states with a broad mandate similar to that of the UN, including peace and security, and economic integration. The OAU did not have a strong focus on peace and security during the Cold War as it focused on defending members' newly granted state sovereignty, especially territorial integrity, through the principle of **non-interference**.

While it attempted to respond to crises in the 1990s, it was limited by its organisational structure and capacity. In 2002 the OAU was restructured as the AU to respond to the dramatic increase in intra-state conflict, backed by the realisation that the UN was unable to address African problems.

The AU was given not one mandate but 14:

1. achieve unity among African states;
2. defend their sovereignty;
3. promote their political and economic integration;

4. defend common African positions;
5. encourage international cooperation;
6. promote continental peace and security;
7. promote democratic principles;
8. promote and protect human rights;
9. establish conditions for international economic engagement;
10. promote sustainable development;
11. promote cooperation to achieve higher living standards;
12. harmonise with regional economic communities to achieve the Union's objectives;
13. facilitate research and development in science and technology;
14. work with international partners to eradicate disease and promote good health (AU Constitutive Act: 2000, Article 3).

As can been seen from its multifaceted mandate, the AU covers all interactions between member states and those outside the AU. It functions both as a forum IO and as a service one, with a range of sub-committees designed to further its work. The AU's structures borrow from the EU (see Chapter 8) and the UN. The AU was to have nine main organs.

(1) The Assembly is the primary decision-making body. All 55 African states are members, represented equally (as with the other organs). It determines the overall policy direction. Votes are passed consensually or by a two-thirds majority.

There are concerns that the decision-making process is chaotic and that states lack the political will to enforce decisions once they have been made. The Assembly has been unable to respond effectively to members' internal instability, including the cases of Madagascar in 2002, Zimbabwe in 2008, Libya in 2011 and Egypt in 2011 and 2013. There are also no procedures for implementing its R2P (see page 45).

(2) The Executive Council is made up of the member states' Ministers of Foreign Affairs. The Executive is responsible for implementing a broad range of activities delegated to it by the Assembly. Membership and voting rules are the same as for the Assembly.

(3) A Permanent Representatives Committee is to facilitate the work of the Executive Council.

(4) The AU Commission is the secretariat of the IO under the Chairperson. The Commission undertakes the everyday operations of the AU.

There is concern that power in the AU has become centralised in the secretariat, with decisions regarding peace and security coming from here rather than the Peace and Security Council (see below, page 49). Operational problems continue to hamper its effectiveness (Makinda *et al.* 2016).

(5) The Constitutive Act provided for a range of Specialised Technical Committees, although many of them have yet to be realised.

(6) The AU's Economic, Social and Cultural Council (ECOSOCC) was established in 2004 to have advisory powers, and is comprised of civil society groups. ECOSOCC can provide input into the Executive Council, which prepares items for Assembly summits.

(7) A Pan-African Parliament, which has been ratified by 50 member states. The Parliament is currently made up of over 260 members elected by their own parliaments. The Parliament has a mandate to provide advice and consultation to the Assembly and ECOSOCC.

It first met in 2004. It has yet to acquire legislative powers similar to those of the European Parliament.

(8) The Constitutive Act also provides for a Court of Justice.

The AU has oversight of the African Commission on Human and Peoples' Rights (which upholds the African Charter on Human and Peoples' Rights) and the African Court of Human and Peoples' Rights, which was ratified in 2005. In 2008 the African Court of Human and Peoples' Rights was merged with the Court of Justice of the African Union to become the African Court of Justice and Human Rights. It has yet to be ratified.

(9) The Constitutive Act envisaged financial institutions to further African integration, such as an African Central Bank, an African Investment Bank and an African Monetary Fund, but these have not yet been established.

The AU organs are ambitious and require a long-term commitment to integration, the rule of law, democracy, human rights and good governance. The AU's primary difficulty is a dire lack of resources (from member states' assessed contributions and voluntary funding) and the political will to realise its integration objectives.

The Peace and Security Council (PSC) was created by protocol in 2004 to be the collective security arm of the AU, with a mandate for the prevention, management and resolution of conflicts. The PSC's remit is far-reaching, encompassing an early-warning system, peace-building, peacekeeping and enforcement. It surpasses the OAU by allowing a stand-by force and intervention. Intervention can be agreed upon only in grave circumstances, specifically war crimes, genocide and crimes against humanity. The Council meets in continuous session, and is comprised of 15 members with seats allocated by regional representation and national rotation. They are elected by the Executive and endorsed by the Assembly. The organ operates at summit, minister and ambassador levels.

As the primary security unit within the AU, the PSC has undertaken peace operations in Burundi (2003–2004), Sudan (2004–present), the Comoros (2006, 2008) and Somalia (2007–present), with a short stint in Mali (2013). Except for the Comoros, the AU has either transitioned operations over to the UN or worked with the UN and other regional IOs (in Sudan). Owing to the AU's lack of trained peacekeepers, equipment and logistical support, the UN agreed to strengthen its capacity to undertake peace operations.

The Problem: The Changing Nature of Weapons and Conflict

The problem for peace and security IOs is the changing technology used for warfare and the changing nature of conflict. The UN was created in response to **war** between states. However, the UN was impeded almost from its inception by the threat of nuclear weapons and the Cold War (see pages 51–52), and by the proliferation of **intra-state** conflict.

Intra-state Conflict

Intra-state conflict was the predominant form of conflict in the post-1945 period. Intra-state wars include those fought against foreign occupants, those fought by separatist minorities and those fought against native incumbents. Many of these were wars of independence such as the French wars in Algeria and Vietnam. Once they had become independent, many new states were unstable, leading to civil wars. In all of these cases control of the state is usually the prime goal. The tactics and technology used for these wars differ. There are few decisive battles; combat is characterised by attrition, terror, psychology and actions against civilians. Wars are fought by mercenaries, trained soldiers, professional killers, volunteers, terrorists, criminals and civilians, including children. Wars depend on groups acquiring external support for arms and finance, or they battle for resources to fund their efforts. Weapons include conventional light arms, anti-personnel landmines, rocket launchers and bombs such as improvised explosive devices (IEDs).

Since the end of WWII conflicts have overwhelmingly been intra-state rather than inter-state conflicts (Pettersson and Wallensteen 2015: 539). Yet the number of intra-state wars has declined. Between 1989 and 2002, 100 conflicts ended peacefully. Until the terrorist attack of 11 September 2001 against the United States, the majority of the UN's efforts in the post-Cold War period had been directed towards peacekeeping.

Terrorism

On 11 September 2001, al-Qaeda, a terrorist network that espouses a radical interpretation of the Koran that advocates Jihad (holy war), hijacked commercial airlines and used them as suicide bombs by crashing them into the World Trade Center in New York, the Pentagon in Washington, D.C., and a field in Pennsylvania (it is thought that the hijackers of this aircraft had intended to target the White House). This is considered to be the largest terrorist attack in modern history, killing nearly 3,000 people in the World Trade Center alone. On 12 September 2001 the UNSC legitimised the United States' right to self-defence in Resolution 1368. The United States invaded Afghanistan on intelligence that it was harbouring al-Qaeda.

From 1948 the UNSC's response to terrorist attacks had been on a case-by-case basis. Resolutions on terrorism were punitive and employed sanctions. These would be monitored by the 1267 Committee (named after the resolution). In 1999 the UNSC went beyond these measures, passing Resolution 1269 to condemn all terrorist acts and calling on all member states to adopt conventions against terrorism and refrain from activities that might aid terrorists. This would be backed by a more strongly worded resolution, Resolution 1368, after 2001, which also created the UNSC's Counter-Terrorism Committee (CTC). The CTC would be further institutionalised by Resolution 1535, by creating a Counter-Terrorism Executive Directorate, which was operationalised in 2005, that increased its powers and staffing.

Nuclear Weapons

The United States dropped atomic bombs on Japan six weeks after the signing of the UN Charter. Over the decades the relationship between the Soviet Union and the United States waxed and waned, but was maintained on the basis of the nuclear deterrent stopping outright conflict. The fear throughout the Cold War was that intervention of the superpowers in intra-state wars in Africa, Asia, the Middle East and Latin America (proxy wars) could trigger outright conflict leading to nuclear annihilation.

By 1964 all of the UNSC's P-5 had acquired nuclear weapons. In order to stop the nuclear arms race from spreading, the P-5 promoted the nuclear Non-Proliferation Treaty (NPT). The NPT, which was opened for signature in 1968, entered into force in 1970. It is a landmark international treaty, which aims to prevent the spread of nuclear weapons and technology, to promote cooperation in the peaceful use of nuclear energy, and to achieve nuclear disarmament by the nuclear-weapon states.

Over time, other states would attempt to acquire such weapons, including Israel, Iran, Iraq, Libya and North Korea. The NPT served as a buffer: by agreeing not to seek nuclear weapons, non-nuclear signatories would be able to gain the benefits of nuclear energy (see Box 3.2). A total of 191 parties have joined the NPT. It is the most universal arms limitation and disarmament agreement. However, in 1998 both India and Pakistan set off nuclear tests. Neither of them contravened the NPT because they were not party to the convention.

Box 3.2 The International Atomic Energy Agency

The IAEA was created in 1957 during the nuclear arms race. Under the auspices of the UN, the IAEA is mandated to facilitate atomic energy for peace, health and prosperity throughout the world. Nuclear technology is 'dual-use', meaning that it can be used for peaceful nuclear energy or to build weapons. The IAEA was given seven functions, namely to

1. facilitate research and the application of atomic energy for peaceful purposes;
2. provide the material, services, equipment and facilities for research and development on atomic energy and its use;
3. foster the scientific exchange of information;
4. encourage the exchange and training of scientists;
5. establish and administer safeguards for ensuring fissionable and other materials are not used for military purposes;
6. design and implement safety standards for public health;
7. acquire facilities needed to implement its activities.

The IAEA is based in Vienna and is comprised of over 4,000 staff headed by a Director General. The organisation has 169 member states that comprise the General Conference, with equal votes. The Board of Governors is the main decision-making body. The Director General is under the authority of the Board. The Board has 35 members, constituted by the 10 members most advanced in atomic energy technology plus the members most advanced in the technology of atomic energy by region.

Like other UN agencies, the IAEA's budget is derived from member states' assessed contributions, which fund its regular budget, and the extrabudgetary commitments which are volunteered by members and other donors. Its 2017 budget was €359.3 million, which is zero real growth over its 2016 budget (IAEA 2017). The Director General has previously noted that starving the IAEA will impede its ability to meet its mandate (Brown 2015).

As a technical agency, the IAEA has discretion in verifying states' commitments to the peaceful use of nuclear energy and upholding the NPT and other WMD conventions. There is evidence that using the IAEA to spread dual-use technology places states within reach of acquiring nuclear weapon capacity, which would otherwise have remained far beyond their capability (Fuhrmann 2012).

The IO hit the international headlines when the United States and Britain argued that Iraq had WMD and should be invaded. The UNSC passed Resolution 1441 to send into Iraq the IAEA weapons inspectors, who had withdrawn in 1998 after destroying its nuclear weapons programme. The IAEA reported to the UNSC that there was no evidence of a resumption of a WMD programme. The Director General, Mohamed ElBaradei, and the IAEA secretariat won the Nobel Peace Prize in 2005 for withstanding pressure in order to try to prevent war.

With the unravelling of the Soviet Union, fears escalated that nuclear and other WMD could fall into the hands of rogue states or terrorists. Concerns over the acquisition of nuclear weapons by actors that previously did not possess them have become a central concern to policy-makers around the world. In 2017 the Nuclear Weapon Ban Treaty was passed, and it is now open for signature by states.

Most negotiations for arms reduction take place outside the UNSC but may be backed by UN sanctions. For example, in 2015 the United States, UK, Russia, France, China and Germany reached an agreement to lift economic sanctions against Iran if it stopped its ongoing efforts to develop advanced nuclear industrial capabilities consistent with a weapons programme.

Disarmament

The UN Charter references disarmament only three times (Articles 11, 26 and 47). Instead, the collective use of force was seen to be the primary means for ensuring peace. The UN has a Disarmament Commission that began under the UNSC in 1952 to prepare treaty proposals on disarmament. In 1960 it was devolved to the UNGA to prepare disarmament recommendations. The Commission is supported by the Office for Disarmament Affairs, which was established in 1982. Even after the Cold War, no agreement has been reached by the Commission. Where disarmament has become prominent over the past 20 years is in peacekeeping operations: UN missions seek to disarm, demobilise and reintegrate forces after conflict.

The UN is a visible forum to discuss arms limitation conventions, including the Convention on Anti-personnel Landmines (1997), the Cluster Munitions Convention (2010) and the Arms Trade Treaty (2014). In 2015 the UNGA passed a resolution on small and light arms. Owing to their exceptional impact, states have signed specific conventions against the use of chemical, biological and nuclear weapons. Non-proliferation conventions also include the Seabed Arms Control Treaty (1972), an Outer Space Treaty (1967) and the Partial (1963) and Comprehensive Nuclear Test Ban Treaties (the latter has not entered into force since the UNGA adopted it in 1996).

The majority of weapons stockpile reductions have been agreed bilaterally between the superpowers, such as by means of the Strategic Offensive Reductions Treaty (SORT) in 2002, which established bilateral strategic nuclear arms reductions. These bilateral efforts would be endorsed by UNSC Resolution 1540 and its subsequent committee in 2004 to prevent the spread of WMD to terrorists. These would be backed by Resolutions 1566 and 1624 further specifying member states' obligations.

Explaining Peace and Security IOs' Behaviour

The main theoretical explanations for peace and security IOs' behaviour tend to rest on IR theories. However, more recent work uses the P–A model to explain their behaviour, and there are nuanced organisational culture accounts that deepen our understanding of the organisational constraints under which decisions are made.

IR Theory Accounts of Peace and Security IOs' Behaviour

The UN was built on **liberal internationalist** ideals. It makes a moral determination as to when a conflict is just. In modern international law there are only two just reasons for states to use force. The first is self-defence against aggression (Article 51 of the UN Charter). The second is the principle of collective security enshrined in Chapter VII (Articles 41 and 42) of the UN Charter.

The just recourse to war or **jus ad bellum** includes the following components. The state should have a just intention. The state should publicly declare why war is necessary, and how war might be ended. War is just if it is considered a last resort. War is not just if there is no reasonable hope of success. Killing is acceptable if the reason for war is lawful. There should be a reasonable link between the objectives for war and the means to achieve them. States should accept peace once their objectives have been achieved. Other components to just war are based on the means through which war is waged (**jus in bello**).

IR theories have attempted to identify when states choose to cooperate through IOs such as the UN to achieve their interests. Throughout the Cold War realpolitik was evident. Peace and security IOs were sidelined as the primary vehicles for determining whether to go to war. States were engaged in **security dilemmas** as a result of which conflict was deemed inevitable. Liberalism was considered idealistic. Liberal internationalist sentiments surged in the post-Cold War period but deflated after UN failures. The unilateralist bent of the United States under Presidents George W. Bush and Trump reinforced perceptions that the UN and NATO remain tools to be used by the powerful only when it suits them. Most evidently, power politics impedes reform of the UNSC.

Liberal internationalist arguments regarding the UN have articulated the importance of the UNSC for bestowing legitimacy (Hurd 2005) even when it is constrained in its problem-solving capacity (Prantl 2005).

The UN can be used to help sway states to accept the hegemon's determinations (Thompson 2006). The UN provides a forum for powerful states to justify their position to less powerful states. The United States went to great lengths to justify its intention to invade Iraq in the UNSC rather than bypass it. In 2003 the United States built a legal case for war that was based on past UNSC resolutions. For liberal internationalists this demonstrates the importance of the UN: in previous decades exhortations by the hegemon in the UN were unnecessary.

International cooperation on peace and security reveals bargaining as per **neorealism** and **neoliberal institutionalism**. Owing to the importance of the UNSC's stamp of approval, powerful states will trade aid for votes in their favour on the UN Security Council (Vreeland and Dreher 2014). The US invasion of Iraq also divided Europe, raising questions as to the strength of the North Atlantic Alliance and European states' dependence on the US security umbrella. This raised the question of relative or absolute gains for maintaining the alliance. In using NATO to legitimise the US intervention in Afghanistan, the extent to which European allies free-ride on US military capability was also revealed.

However, the biggest debate over the role of peace and security IOs came from the neorealist attack on NATO. After the Cold War, leading neorealist John Mearsheimer (1994–1995) wrote that NATO should either disappear or reconstitute itself in the light of the changing balance of power. In fact, neither occurred, although NATO did expand to take on new members and missions. This demonstrated the weakness of the neorealist articulation of institutions, and shored up the neoliberal institutionalist position that IOs can facilitate long-term cooperation at the expense of short-term gains.

Meanwhile, constructivists have argued that collective ideas can create **security communities**. Constructivists argue that IOs like NATO and ASEAN exemplify a new means through which security dilemmas can be overcome (Acharya 2001; Deutsch 1957). Cooperating within IOs enables states to transcend suspicion to create shared understandings and identities that embrace peaceful means for resolving disputes.

Explaining Peace and Security IOs' Behaviour through IO-Specific Theories

P–A model scholars have examined how states interact with peace and security IOs. For example, international relations scholars David Auerswald and Stephen Saideman (2014) argue that NATO's military operations in Afghanistan can only be understood through the constraints contributing states placed on their forces within the NATO alliance. In Afghanistan, extensive principal oversight determined that troops were rewarded for obeying national orders, even if this was at the expense of the multilateral mission.

Insufficient principal oversight of the IAEA, along with its technical expertise and information, has also been used to argue that the IO is engaged in agency **slack**. The result of this is that its technical cooperation is more likely to lower the costs of acquiring a nuclear weapons programme for recipient states and therefore increase the likelihood that a nuclear weapons programme will succeed (Brown and Kaplow 2014).

Constructivist Organisational Culture Accounts of Peace and Security IOs

Organisational cultural accounts of IOs' behaviour do not compete with P–A model or IR theory explanations. They seek to identify how certain ways of doing things become normal. Why do UN efforts to address conflicts all over the world look the same? And why does the UN regularly fail to achieve its objectives in conflict zones? Answers to both questions lie in the fact that the decision-making practices of the UN have built over time on an international expatriate community working to address conflicts. Practitioner and scholar Séverine Autesserre (2014) argues that the shared practices, habits and rituals of those who intervene in conflict zones are counterproductive, to the point of undermining the efficacy of the IO's actions. Despite a long-held recognition that these responses do not work, and do not include local actors in the conflict, they persist, even when UN actions have unintended consequences, including worsening the situation.

NGOs also operate in specific ways that may interfere with meeting their mandate. The ICRC has a specific culture, which is state-centric, legalistic and bureaucratic, which limits its ability to protect those it seeks to assist (Bradley 2016).

Competition over Minimising and Halting Conflict: NGOs and Private Military Companies

Both non- and for-profit organisations seek to contribute to international peace. NGOs and modern private military companies (PMCs) are examined here. NGOs have been operating in the field since the early missionaries. In the modern form, NGOs, foremost amongst them the International Committee of the Red Cross (ICRC) and Médecins Sans Frontières (MSF, see Chapter 5), have established their own niche in providing humanitarian assistance for non-combatants in conflict situations. By one estimate there are over 200,000 international humanitarian NGOs operating (Barnett 2011).

NGOs are also strong advocates for banning weapons. A transnational coalition was responsible for the Convention on the Prohibition of the Use, Stockpiling, Production and Transfer of Anti-personnel Mines and on Their Destruction (the Ottawa Treaty). It has 162 signatories. In 1997 its organiser, Jody Williams, won the Nobel Peace Prize. In 2017 the International Campaign to Abolish Nuclear Weapons won the Nobel Peace Prize for pressuring states to adopt the UN Treaty on the Prohibition of Nuclear Weapons. At the time of writing, 53 states have signed the treaty.

NGOs have been active in establishing the legal conduct of states in relation to non-combatants during war. The most influential NGO is the ICRC (on Amnesty International and Human Rights Watch see Chapter 4). It has visited more detainees than any other NGO. The ICRC was established in 1863 in order to provide humanitarian protection for victims of armed conflict. Its functions expanded from caring for the wounded and sick during war to cover prisoners of war, civilians, political prisoners and families separated by war. It provides emergency humanitarian assistance and relief, visits detainees, spreads knowledge, and helps develop international humanitarian law. It is a 'guardian of international humanitarian law' for establishing the Geneva Conventions that legalise the protection of victims during war (see Chapter 5). It has won four Nobel Peace Prizes for its efforts (Forsythe 2005).

The ICRC is unusual in that it is a private voluntary organisation whose primary decision-making body, its Assembly, is comprised of Swiss nationals. The Assembly has a smaller Assembly Council that takes strategic decisions. The President is the international face of the IO, conducting humanitarian diplomacy and ensuring the functioning of the organisation. The distinction between state and non-state actors blurs in that state delegates attend, sign and ratify the Geneva Conventions for armed conflict created and monitored by the ICRC. The organisation has from the beginning endorsed three principles to undertake its humanitarian operations: its independence, its neutrality and its impartiality.

Contributions to the ICRC are voluntary, with 84 per cent generated by state parties to the Geneva Conventions. The rest comes from IOs (EU), the private sector and national Red Cross and Red Crescent societies. In 2017 its budget surpassed two billion Swiss francs, up from 1.67 billion in 2016. The ICRC is interesting as it both spearheads and is separate from the Red Cross humanitarian movement (Forsythe 2005). It has a staff of over 2,000 and operates in over 80 states.

While humanitarian NGOs have altered the landscape of armed conflict, their impact may also have an adverse effect. Refugee camps spring up to provide relief to non-combatants. These may be used by opposing forces to continue the conflict. This was most notable in the Rwandan genocide, where combatants used humanitarian resources provided by NGOs to continue the slaughter (on

Rwanda see Chapter 4). This creates a paradox where humanitarian action may help prolong the suffering it was intended to alleviate (Terry 2002).

For-profit organisations also operate in war. Mercenaries have existed since the twelfth century, but over time their presence became morally repugnant. By the nineteenth century a strong norm had emerged that using mercenaries, or those using force for personal gain, was abhorrent. States' increasingly turned to using citizen armies (Percy 2007). Mercenaries played roles in wars on the African continent during the 1960s, but the norm against their use largely held.

However, there has been a dramatic shift in the types of state-sanctioned actors engaged in intra-state warfare. After the Cold War states began outsourcing their security to PMCs, firms like Blackwater, Sandline International, Halliburton and Triple Canopy, which charge for their military services and advice, including combat. In the 1990 Gulf War the ratio of US forces to PMC staff was 50:1. By the 2003 Iraq war this ratio was 10:1 (Isenberg 2007: 83). The increased use of PMCs has enabled embattled developing states mired in conflict to purchase firepower to train their forces and supplement their troops in Angola, Côte d'Ivoire, Liberia, Sierra Leone and Papua New Guinea (Varin 2015).

PMCs have been instrumental in changing the state of conflict towards resolution in Sierra Leone (Executive Outcomes) and in Bosnia (Military Professional Resources Incorporated). Of course, contracting organisations to undertake state security raises ethical questions about the transparency and accountability of their operations, as well as the extent to which they can be controlled. For example, PMC staff were implicated in the torture of prisoners in Abu Ghraib in Iraq in 2003, but it was not clear which laws and rules of engagement applied, and only junior staff were prosecuted.

Chapter Summary

How to combat threats to international peace and security is the remit of the UN. Over time, the changing nature of weapons and conflict has left it overstretched and frequently unable to respond. During the Cold War the UNSC was stymied, leaving the UNGA and the Secretary General to come up with inventive ways to address different situations. From the 1990s it would grapple with peacekeeping, enforcement and humanitarian intervention under R2P. The UN remains the arbiter of what constitutes a just war. Yet it has also devolved responsibility to NATO, the AU and other regional organisations. This chapter outlined the mandate, function and structure of these IOs while examining a range of threats from nuclear war to terrorism. While IR theories identify the basis for cooperation according to liberal internationalist precepts, and provide realist identification of the causes for conflict, newer P–A model and constructivist organisational culture approaches also reveal how inappropriate decision-making at the IO level may still lead to poor outcomes even when IOs are ostensibly implementing laudable policy mandates from states.

Guiding Questions

1. What are the strengths and weaknesses of the UN in responding to armed conflict?
2. Why has NATO lasted so long?
3. Can the AU adequately respond to security breaches?
4. Which theory best explains how IOs respond to international peace and security?
5. Can IOs adequately address the proliferation of weapons?

Further References

Online Resources

Global Policy Forum: www.globalpolicy.org/home.html. An independent policy watchdog that analyses UN reform.
Security Council Report: www.securitycouncilreport.org/index.php. A channel to provide greater transparency into the UNSC's work.

Further Reading

Autesserre, S., 2014, *Peaceland: Conflict Resolution and the Everyday Politics of International Intervention*, Cambridge, Cambridge University Press.
Bradley, M., 2016, *Protecting Civilians in War: The ICRC, UNHCR, and their Limitations in Internal Armed Conflict*, Oxford, Oxford University Press.
Chesterman, S., 2007, *Secretary or General? The UN Secretary General in World Politics*, Cambridge, Cambridge University Press.
Coleman, K., 2007, *International Organisations and Peace Enforcement: The Politics of International Legitimacy*, Cambridge, Cambridge University Press.

Doyle, M., and N. Sambanis, 2006, *Making War and Building Peace: United Nations Peace Operations*, Princeton, NJ, Princeton University Press.

Forsythe, D. P., and B. A. Rieffer-Flanagan, 2007, *The International Committee of the Red Cross: A Neutral Humanitarian Actor*, London and New York, Routledge.

Luck, E., 2006, *UN Security Council: Practice and Promise*, London and New York, Routledge.

Malone, D. M. (ed.), 2004b, *The UN Security Council: From the Cold War to the 21ˢᵗ Century*, Boulder, CO, Lynne Rienner.

Prantl, J., 2006, *The UN Security Council and Informal Groups of States: Complementing or Competing for Governance?*, Oxford, Oxford University Press.

Wheeler, N., 2002, *Saving Strangers: Humanitarian Intervention in International Society*, Oxford, Oxford University Press.

4   Protecting Human Rights

Introduction

Never again. In 1945, the 50 states meeting in San Francisco to create the UN vowed never to repeat the atrocities stemming from two world wars and the Holocaust. The **genocide** perpetrated by Nazi Germany and the other Axis powers in Europe led to the death of six million Jews and numerous members of other groups. Therefore, **human rights** were a prominent feature of the new UN, appearing seven times in the Charter. As one of its principal purposes, the UN seeks to encourage 'respect for human rights and for fundamental freedoms for all' (United Nations 1948a, Article I (3)). Despite the creation of the UN

Commission on Human Rights, the endorsement of the Universal Declaration of Human Rights (UDHR) and the adoption of the Convention on the Prevention and Punishment of the Crime of Genocide in 1948, little was achieved in the decades immediately after. The world continued to turn a blind eye to genocide in Cambodia in the 1970s, Rwanda in the 1990s and Sudan in the 2000s. Yet human rights, including, but not limited to, the right to life, liberty, work, social security, freedom of privacy, thought, expression and association, are now major concerns in international relations. How human rights have been accepted as a problem to be addressed internationally is examined in relation to the organisations that promote human rights. The extension of the rights to be protected has come about as a result of the concerted action of organisations such as the UN, NGOs and states.

This chapter will examine the following issues.

- The mandate, structure and function of the UN Human Rights Commission (later Council), the Office of the High Commissioner for Human Rights (OHCHR) and the UN High Commissioner for Refugees (UNHCR), with discussion of regional organisations throughout.
- The International Criminal Court (ICC) that has the power to enforce specific human rights.
- The problem of protecting human rights when states diverge over whether human rights exist and should be protected.
- How traditional IR theories counterpose IO-specific theories for analysing why human rights IOs behave the way they do.
- Prominent competition for promoting and protecting human rights between international NGOs like Amnesty International (AI) and Human Rights Watch (HRW).

The Mandate, Function and Structure of the United Nations Human Rights Council, the OHCHR and International Courts

The international human rights **regime** is an increasingly dense legal framework. However, enforcement of human rights predominantly remains with states. Inter-state cooperation is contentious because **sovereign** states have the political authority to determine what happens within their territory and to their people. Nonetheless, states have created a number of bodies to advance human rights.

From the Commission on Human Rights (CHR) to the Human Rights Council (HRC)

The UN constitutes specific organisational units that have particular mandates. However, there are also cross-cutting themes, such as human rights, that now must be addressed by all bodies. The UN Charter references human rights, but does not specify what they are. This was left to diplomatic efforts to prescribe. Article 68 of the UN Charter empowers the UN to establish commissions for economic, social and human rights promotion. In 1946, the Economic and Social Council of the UN (ECOSOC) created the Commission on Human Rights (CHR) with a mandate to set the international agenda on human rights, provide a forum for debating human rights, and draft resolutions. Yet the CHR initially limited its own activities to human rights promotion, not protection.

The CHR's functions would evolve over time: from primarily standard-setting (1946–1966), to reporting human rights violations (1967–1979), to providing states with advice on how to better protect human rights (1980s onwards). The CHR operated until 2006, when it was replaced by the Human Rights Council (HRC, see pages 67–68). In terms of its structure, the CHR had 53 member states drawn from the United Nations General Assembly (UNGA). It had an annual session in March and April for six weeks in Geneva, with over 3,000 delegates from member and observer states and NGOs participating. This made it the largest policy-making body on international human rights. It was considered to have a high diplomatic importance, with heads of states addressing the CHR.

The CHR's early years were spent promoting and drafting standards, including the Universal Declaration on Human Rights (UDHR). The UDHR is the most authoritative statement of international human rights and comprises 30 articles of soft (non-enforceable) law. The UDHR recognises the universality, indivisibility and inalienability of the rights of all people as the foundation of equality, freedom, justice and peace in the world. In adopting the UDHR, states recognised the legitimacy of the rights of individuals within international relations. The UDHR is the cornerstone of the UN's human rights framework and was to be the first of three instruments constituting an International Bill of Human Rights. The second instrument was to establish binding human rights and the third was to be focused on implementation (Ramcharan 2008). However, the second instrument was separated into two: the International Convention on Civil and

Political Rights (ICCPR), promoted by the United States, and the International Convention on Economic, Social and Cultural Rights (ICESCR), advocated by the Soviet Union. These were adopted by the UNGA in 1966, and entered into force in 1976 when enough states had ratified them.

The CHR was the initiator of covenants and treaties, providing a forum for negotiations, drafting and their establishment. Many conventions begin as declarations which are presented to the UNGA for adoption (after being discussed in the UNGA's third committee on Social, Humanitarian and Cultural Issues). For example, in 2007 the UNGA passed the Declaration on the Rights of Indigenous Peoples. If the UNGA so decides, the (now) Human Rights Council may then draft the declaration into a convention for ratification and accession by member states. Once enough member states have ratified the convention, it will enter into force and become binding on those signatories. The UN is the locus for 10 human rights conventions and optional protocols (Box 4.1). The treaties resulted from the concerted efforts of specialised human rights advocates (on indigenous peoples, for example). International law would also emerge

---

Box 4.1 The UN Human Rights Conventions

1. Convention on the Prevention and Punishment of the Crime of Genocide (Genocide Convention, 1948)
2. International Convention on the Elimination of All Forms of Racial Discrimination (CERD, 1965)
3. International Convention on Civil and Political Rights (ICCPR, 1966)
4. International Convention on Economic, Social and Cultural Rights (ICESCR, 1966)
5. Convention on the Elimination of All Forms of Discrimination against Women (CEDAW, 1979)
6. Convention against Torture and Other Cruel, Inhuman or Degrading Treatment or Punishment (CAT, 1984)
7. Convention on the Rights of the Child (CRC, 1989)
8. International Convention on the Protection of the Rights of All Migrant Workers and Members of Their Families (ICMW, 1990)
9. International Convention for the Protection of All Persons from Enforced Disappearance (CPED, 2006)
10. Convention on the Rights of Persons with Disabilities (CRPD, 2006)

regionally: the European Convention on Human Rights and Fundamental Freedoms in 1953; the Inter-American Convention in 1969; the African Charter on Human and Peoples' Rights in 1986; and the ASEAN Declaration on Human Rights in 2012.

Of these UN conventions, nine would have specific treaty bodies created to maintain and enforce their provisions (Box 4.2), while the Genocide Convention is enforced by the International Criminal Court (see pages 71–74). The regional

Box 4.2 The UN Human Rights Treaty Bodies

There are nine human rights treaty bodies (committees), which were established by their convention or by ECOSOC. The committees are mandated to promote and enforce the treaty. Once a state has ratified a convention, it is required to submit periodic reports to the committee for review. However, states may make reservations, understandings and declarations that limit what they agree to be bound by.

The bodies function by assisting states in fulfilling their treaty obligations by offering views, recommendations and general comments. The treaty bodies comprise between 10 and 18 experts. These are individuals acting independently who have a recognised competence in human rights. They are elected by state parties. Some of the treaty bodies accept complaints from individuals about specific violations, which the treaty body may then investigate. NGOs are also allowed to submit parallel or shadow reports to most of the treaty bodies to provide a fuller picture of states' compliance. The treaty body then makes concluding observations on a state's treaty adherence. To date, 80 per cent of UN members have ratified four or more of the human rights treaties.

The treaty compliance system has been criticised for not being efficient or effective, with states providing inaccurate or incomplete reports, or no report at all, while the treaty bodies themselves are under-resourced and may contribute to overlapping jurisprudence and forum shopping. Although these treaties are fundamental to the system of human rights protection internationally, scholars have identified that compliance with the treaties rests on local advocates taking up the recommendations of the committee in order to change states' practices (Hafner-Burton 2013; Krommendijk 2015). The ability of a state to implement human rights treaties may also depend on the efficiency of that state's bureaucracy (Cole 2015).

conventions are backed by the European Commission on Human Rights, the Inter-American Commission on Human Rights, the African Commission on Human and Peoples' Rights, and the ASEAN Intergovernmental Commission on Human Rights.

From 1967, the CHR began to focus on developing fact-finding mechanisms and procedures for identifying human rights violations around the world. The commission established 'special procedures' to investigate and issue public reports on situations of gross human rights violations in states or on human rights generally. It could do so by appointing Special Rapporteurs, independent experts, special representatives and working groups. Complaints by states that opposed being labelled human rights violators increased throughout the 1970s. In the 1980s, the CHR began to focus on technical assistance to states to overcome obstacles to realising human rights.

The CHR began to undertake thematic and country mandates. The former included issues such as human trafficking. Country mandates included ones for Afghanistan, Bosnia-Herzegovina, Burundi, Cambodia, the Democratic Republic of Congo, Haiti, Iraq, Myanmar, Palestinian Territories occupied since 1967 and Somalia. The country mandates have been more effective than thematic mandates, with states responding when explicitly identified.

Despite being the central architect of human rights work in the UN, the CHR lost credibility. While it was able to provide important recommendations to states, it also began to resemble a club where friendships lead to wrong-doing being overlooked. This undermined its reputation. The Commission became known for having a record of double standards, such as having human rights perpetrators as members, including Sudan and Saudi Arabia. This came to a head when Libya, known for its human rights violations, was elected chair of the commission in 2003. Although human rights violations were often identified by the CHR, only politically isolated states were denounced for their abuses, because they were easy targets (Lebovic and Voeten 2006).

In the light of broader UN reforms, in 2005 the UN Secretary General Kofi Annan proposed a revitalised body bolstered to a council akin to the UNSC and ECOSOC. The new Human Rights Council (HRC), which was established by UNGA Resolution 60/251, was mandated to be responsible for promoting the protection of all human rights for all; to address situations of human rights violations; and to make recommendations. It should also promote effective coordination and the mainstreaming of human rights within the UN system (UNGA, 2006).

It was given five functions:

1. contribute to the prevention of human rights violations through cooperation and dialogue;
2. assume the responsibilities and role of the CHR;
3. work with states, national human rights institutions and NGOs on human rights;
4. make recommendations to promote and protect human rights;
5. report to the UNGA (UNGA, 2006).

Structurally, the Council did not achieve its ambitions, but it did become more authoritative as a subsidiary body under the UNGA. It now meets three times per year. Its 47 members are elected by a simple majority of the UNGA according to regional representation. Like the CHR, the HRC does not debar human rights violators from being elected to the HCR, a fundamental weakness that has allowed the same voting practices that beleaguered the CHR to reappear.

The HRC maintains the CHR's special procedures. It also has an advisory committee which provides expertise on human rights, and a complaint procedure to accept individual submissions on human rights violations. Kofi Annan was instrumental in devising a new process for the HRC, the Universal Periodic Review (UPR), which enables states to review other states' human rights records every five years. The UPR, which has been approved by the UNGA, is a means of positive reinforcement rather than shaming: it is meant to be cooperative and non-confrontational. It also aimed to streamline the process so as not to overburden states or consume too much time and resources (McMahon and Aschiero 2012). Indeed, states have only three minutes to present their recommendations! As might be expected, states use these recommendations to reciprocate friendly comments to like-minded states. States tend to vote according to their own position on human rights, but members of some blocs such as the European Union respond alike (Hug and Lukács 2014). In sum, the HRC's work remains highly politicised, and it does not have the power to enforce human rights.

The Office of the High Commissioner for Human Rights (OHCHR)

In June 1993, states met at the World Conference on Human Rights in Vienna to review and assess all the progress that had been made in the field of human rights. The main discussion, attended by specialists, states and NGOs, was about the adequacy of the IHRR under the UN. An increasing number of states questioned the direction of the IHRR (as will be discussed below). Despite this, 171 states signed the Vienna Declaration and Programme of Action (VDPA), which emphasises the universality of human rights, stresses the right to development, women's and indigenous rights, and the problems of ethnic cleansing and systematic rape (as the war in the former Yugoslavia unfolded). It led to the establishment of the Office of the High Commissioner for Human Rights (OHCHR).

The idea of locating authority for human rights within an individual has a long genesis. The UN High Commissioner for Human Rights was given the mandate to be the official with principal responsibility for human rights activities by the UN. The Commissioner works under the Secretary General but abides by the decisions of the UNGA and ECOSOC (UNGA 1993b). The High Commissioner for Human Rights has a four-year term, and is appointed by the UNSG with approval from the UNGA, on the basis of personal integrity and human rights expertise. The position also rotates regionally.

The High Commissioner for Human Rights was given 11 functions, including to

1. promote and protect all civil, cultural, economic, political and social rights,
2. coordinate among the UN bodies,
3. streamline the UN's human rights machinery,
4. advance education on human rights,
5. undertake tasks requested by other UN bodies,
6. work with regional human rights bodies,
7. provide advice and technical assistance to states,
8. seek to remove obstacles to the furtherance of human rights,
9. promote and protect the right to development,
10. engage with states through a dialogue on human rights,
11. enhance international cooperation on human rights (UNGA 1993a).

The VDPA incorporated identification of the interdependence and mutual reinforcement of democracy, development and respect for human rights. This recognition of the importance both of democracy and of the right to development in the Vienna Declaration indicates that the concerns both of the **Global North** and of the **Global South** were addressed (see Chapter 9).

Structurally, the High Commissioner for Human Rights is in charge of the OHCHR, which sits within the Office of the UNSG. It is up to the UNSG to ensure adequate resources for the OHCHR, and like other UN bodies it relies on voluntary member contributions as well as donations from IOs, foundations and individuals. The financial resources of the OHCHR are severely limited

(UN OHCHR 2017b); compare this with the resources of the WHO in Chapter 5 and the World Bank in Chapter 9). The OHCHR has over 1,000 staff in four divisions: a research and right-to-development division; a division supporting the work of the human rights treaty bodies (Box 4.2); a field operation and technical cooperation division that also engages with states on human rights; and a division that supports the HRC. It maintains 13 country and 13 regional offices around the world, with 689 human rights officers working in peace missions and political offices (UN OHRHC 2017a).

The OHCHR has a broad mandate, and the High Commissioner's role is vague in terms of who the 'clients' are. Are they member states or victims of human rights abuses? The activities of the OHCHR are heavily dependent on the individual commissioner. The second UN High Commissioner for Human Rights, Mary Robinson (1997–2002), was effective in promoting the right to development as per developing states' needs, while promising to 'stand up to bullies' (Mertus 2009). Human rights officers are appointed on the basis of their integrity and expertise, and much work for the UN is done without payment. Support for international human rights is dependent on the willingness of individuals to promote and protect them.

The OHCHR has sought to improve the level of competence of human rights officers working in UN peace missions. It played an active role in promoting human rights in Bosnia-Herzegovina and Rwanda. However, constraints imposed by resource problems meant that its presence in 1994 did little to stop the Rwandan genocide.

The OHCHR supports National Human Rights Institutions (NHRIs), which may be hybrid state–non-state institutions that promote competence and adherence to international human rights norms domestically. Of course, these vary significantly in how they perceive human rights and whether they defend them. After promoting human rights, the next step is to protect them. The rise and power of international courts is therefore of vital importance.

International Courts

The rise of international courts has been slow but steady. The first such court was the Permanent Court of Arbitration, which emerged from the Hague Conference of 1899; the League of Nations would follow with the Permanent Court of International Justice (see Chapter 1). The International Court of Justice (ICJ) was created in 1945 as a principal organ of the UN regarding the pacific settlement of disputes (United Nations 1948a). The ICJ is mandated to use international law to settle disputes between states if they are willing to accept the ICJ's jurisdiction. It also provides advisory opinions on legal issues as requested by UN agencies. The ICJ functions to uphold international treaties, conventions, custom and the general principles of law. The law on which the ICJ deliberates remains contested, undermining the ICJ's influence on international relations. Although the ICJ is not geared to focus on individual human rights, it increasingly addresses the human rights conventions that states adhere to, and its advisory opinions have opened the way for protecting human rights. Moreover, the UN Security Council increasingly recognises the infringement of human rights as a threat to international peace and stability, especially through the Responsibility to Protect principle (see Chapter 3).

In terms of inter-state disputes, the number of courts, such as the European Court of Justice, and arbitration processes continues to grow, prompting scholars to acknowledge the legalisation of world politics (Goldstein *et al.* 2001). International courts have emerged to uphold regional human rights treaties: the European Court of Human Rights, the Inter-American Court of Human Rights and the African Court of Human and Peoples' Rights. Political scientist Karen Alter (2014) argues that the rising prominence and power of international courts since the end of the Cold War stems from the fact that states are more willing to delegate to them. This also enables international courts to empower those who wish to uphold the law transnationally and internationally.

The International Criminal Court

The earliest proposal for an international criminal court was floated in 1872 by Gustave Moynier, one of the founding members of the International Committee of the Red Cross (see Chapter 3), after the Franco-Prussian war. Yet non-permanent tribunals were established in the aftermath of war on an ad hoc basis throughout the twentieth century. For example, the Peace Treaty of Versailles created a criminal tribunal to prosecute Germany's Kaiser Wilhelm. After WWII, international war crimes were prosecuted by the International Military Tribunal in Nuremberg and the International Military Tribunal for the Far East in Tokyo. This would be followed in the 1990s by the ad hoc International Criminal Tribunal for the Former Yugoslavia (ICTFY) and the International Criminal Tribunal for Rwanda (ICTR).

The UN Charter does not refer to international criminal courts: it was presumed that the powers granted within Chapter VII to remove threats to international peace and security were sufficient to create such courts. The

Box 4.3 The Geneva Conventions

Prior to 1948 there were isolated attempts to establish some limitations on the impact of states on individuals. The first Geneva Convention (I) aimed to ameliorate the condition of the wounded in war. It was adopted at the Geneva Conference in 1864, at which 16 states were represented. It was superseded by later conventions in 1906, 1929 and 1949. There are now four Geneva conventions, which constitute the Geneva laws: Geneva Convention II on the Amelioration of the Condition of the Wounded, Sick and Shipwrecked Members of Armed forces at Sea; Geneva Convention III concerning the Treatment of Prisoners of War; and Geneva Convention IV on the Protection of Civilian Persons in Time of War. These are a collection of conventions established by states to uphold international humanitarian law, or the rights of individuals during conflict (distinct from broader international human rights law).

UNSC gave the ICTFY and ICTR jurisdiction to investigate crimes of genocide, crimes against humanity and violations of the Geneva Conventions (Box 4.3). Concerns over the costs and inefficiencies of these ad hoc tribunals arose. Later, the UNSC moved towards hybrid (international–local) courts rather than creating more tribunals in post-conflict states such as Bosnia-Herzegovina, Cambodia, East Timor, Kosovo and Sierra Leone.

Legal scholar Dominic McGoldrick argues that the ICC is a belated response to the trauma of the twentieth century, including two world wars, genocide, the fear of nuclear fallout during the Cold War and atrocities committed in warzones globally (McGoldrick *et al.* 2004). With the promotion of the Genocide Convention in the late 1940s, the idea of a permanent court was floated within the UN. Acting under the authority of the UNGA, the International Law Commission prepared draft proposals for an international criminal court in the 1950s, but these proposals were hamstrung over the definition of the crime of aggression. Work resumed in 1989, later galvanised by the genocide in the former Yugoslavia and Rwanda. In 1994, the International Law Commission prepared a draft statute and the UNGA convened the United Nations Conference of Plenipotentiaries on the Establishment of an International Criminal Court (ICC) in 1998. At this conference 120 states voted for the ICC; seven states voted against, including the United States and China. The conference ended with the promulgation of the Rome Statute of the International Criminal Court (United

Nations 1998). In 2002 the 60th state ratified the Rome Statute, bringing it into force.

This was a watershed: it was the first permanent treaty-based international criminal court. The Rome Statute sets out the Court's jurisdiction, structure and functions. The ICC's mandate is to have jurisdiction over four areas of international criminal law: **genocide**, crimes against humanity, war crimes and crimes of aggression. Debates over what the crime of aggression entailed went on until 2010, when an amendment to the Rome Statute defined it as the use of armed force by one state against another (United Nations 2010: Article 2, point 2).

The ICC functions as a complement to national courts, meaning that the latter retain jurisdiction over genocide, crimes against humanity and war crimes. If a case is being considered by a country with jurisdiction over it, the ICC cannot act unless the country is unwilling or unable genuinely to investigate or prosecute. A country may be 'unwilling' if it is clearly shielding someone from responsibility for ICC crimes, as in cases like Rwanda, where the atrocities were state-orchestrated. A country may be 'unable' when its legal system has collapsed, as was the case in Cambodia where the national court system was destroyed. Crimes committed before 2002 cannot be brought before the court.

A case may be opened by referral from member states or the UNSC may refer situations to the ICC Prosecutor for investigation. Or the ICC prosecutor may institute legal proceedings if a crime is alleged to have occurred in an ICC member state, or in a non-member state if the latter is willing to recognise the ICC's jurisdiction. The perpetrator must also be a national of a member state. The UNSC may also ask for a deferral of an investigation for up to 12 months, raising questions about political interference of the permanent members of the UNSC in the workings of the court.

The ICC is located in The Hague, with six field offices where investigations are under way. It has over 800 staff, and in 2016 its budget was €139.5 million. Structurally, the ICC has three principal organs: the Assembly of State Parties, the Court itself and a Trust Fund for Victims, which provides support and reparations. The 124 member states that ratified and acceded to the Rome Statute form the Assembly of State Parties (ASP). This is the ICC's primary administrative and decision-making body. The ASP meets annually, and each state has one vote, although decisions are made by consensus.

The Assembly of State Parties has a Bureau, consisting of a President, two Vice Presidents and 18 members elected by the Assembly for a three-year term. They are elected according to equitable geographical distribution and the adequate representation of the principal legal systems of the world. The Assembly of State Parties determines the adoption of normative texts, sets the budget and elects the judges, the prosecutor and deputy prosecutors. A permanent secretariat was created in 2003 (ICC 2017).

The court itself is comprised of four organs:

1. the presidency, comprised of three judges elected by the court's 18 judges to supervise the work of the court;
2. the judicial division, comprised of the 18 judges of the ICC;
3. the Office of the Prosecutor;
4. the registry which provides support to the court.

To date, 24 cases have come before the court. It has issued 30 arrest warrants and nine summons to appear, and has returned six verdicts. In three cases charges against individuals were dropped owing to their deaths (ICC 2017). While there are criticisms over the workings of the ICC regarding the time cases take and their procedures, the creation of the ICC is a major step forwards for upholding international law. The basis for creating a legal system to protect human rights is examined next.

The Problem: Promoting, Protecting and Expanding Human Rights Internationally

Human rights have a **liberal** philosophical basis. Although all major religions and ideologies recognise human dignity, liberal philosophy argued that these were rights to be codified within a legal system. States should uphold these rights in order to realise the equality and autonomy of individuals. Three fault-lines therefore emerged in attempting to realise human rights at the international level: first, the demand that states accept and recognise that human rights should be codified into international law, usurping the traditional prerogative of sovereign states; second, that all rights are indivisible when states promote some rights over others; and third, that all states should accept the spread of Western liberal values through adopting and ratifying international human rights law. Each would impede the recognition of human rights internationally.

First, the promotion and protection of human rights undermines the traditional sovereign right of states to have political authority within their own territories, including over their people. Article 2 (7) of the UN Charter upholds states' right to **non-interference** (United Nations 1948a). This was particularly important for states that had realised their independence only after decolonisation. States have strongly defended this right, including overlooking atrocities committed by other states against their own people, such as the genocide perpetrated by the Pol Pot regime in Cambodia in the 1970s. Dictators were able to act with impunity to eradicate people by any means. The invasion of Cambodia by Vietnam to stop the genocide in 1978 was widely denounced, not only because of the strength of adherence to the principle of non-interference but also owing to **Cold War** politics. States' responses began to change after the collapse of the Soviet Union, but the UN did not act quickly enough to halt the genocide in the former Yugoslavia and Rwanda. How and why the UN reacted to these events is discussed in the theory section.

Second, the rights outlined in the UDHR remain contested. Western liberal states championed the civil and political rights of the individual, so-called 'first-generation rights'. Communist states argued that economic rights were more important and pushed heavily for 'second-generation rights'. The contestation over the primacy of these rights led to the separate covenants. While the United States has not ratified the ICESCR, developing states have tried to use the CHR to emphasise economic rights. Developing countries have tried to promote the rights of the community to develop, 'third-generation rights', in contrast to the negative rights of the individual espoused by liberal democratic states. Others argue that women's and indigenous peoples' rights need specific protections beyond the main covenants. The indivisibility of these rights can be debated in terms of different lines of inquiry: religious, ideological and philosophical. Each raises questions about the role of the state in promoting and protecting human rights.

The third point of debate is whether there are universal values that apply worldwide, despite the major differences of religions, cultures and experiences. At the Vienna Conference in 1993, 10 states, namely China, Cuba, Syria, Indonesia, Iran, Pakistan, Vietnam, Malaysia, Singapore and Yemen, opposed what they saw as the Western-centric nature of the IHRR. They argued that the IHRR overlooks important distinctions, such as the right to self-determination and development.

Part of this discussion was the 'Asian Values' debate, where states such as Singapore, then under Lee Kuan Yew, and Malaysia under Mohammed Mahathir argued that the collective values of the family and the community were overshadowed by the focus on the rights of the individual. Asian values, they argued, led to regionally specific Asian-style democracies that could help guide national development and prosperity. The Vienna Conference sought an end to the debate over cultural relativism, with states agreeing that it is the duty of states to promote and protect all human rights (UNGA 1993a: Article 1 (5)).

Although states have increasingly agreed that human rights are important and need to be protected, their actions frequently do not match this commitment. Australia flouts international refugee law by imprisoning people in offshore detainment facilities. The United States, supported by its allies, has engaged in torture, rendition and practices that contravene the Geneva Conventions at its Guantánamo Bay detention camp. Russia has cracked down on dissidents, with suspicious deaths of journalists and feminists. In 2014, Uganda passed an anti-homosexual law, although this was later overturned. These are just a few examples. No state is above censure. How does your state fare in upholding and protecting human rights? Owing to the failures of states to protect human rights, NGOs have tried to shame and persuade states to follow international human rights standards in order to improve compliance.

Explaining Human Rights IOs' Behaviour

The IR and IO-specific theoretical approaches provide alternative lenses through which to explain how and why human rights IOs behave.

International Relations Theoretical Explanations of Human Rights IOs' Behaviour

The main theoretical divide when discussing human rights internationally has been between **liberal internationalism** and realism. For liberal internationalism, the entire point of creating international law, and IOs to uphold that law, is to protect the freedoms and equality of individuals. The liberal international approach seeks to advance the protection of human rights primarily through the advancement of international law. Promoting even soft, non-binding, international law, such as the UDHR, is important because it may become customary international law over time. This means that most states treat it as though it is law and abide by it. Thus, the UN's human rights focus has been to create and enforce international law as the primary means of advancing individual rights and freedoms. Most research on international human rights therefore advances the normative position that these are rights worth protecting. **Liberal** and **constructivist** approaches examine why states hold the perspective on human rights they do.

Human rights have generally been accorded a low priority by **realists** who argue that they should remain the primary concern of sovereign states. This means that there is a fundamental tension within the UN: it is designed to promote the rights of individuals, but is comprised of sovereign states. Of course, how states view human rights has changed over time: the United States increasingly made it part of its foreign policy from the 1970s onwards, as have other Western liberal 'steward' states (Hafner-Burton 2013). This has led the UN to recognise that protecting human rights is increasingly fundamental to its two other pillars: upholding peace and security, and promoting economic and social development. Although states have accepted the VDPA and many of the UN human rights treaties, there remains a fundamental difficulty for states in applying them. Arguably, a realist approach can still explain the behaviour of states that declare that human rights are important: for example, the United States promotes human rights abroad, but may not uphold them domestically.

Tensions remain between states over the universality of human rights being advocated by Western states. The North–South divide means that human rights becomes yet another issue over which states compete, leading to bloc voting in the HRC. When the new HRC was designed, it was quite late into the negotiations before the regional representation and the rotation of members of the body was discussed. According to the UN regional allocation formula, more seats would go to Asian and African states, and the permanent five members of the UNSC would lose their de facto permanent membership.

Regional representation determines which states' preferences could influence the HRC's operations. The more numerous developing states preferred cooperative approaches to addressing human rights, whereas Western states wanted specific resolutions to tackle human rights violations. This speaks to the problem of international cooperation as identified by **neoliberal institutionalist** and **neorealist** approaches. Although states agreed to cooperate, they had differing preferences for achieving human rights. The **neoliberal institutionalist** approach also emphasises the importance of IOs providing information. On the basis of CHR information, other IOs such as the World Bank would provide less multilateral aid to states known to be violating human rights (Lebovic and Voeten 2009).

States tend to behave **rationally** to achieve their interests on the Council. States with poor human rights records have become much more vocal on the

Council after the loss of moral rectitude by Western states abusing human rights in fighting their war on terror. This has led to a decline in the number of country mandates being undertaken by the Council as well as attempts to restrict the activities of the Special Rapporteurs, thus constraining the UN's activities in protecting human rights. However, it is unclear how cohesive voting blocs within the Council are (Richardson 2015).

Power politics also infuses debates over the ICC. Indeed, three of the permanent five members of the UNSC will not ratify it: the United States, China and Russia. The United States was initially in favour of it, but then became a strong opponent of the ICC. It took extraordinary steps to protect itself from the ICC, despite the fact that the ICC is designed to complement national legal systems and must be recognised by the state as having jurisdiction. US opposition may be waning: in 2005 the United States permitted the UNSC to authorise an ICC investigation of Sudanese officials in Darfur in relation to violations of international humanitarian and human rights laws (UNSC Resolution 1593).

In turn, the arrest warrant for Sudanese President Omar al-Bashir by the ICC Prosecutor in 2009 led the AU to oppose the ICC by recommending that states not cooperate with the ICC, while making proposals to limits its actions. This is despite the fact that some African states originally supported it. This highlights the desire of African states to use the ICC when they do not have the capacity to act to prevent atrocities, while wanting to retain state sovereignty. Constructivists have argued that African states are seeking to solidify their identities and interests in unsettled circumstances (Mills 2012).

Approaches to Explaining Human Rights IOs' Behaviour

Both the P–A model and constructivist organisational culture have been used to explain human rights IOs' behaviour. Given the forum status of the CHR and the HRC, there is less room to analyse this body's autonomy in decision-making, while the OHCHR is based on the integrity of the individual appointed rather than on the culture of the office or its delegated powers.

Human rights IOs that have some discretion include international courts. Political scientist Eric Voeten (2007) has analysed the European Court of Human Rights to argue that activist judges who seek to expand the mandate of the court are appointed by EU states that favour integration. In this way, the principal's preferences shape the agent, enabling it to become an activist court. This is contrary to explanations that focus on the judges' legal culture or their home states' human rights. This fits the P–A model, where there is a clear delegated relationship and the preferences of the agent can be compared with those of the principal. However, others argue that the principal–agent relationship must recognise the European courts' independence, which stems from judges' integrity (Alter 2008).

In a quite different vein is the **constructivist organisational culture** literature on human rights IOs. Instead of analysing how member states' preferences do or do not determine the behaviour of IOs, the organisational culture literature has examined the UN, including the UN Secretariat, the UNSC and the United Nations High Commissioner for Refugees (Box 4.4), in accounting for their actions. Political scientist Michael Barnett investigated how the UN responded to the

Box 4.4 The United Nations High Commissioner for Refugees (UNHCR)

The UNHCR, a programme created in 1950, built on international cooperative efforts begun after WWI to staunch the flow of people dislocated during war. The UNHCR was mandated to provide support for states in meeting the 1951 Convention Relating to the Status of Refugees, and to oversee states' implementation of their obligations. In the aftermath of WWII the UNHCR was designed to operate for a limited duration of three years to aid European refugees, backed by voluntary contributions from member states. It was given a restricted mandate to assist people fleeing persecution by their government as a result of events occurring before 1951. Given its circumscribed activities, the UNHCR's continued existence and expanded geographical and longitudinal scope can be explained by the ability of the organisation to increase its autonomy to become a purposive actor in its own right. It was able to generate its own funds through contributions from non-state actors and offer its assistance to refugees in Europe and beyond.

This work was rewarded by the UNHCR being given the Nobel Peace Prize in 1954 and again in 1981. These activities granted the UNHCR 'lead agency' status as the authority on refugees. The UNHCR's functions have expanded over time. Originally the UNHCR was to provide protection to refugees and to find a durable solution to their situation. It now includes providing assistance not just to refugees but also to internally displaced people (those fleeing within states) as well as victims of natural disasters. Its functions are now more akin to those of a broader humanitarian agency, providing relief in complex emergency situations, including Rwanda.

Structurally, the UNHCR reports to the UNGA and is guided in its operations by an Executive Committee comprised of 79 member states and elected from ECOSOC. The High Commissioner, based in Geneva, determines the everyday operations of the refugee agency, which currently has nearly 11,000 staff operating in 130 states, with a budget of $6.54 billion in 2016 (UNHCR 2017).

Constructivist organisational culture scholars argue that the UNHCR's expansion of its activities has been driven by the leadership of the organisation adapting to new circumstances, sometimes in opposition to the wishes of its core principals (Betts 2012). Over time the UNHCR has radically departed from its core beliefs in protecting refugees. Originally it focused on durable solutions based on asylum, third-country resettlement or (voluntary) repatriation. With states increasingly wanting refugees repatriated, the UNHCR developed a 'repatriation culture' that potentially threatened refugees' rights, even when there was no pressure from states. This is evidence of the normalisation of deviance, which subverts the original intention of the IO (Barnett and Finnemore 2004).

Rwandan genocide, arguing that the response of the DPKO and the Secretariat to the events leading up to the genocide was shaped by the organisation's informal culture. Evaluating the role of the UN in the Rwandan genocide is vital, considering how influential the Holocaust was on the design of the UN. States vowed never again. Five decades later, it reoccurred while the UN watched.

The UN in Rwanda

In 1994, approximately 800,000 Tutsi and moderate Hutu were massacred within 100 days. Early reports focused on chaos resulting from the outbreak of civil war. Yet subsequent analysis shows that information was being passed from the limited UN force in Rwanda under General Roméo Dallaire to the DPKO. Once the Secretariat was aware of the killings, the information was not passed on to the UNSC to authorise an intervention (Barnett 2002). Individual decisions within the UN not to respond to the genocide resulted from the UN's informal belief system: that interventions should be impartial, neutral and with the consent of the parties (Barnett 2002; Piiparinen 2008). Bureaucrats within the UN argued that it was legitimate not to intervene in a civil war where there was no peace to keep (see Chapter 3). Compounding the issue was the impact of failure and over-reach resulting from humanitarian intervention in Somalia in 1992–1993.

Staff chose not to speak out, knowing that the member states of the UNSC were not in favour of further risky peacekeeping operations. The UN's reputation was on the line. So staff behaved according to the rules, choosing not to advocate to intervene; those who did were ignored or punished for doing so (Piiparinen 2008). The logical conclusion of such rule-following is IO **dysfunction**: an IO designed to ensure that genocide never took place again watched it happen.

When the extent of the slaughter under way became clear, UNSC members were officially apprised of the situation. But they dithered over how to respond until the carnage concluded with the fleeing into exile of the 'génocidaires', the Hutu-controlled ruling party (MRND), its army and its militia, the Interahamwe. While power politics can explain why the UNSC and the most powerful states did nothing, other theories point to the structural weakness of the UNSC: it was non-transparent, non-representative and unaccountable in its decision-making structure, which allowed states to evade responsibility for their decisions, while weakening the Genocide Convention (Adelman and Suhrke 2004).

Competition over Providing Human Rights: NGOs

While IOs have been fundamental to furthering inter-state cooperation on the promotion and protection of human rights, much of the work in helping states conceive human rights as an international issue can be attributed to NGOs and to the foundations that often fund them. NGOs have played an instrumental role in framing debates and setting the agenda on human rights within the UN, while driving states to publicly acknowledge their human rights abuses and increase compliance with international law.

The number of international human rights NGOs continues to grow, with the majority emerging from the 1970s onwards primarily in the Global North. Over 4,000 NGOs have accredited status with ECOSOC, which enables them to participate to varying degrees in UN meetings, including the HRC. NGOs send representatives who magnify large-scale UN conferences such as the 1993 World Conference on Human Rights in Vienna and the 1995 Fourth World Conference on Women held in Beijing. Although only 248 human rights NGOs had consultative status at Vienna, another 593 participated, and approximately 1,500 NGOs attended.

The degree of access and status of NGOs are different from those of states, but they nonetheless play an important role in highlighting human rights while seeking to influence official deliberations. Indeed, it was the Dutch section of Amnesty International (AI) that circulated the need for a High Commissioner for Human Rights, leading to its eventual adoption. It was also one of the main NGOs that pushed for the creation of the ICC.

NGOs are partners with the UN, but they are also competitors in seeking to prevent or solve human rights abuses. While IOs have frequently focused on drafting, signing and ratifying human rights conventions, human rights NGOs help create demand for human rights. For example, AI has played a vital role in identifying state-sponsored violence, including torture, disappearances and extrajudicial killing. AI's campaign against torture is considered one of the most successful NGO initiatives ever undertaken (Martens 2006).

By documenting such practices, AI could help build opposition to them, thus helping to create a new norm to protect the specific rights of political opponents to states. It would then be drafted into the Convention Against Torture by the UN. NGOs therefore wield significant power in identifying which human rights have international salience worthy of a transnational campaign. Once the issue has been identified, framed, accepted and ratified in international law, NGOs then work tirelessly to hold actors accountable for meeting those rights.

Although there are thousands of international human rights NGOs working in this area, AI and Human Rights Watch (HRW) stand out. AI, as mentioned above, is one of the oldest still operating today. Its mandate is to promote all human rights, and in particular to prevent grave abuses to physical and mental integrity, defend freedom of conscience and expression, and challenge discrimination, through research and action (Amnesty International 2005). In 1961, when human rights was not a well-known or widely used concept, AI began as a voluntary organisation aiming to protect 'Prisoners of Conscience', or people detained for their beliefs or for being different, provided they had not used or advocated violence. AI sought to do so by 'Urgent Actions': immediate letter-writing campaigns to the imprisoned in order to facilitate their release. Doing so broke significant ground for transnational protest movements in seeking to challenge the sovereign prerogative of states to abuse their citizens. By seeking to directly contact prisoners, state-sanctioned abuse was revealed.

Political scientist Anne-Marie Clark argues that AI has global reach because it was built on three attributes: principled moral adherence to upholding universal human rights; acting as a politically impartial neutral actor in international relations (because it does not negotiate with states that are violating human rights); and careful documentation and reporting on human rights violations globally. This contributed to new fact-based concepts about human rights (Clark 2001). AI's efforts to identify states' human rights abuses fit within the concept of 'information politics', where a multitude of factors help generate AI's amplification of abuses in some states and not others (Keck and Sikkink 1998). AI generates credible legitimate information about abuse. AI's success in being the primary human rights NGO from WWII onwards has resulted from its organisational choices and structures that enabled it to establish the political salience of human rights internationally (Wong 2012).

AI is a voluntary organisation, with over 2.2 million members, comprised of national sections that are represented at the International Council. The Council elects nine members to the International Board to provide overall guidance and leadership. Within this, the International Executive Committee is the primary decision-making body. Day-to-day management is undertaken by the International Secretariat in London under the management of the Secretary General and a team of senior directors. Over time, AI has had to grapple with the changing international landscape: the old guard sought to maintain the focus on Prisoners of Conscience rather than issue-specific campaigns that sought to tap into newer protest methods.

In comparison, HRW began by seeking to hold the Soviet Union to its human rights obligations under the 1975 Helsinki Accords, which were agreed at the Conference on Security and Cooperation in Europe. Helsinki Watch was created in 1978 in New York with funding from the Ford Foundation, but other regional watch groups soon followed. In 1988, they all adopted the name Human Rights Watch after a Ford Foundation recommendation. Unlike the volunteer structure of AI, HRW is a professional, smaller and more 'corporate'-styled NGO, with a staff of approximately 400. HRW's mandate is to uphold human dignity and promote human rights for all. It does so through investigating violations of human rights, disseminating information on such abuses, and pressuring those with power in order to secure justice (HRW 2017).

Like AI, HRW began through a letter-writing campaign to support political prisoners. However, it would also lobby governments to pressure states that were violating human rights, and has focused on the advocacy of specific rights such as children's and women's rights, and the rights of those affected by the proliferation and use of arms. HRW is divided into regional groups and thematic divisions and programmes. It has a senior management of 48 staff, and is governed by a Board of Directors. It has a significant resource base, having raised a total of $81 million by 2015 from individuals and foundations.

Its determination to call out the silence of Western governments on human rights abuses and its willingness to engage with states that are violating human rights have made this NGO a powerful force in international human rights. Despite this, it is recognised that not all 'naming and shaming' campaigns work. HRW naming and shaming activities work best in the context of civil and political rights, where violations can be demonstrated, rather than for economic, social and cultural rights where harm is structural but not as visible.

Chapter Summary

One of the UN's principal purposes is to encourage respect for human rights and promote fundamental freedoms for all. From the beginning, the UN was engaged in human rights activities, with the drafting of the UDHR, the creation of the Genocide Convention and the work of the CHR. The Commission was central to the work of the UN and the evolution of human rights conventions. Yet its activities were increasingly overshadowed by the composition of member states sitting on the Commission and the willingness to look the other way regarding gross human rights violations. After being restructured as the HRC the body has improved procedures, yet remains politicised. The establishment of the ICC further progresses the enforcement of human rights, although it too suffers from not being recognised by some powerful states. While power politics and the position of states on issues of human rights are vital to understand why states act the way they do, the actions of some human rights IOs, particularly the courts, the UNHCR and the UN bureaucracy, are best understood through IO-specific explanations.

Guiding Questions

1. Is the HRC an improvement for promoting and protecting human rights over the CHR?
2. What use are the UN human rights treaty bodies?
3. What does the ICC do?
4. Are liberal and realist IR theories on states' human rights mutually exclusive?
5. Do P–A model and organisational culture explanations of human rights IOs' behaviour seek to analyse fundamentally different things?

Further References

Online Resources

Bayevfsky.com: www.bayefsky.com. A great resource from Professor Bayefsky from York University on the various UN human rights treaties and how to access or use the international human rights system.

Genocide Watch Interactive Map: www.genocidewatch.com/ten-stages-of-genocide-world-map. Up-to-date information on states that are in the stages leading up to, or are enacting, genocide.

Human Rights Resource Center: www.hrusa.org/default.shtm. A great resource for human rights education.

Human Rights Voices: www.humanrightsvoices.org/?h=1. A critical view of UN actions in relation to human rights

Project on International Courts and Tribunals: www.pict-pcti.org. A research network hub on the rise of international courts, with contributions by leading scholars and jurists.

Further Reading

Alston, P., and J. Crawford (eds.), 2000, *The Future of Human Rights Treaty Monitoring*, Cambridge, Cambridge University Press.

Alston, P., and F. Mégret (eds.), 2012, *The United Nations and Human Rights: A Critical Appraisal*, second edition, Oxford, Oxford University Press.

Donnelly, J., 2002, *Universal Human Rights in Theory and Practice*, Ithaca, NY, Cornell University Press.

Føllesdal, A., J. Karlsson Schaffer and G. Ulfstein (eds.), 2014, *The Legitimacy of International Human Rights Regimes: Legal, Political and Philosophical Perspectives*, Cambridge, Cambridge University Press.

Freedman, R., 2013, *The United Nations Human Rights Council: A Critique and Early Assessment*, New York, Routledge.

Keller, H., and G. Ulfstein (eds.), 2012, *UN Human Rights Treaty Bodies: Law and Legitimacy*, Cambridge, Cambridge University Press.

Mertus, J. A., 2009, *The United Nations and Human Rights: A Guide for a New Era*, second edition, New York and London, Routledge.

Orchard, P., 2014, *A Right to Flee: Refugees, States, and the Construction of International Cooperation*, Cambridge, Cambridge University Press.

Tomuschat, C., 2014, *Human Rights: Between Idealism and Realism*, third edition, Oxford, Oxford University Press.

Weisburd, A. 2016, *The Failings of the International Court of Justice*, Oxford, Oxford University Press.

Welch, C., 2001, *NGOs and Human Rights: Promise and Performance*, Philadelphia, PA, University of Pennsylvania Press.

5 Providing Global Health

Introduction

On 26 December 2013 a toddler in a small rural town in Guinea developed a fever. Two days later he died. Relatives followed. The fever spread, with more deaths, reaching the capital in February. By early March it was recognised that the deaths were linked, but the disease had not been identified. On 21 March 2014 a World Health Organization (WHO) collaborating centre in France identified the disease as the most lethal strain of the Ebola virus. By the time the WHO had announced an international public health emergency, 29 people had already died and 49 cases had been reported. The disease spread to Liberia and Sierra

Leone before air travellers transmitted it to Nigeria and the United States. The Ebola **epidemic** was the most deadly outbreak of the disease since its first recording in 1976. By April 2016, it had claimed the lives of 11,310 people.

The outbreak would lead to severe criticism of the WHO as the leading international health organisation for not responding quickly and effectively (Kamradt-Scott 2016), compounding criticisms that its visibility should not be taken for capability (Smith 2009). Since the virus is thought to have been transmitted from bats coming into contact with humans after losing their habitat, the Ebola outbreak is just one of the diseases increasingly crossing from animals to humans before spreading internationally. Others include bovine spongiform encephalopathy (BSE) or 'mad cow disease' from the 1990s, severe acute respiratory syndrome (SARS) in 2003, H5N1 'avian flu' in 2004, H1N1 'swine flu' in 2009 and, most recently, the Zika virus. The latter was spread rapidly across 33 mainly Latin American states during 2015 and 2016 by mosquitos. The disease affected between half a million and 1.4 million people in Brazil alone, with a link suspected between the virus and birth defects, and the virus acted as a trigger for Guillain–Barré syndrome, which leads to paralysis and death.

This chapter examines

- the mandate, structure and function of the WHO, the UN Children's Fund (UNICEF) and UNAIDS, which was created in response to the global HIV/AIDS epidemic, with a box on the UN Population Fund (UNFPA);
- the problem these IOs are tasked with solving;
- how scholars seek to explain health IOs' behaviour using a range of IR and IO-specific theoretical approaches;
- competitors to traditional health IOs, including philanthropists, hybrid IOs, such as the Global Alliance for Vaccines and Immunization (GAVI), and NGOs such as Save the Children and Médecins Sans Frontières (MSF).

The Mandate, Function and Structure of the WHO, UNICEF and UNAIDS

Health covers a range of concerns ranging from individual physical and mental well-being to social concerns regarding public hygiene and sanitation, preventing and managing the outbreak of diseases and their spread, and the threat of biological warfare and bioterrorist attacks. Much of the heavy lifting is done at the international level by the WHO and a number of UN agencies (the World Bank is analysed in Chapter 9). How states and IOs frame health shapes their responses to ill-health. Understanding how health IOs operate is vital for effectively addressing international health problems.

The WHO

In 1948 the WHO was established as a special agency of the UN. Its foundation was built on inter-state cooperation arising in the mid 1800s. As trade, commerce and travel increased with industrialisation, so did efforts to contain the spread of diseases using scientific, medical and technological advances. The first International Sanitary Conference, comprised of 12 governments, was held in 1851 in Paris to discuss the nature of epidemic diseases, particularly cholera, which had swept Europe 20 years before. Little was achieved because there was no scientific consensus on how communicable diseases were transmitted, and major trading states had competing quarantine practices. The rise of multilateral conferences in part resulted from the need for states to collectively address the spread of 'exotic' diseases arising from imperialism and international commerce, via a system of quarantine.

Nine more International Sanitation Conferences were held in the nineteenth century but it was not until 1903 that the first International Sanitation Convention was established and the idea of a permanent IO to address the spread of diseases gained momentum. In 1907, 12 states signed the Rome Agreement establishing the Office International d'Hygiène Publique (OIHP), including tackling the spread of cholera, plague and yellow fever.

Member states wanted to ensure that the new IO would not be controlled by a single state and could act for the **public good**. The OIHP was controlled by a Permanent Committee of member states, on which technical representatives rather than diplomats would sit, although this was broadly interpreted. Sixty states signed the Rome Agreement, and the OIHP lasted for 40 years. While the OIHP existed prior to the League of Nations, it was agreed that the OIHP should come under the authority of the League as all IOs established by international treaties preceding it should (League of Nations 1924: Article 24). The OIHP and a new Health Organisation of the League were connected in complex bureaucratic ways, with both vying for control; on the latter see Weindling (1995). They effectively halted operations during WWII.

A universal international health organisation was proposed by China and Brazil during the 1945 San Francisco conference establishing the UN. The WHO's mandate is to attain the highest possible level of health for all people (WHO 2006: Chapter I, Article 1). This **liberal internationalist** vision represents a fundamental aspiration for humanity. The WHO recognised health as a global public good and as a human right. The WHO was given 22 functions to enact its mandate, including to act as the directing and coordinating authority on international health work. It was to have both forum and service functions by being the locus for discussions on international health as well as providing assistance directly to states. In keeping with medical trends, the WHO exemplified the focus on prevention rather than finding a cure or focusing on quarantine, which had been the basis for the OIHP.

The WHO took up some of the functions of the previous health IOs. It continued to publish *The Bulletin*, a monthly journal for information dissemination from the OIHP. In 1951 it drafted and approved the International Sanitary Regulations; these originated from the 13 International Sanitary Conventions held previously. They were renamed the International Health Regulations (IHR) in 1969. They have legal authority, requiring the reporting by states of outbreaks of infectious diseases: smallpox, yellow fever, cholera, plague, typhus and relapsing fever. The instruments are binding, but states could opt out if other members approved. Despite attempts to strengthen the regulations and with some modification as to which communicable diseases were covered, the regulations remained relatively unchanged after 1969.

In terms of its structure, the WHO is comprised of three components. The first is the World Health Assembly (WHA), on which all 194 member states are represented equally. Each state has one vote. Up to three delegates with technical competence in health are sent from each state. The WHA meets annually and has the capacity to elect the Executive Board and the Director General, and to determine the policies of the WHO. The WHA elects a 34-member Executive Board for a three-year term to act as the executive organ of the WHA. By gentlemen's agreement, at least three of the UNSC members are meant to be represented on the Executive Board. The Board is made up of technically qualified specialists, making it a **functional** IO. The Executive Board meets biannually to facilitate the WHA's work, oversees the WHA's budget, and may direct the Director General to respond to **pandemics**.

The Director General and the Secretariat, based in Geneva, manage the daily affairs of the WHO's 7,000-strong staff across the six regional offices, for Africa, the Americas, the Eastern Mediterranean, Europe, Southeast Asia and the Western Pacific, and 149 country and liaison offices. The regional organs of the WHO were initially controversial; they derived from the refusal of the Pan American Sanitary Bureau to be absorbed by the WHO (it had existed as long as the OIHP). The WHO's constitution stated that it should be integrated in due course, rather than the WHO taking it over as had been the case with the OIHP and the League's operations. This facilitated the rise of regional offices of the WHO, making it highly decentralised compared with the IMF and the World Bank (see Chapters 6 and 9), with a degree of discretionary decision-making at the regional level. How this affects the WHO's operations is discussed in the theory section below.

The WHO has a biennium budget of $4.4 billion for 2018–2019 (or $2.2 billion per annum) (WHO 2017b). This is tiny compared with IOs like the World Bank (see Chapter 9), or the financing of national health systems. Of note is the varied source of income from which the WHO conducts its work. It has a regular budget derived from member states' contributions; voluntary or extra-budgetary funds from member states; and a small income from other parts of the UN (such as the UNDP and UNICEF) and the World Bank. In terms of budget, the WHO has consistently faced budgetary pressure from its donor member states, which have used non-payment of their contributions to express dissatis-faction (see page 101). In 1982 the WHA approved a policy of zero real growth for the WHO's regular budget. The United States, one of the WHO's major donors, also refused to pay four-fifths of its assessed contributions in 1985. It then pushed for a policy of zero nominal growth for the IO in 1993 in opposition to the WHO's purported politicisation.

The effect of starving the WHO of income has been that it has had to use extra-budgetary funds to cover its core budget. Extrabudgetary funding has increased from 25 per cent of its funds in 1971 to over 70 per cent of its budget today. Extrabudgetary funds can be earmarked, reducing the discretion of the IO to determine where its funds will go in meeting its mandate. Donor member states have identified that the use of extrabudgetary funds had the effect of directing the WHO's policy agenda towards disease-eradication programmes.

In the 1990s the WHO sought to raise additional finance from non-state actors, including the private sector, raising questions over its ability to with-stand pressure from corporate lobbying. By the 1990s the World Bank was one of the largest sources of financing for developing countries' health programmes. Other UN funds focusing on health as part of their operations also had to find new ways to raise funds.

UNICEF

In 1946 the UNGA passed Resolution 57 (I) to create the United Nations Children's Fund (UNICEF) with a mandate to provide emergency assistance and health services to children in war-torn states. In 1950 UNGA Resolution 417 (V) extended its mandate to include children in developing states. In 1953 it was made a permanent fund, and its mandate was again extended to provide assistance for long-term benefits to children everywhere. In the 1960s it shifted from its emergency supply to a country programme approach, and it now operates in 190 states. It functions to provide programmes and emergency relief across the following areas:

- adolescent development,
- child protection,
- communication for development,
- early-childhood development,
- education,
- environmental and climate change,
- gender,
- health,
- HIV/AIDS,
- human rights,
- immunisation,
- innovation,
- nutrition,
- planning,
- monitoring and evaluation,
- water, sanitation and hygiene,
- social and economic policy,
- social inclusion,
- emergencies and humanitarian affairs (UNICEF 2017).

UNICEF's work on maternal and child health and welfare in emergencies, and in developing states, intersects with the activities of other UN agencies: the WHO on health; the FAO on food and nutrition; UNESCO on education; and the ILO on child labour. Owing to this, it has had to defend its operations in turf battles with these agencies, which opposed its operations from the beginning.

In the 1950s UNICEF worked with the WHO to cure millions of children of yaws through a worldwide campaign providing penicillin. In 1965 it was awarded the Nobel Peace Prize for its work. In 1970 it worked with the WHO to formulate the Alma Ata Declaration of Health for All by the Year 2000 and to devise its implementation strategy through a primary health-care approach (see pages 94–95). In 1987 it released its *Adjustment with a Human Face* report, which galvanised opposition to the structural adjustment policies of the IMF and World Bank on the basis of their harmful impacts on women and children (see Chapter 6). It has also contributed to international human rights law by initiating the Convention on the Rights of the Child, which came into being in 1990, the same year as a World Summit for Children was held in New York.

Structurally, UNICEF is directed by its Executive Board, which is comprised of 36 member states of the UNGA and determined by regional representation. The members of the Executive Board are elected for three-year terms by the UN Economic and Social Council (ECOSOC). The Executive Board is the primary decision-making body of the agency. It oversees the implementation of the UNGA's and ECOSOC's policy agenda. The president and four vice-presidents are elected from the Executive Board to constitute the Bureau. This is determined by regional representation, with the president rotating annually. The Bureau facilitates negotiations at the Executive Board sessions by liaising between the secretariat and the regional groups.

The secretariat and staff of UNICEF are under the management of the Executive Director, who has a five-year term and is appointed by the UN Secretary General. The Executive Director manages over 5,600 staff in eight regional offices and over 150 country offices. UNICEF has a budget of nearly $4 billion derived from voluntary contributions from member states, other IOs, NGOs, foundations, corporations and individuals. It also raises funds via the sale of greeting cards and through funding initiatives such as its 'Change for Good' requests for donations of foreign currency from air travellers.

As with other UN agencies, it struggles with the shift to earmarked contributions from its members, which designate how funds must be spent. It is considered one of the more successful UN programmes because it is well known and highly regarded in developed and developing states alike, through its Goodwill Ambassadors and through National Committees in industrialised states comprised of civil society groups that raise funds for, and awareness of, its work.

UNAIDS

While the WHO and UNICEF are old IOs created in the aftermath of WWII, the Joint United Nations Programme on HIV/AIDS (UNAIDS) is relatively recent. It was established in 1996 to combat the human immunodeficiency virus (HIV) epidemic, which causes acquired immunodeficiency syndrome (AIDS). The virus, which was first reported in 1981 in the United States, was recognised as spreading via contact with an infected person's body fluids through high-risk behaviour, such as sex without use of a condom with multiple partners, and the sharing of needles when injecting drugs. The virus spread fast, but the symptoms of the disease would take time to emerge, causing social panic regarding how it ought to be addressed when the symptoms did emerge. The WHO estimated that there were 36.7 million people worldwide living with HIV at the end of 2016. The disease has had major impacts on populations in developing countries and their prospects for economic growth and development. The social stigma of how the disease is spread has made responses to its prevention and management extremely difficult.

The WHO established a number of initiatives to address the spread of HIV/AIDS, such as the Special (later Global) Programme on AIDS from 1987. This early programme took a social medical approach while prioritising human rights (see page 94). UNAIDS grew out of the broad perception that the WHO was unable to address the epidemic because it viewed HIV/AIDS as just one of the diseases it tackled.

The WHO was overwhelmed by the nature of the problem, given its limited resources, and had to contend with the numerous rival initiatives for coordinating a UN response to the epidemic begun by donor member states. In 1995, WHO Director General Nakajima cut back the Global Programme to better integrate it within the WHO, leaving a vacuum for a joint programme comprised of multiple agencies across the UN to fill. The WHO subsequently outsourced its HIV/AIDS work to UNAIDS until 2001, when it reopened its HIV programme. It then had to live with being only one of multiple UNAIDS funders.

UNAIDS has a mandate to be the leading agency to coordinate the UN's response to HIV/AIDS. The joint programme, brought into being via ECOSOC Resolution 1994/24, was to be co-sponsored by the WHO, UNDP, UNICEF, UNESCO, UNFPA and the World Bank (on ECOSOC see Chapter 9). The resolution gave UNAIDS six functions:

1. provide global leadership;
2. promote global consensus on policy and programmatic approaches;
3. strengthen the capacity of the UN to monitor trends and ensure appropriate and effective policies and strategies at the country level;
4. help develop and implement comprehensive national strategies;

5. promote political and social mobilisation to prevent and respond to HIV/
   AIDS;
6. advocate greater political commitment through the mobilisation and allocation of adequate resources (ECOSOC 1994: Objective I (3)).

The structure of the agency is unique within the UN – creating an innovative
and informal partnership of its now 10 co-sponsor IOs, NGOs, member states
and corporations. The governing body of UNAIDS is the Programme Coordination Board (PCB), which is comprised of 22 ECOSOC member states that rotate
annually according to UN regional groupings, the co-sponsors and five regional
NGO representatives. The 10 co-sponsors and the UNAIDS Secretariat constitute
the Committee of Cosponsoring Organizations, which reports to the PCB. The
Committee of Cosponsoring Organizations meets at least annually to determine
the allocation of resources among the co-sponsors. The work of UNAIDS undertaken by each of the co-sponsors is determined by their area of specialisation. As
with UNICEF, the contributions to UNAIDS are voluntary. Its proposed budget
for the 2018/2019 financial year is $562 million (UNAIDS 2017b: 34).

The UNAIDS Secretariat is run by the UNAIDS Executive Director. This position is at the level of an under-secretary-general within the UN. The secretariat
has grown: there are country representatives and offices in over 60 countries,
with focal points in 20 more states. It also has liaison offices in donor states. As
global health scholar Franklyn Lisk points out, 'the secretariat has expanded to
become a recognized entity within the UN system and has taken on the character
of a separate UN specialized agency in all but name' (Lisk 2009: 36–37).

The Problem: Health for All, the Global Spread of Communicable Diseases and Bioterrorism

From the very beginning IOs have had to determine how they would tackle the
problem of health. The WHO had to identify how it would seek to achieve its aim
to attain the highest possible level of health for all people. Over time different
approaches would emerge: the social medicine approach highlighted the social
basis for ill-health, including poor nutrition and lack of sanitation, access to
clean water and affordable care. The means to address this is seen as costly
interventions to build advanced health systems for states. This is called a
horizontal approach to health provision. The alternative was a focus on disease

eradication, which is based on a biomedical approach that can target specific diseases and uses costly medication. This is called the vertical approach. Both have advantages and weaknesses. As the lead international agency with a broad mandate but limited financing, the WHO had to identify the best means of promoting health. For many decades it sought to do both. This led to a panoply of programmes, most with limited funding. Since the late 1990s, the WHO has used a 'diagonal' approach that tried to strengthen health systems while using the voluntary funding to target specific health issues. Debates also ensued as to whether the WHO should focus on clarifying norms and scientific regulations on health or whether it should be a technical assistance agency for its member states like other UN agencies. Owing to the smallness of its budget, it could not do both.

Generally the WHO has favoured the biomedical approach. It would launch a range of disease-eradication programmes, including the International Tuberculosis Campaign (1947–1951); the Malaria Eradication Programme (1955–1970); the Smallpox Eradication Programme (1967–1980); the Expanded Programme on Immunization (from 1974); the Onchocerciasis Control Programme (1974–); the Global Programme on AIDS (1987–1996); the Polio Eradication Initiative (1988–); the Leprosy Elimination Strategy (1991–); and the Global Programme to Eliminate Guinea Worm (1997–).

The WHO's most successful programme is the eradication of smallpox, which was achieved in 1980. The WHO continues to fight polio, the eradication of which is nearly complete, although small outbreaks continue to be reported in Pakistan and Afghanistan. However, it has faced considerable criticism for its failure to eradicate malaria despite the significant funds that it has spent on the programme. This led to declining support for its efforts, while a proliferation of increasingly drug-resistant strains led to reinfection of populations that had for a time been free of malaria. In 1998 the WHO would push the Malaria 'Rollback' Programme rather than eradication, in partnership with the World Bank, UNDP and UNICEF.

Meanwhile, the WHO continued to advance the idea that health is a universal human right. In 1978 the WHO and UNICEF adopted the Alma Ata Declaration of Health for All by the Year 2000. This was followed in 1981 by the strategy to make the goal a reality, but efforts to do so were radically undermined by North–South politics (see pages 102–103) and the support for **neoliberal economic policies** by donor states and IOs such as the World Bank. The neoliberal focus meant that states with weak national health systems were nonetheless encouraged to privatise health provision while implementing cost-recovery and fee-for-service systems, meaning that individual service users had to pay for their treatment. Efforts to resurrect the Health for All aim in the mid 1990s failed to gain traction due to **globalisation** and entrenched neoliberal economic ideas.

This is not to suggest that non-communicable diseases were ignored. In the late 1990s Director General Gro Harlem Bruntland pressed the WHO to make more of its regulations legally binding, specifically championing tobacco control. The use of tobacco has major health implications and was seen as a potential time bomb for developing states' health systems. This shift was contentious because health effects from smoking are considered 'lifestyle diseases', in contrast to the communicable diseases that have been the main thrust of WHO efforts. Nonetheless, in 2003 the WHA approved the Framework Convention on Tobacco Control, which bans the advertising of tobacco products, as well as requiring health warnings on packaging.

This brought the WHO into direct conflict with the tobacco industry. The WHO would also come into conflict with the producers of breast-milk substitutes and of sugary foods over establishing health codes for their use and marketing in developing states. Under Director General Margaret Chan (2006–2017) Universal Health Care coverage was made a priority.

In the 1980s and 1990s the return of tuberculosis and the spread of West Nile virus, Ebola and HIV/AIDS turned member states' attention to the outbreaks of new and resurgent infectious diseases. This shifted the WHO towards viewing health within a global security framework, to protect states from the spread of infectious diseases. The WHO was asked to provide strategies to detect and respond to infectious diseases. In 1997 the WHO established an outbreak-verification system as a surveillance mechanism to globally monitor disease outbreaks. In 2000 it upgraded this to the Global Outbreak Alert and Response Network (GOARN) to detect, verify and contain epidemics. This gave the WHO advance warning of unusual events prior to the uncontrolled spread of an infectious disease outbreak.

SARS was the first 'post-Westphalian' pathogen with a rapid onset and possible global transmission of an unknown disease. It emerged in the Chinese Province of Guangdong, and spread via the air travel of infected people. SARS would lead to 8,422 infections and 916 deaths. The WHO publicly imposed level-three travel advisories on Beijing, Shanxi Province and Toronto. The advisories were based on the severity of the outbreak; whether the disease spread via the general population or was confined in transmission; and the ability of the member state to contain it. The SARS epidemic tested the global health security framework, and it quickly contained the epidemic.

The SARS outbreak, along with the fear of the use of chemical and biological weapons, helped advance the redrafting of the International Health Regulations, which had begun in the mid 1990s. States were increasingly attuned to the possibility of chemical and biological warfare and bioterrorism, including domestic attacks (the sarin gas attack in Tokyo in 1995 and an anthrax attack in the United States in 2001). The new IHR passed in 2005 were implemented in 2007. They delimit the WHO's power, role and responsibilities by restricting its ability to improvise as it did with SARS.

The revised IHR aimed to remove disincentives for states to notify the WHO of events which may develop into epidemics. States were not reporting outbreaks, fearing negative impacts on travel, trade and commerce, with dramatic impacts on their economy. Not reporting, of course, enables the spread of infectious diseases (for example, a plague outbreak in India in 1994 led to over 5,000 suspected cases and 53 deaths).

The WHO's Global Health Security Strategy is comprised of three prongs. First, it seeks to contain known communicable diseases through supporting national surveillance and response mechanisms, backed by laboratory and diagnostic facilities. Second, it aims to respond to events like avian flu or the release of biological agents and acts of bioterrorism through the collaboration of operating verification systems, GOARN, WHO collaborating centres, other UN agencies and states' intelligence networks. Third, it helps to improve national preparedness through plans, surveillance and verification systems to manage the spread of infectious diseases.

In sum, there are various ways in which health can be understood and therefore tackled. There are many causes of ill-health, and IOs need to identify how they will address the problem. Given the limited budget and the proclivities of member states, IOs like the WHO have to prioritise which forms of ill-health they will address and how. Cleavages between social medicine and a biomedical approach remain, as do tensions within the WHO over its norm-setting role compared with providing technical assistance to its members.

Explanations of Health IOs' Behaviour

In seeking to explain whether or not the WHO is successful in meeting its mandate, we need to go beyond whether it helps people attain the highest possible level of health. Different theoretical approaches can identify whether there are problems with attempting to cooperate on issues of international or global health within a system of sovereign states, whether cooperation enables states to achieve relative or absolute gains, whether difficulties lie in the delegation to a wayward agent, or even whether the organisation's culture impedes its activities.

IR Theoretical Explanations of Health IOs' Behaviour

Many of the early studies of health IOs did not employ an explicit theoretical frame to explain their behaviour. Indeed, some are firsthand accounts of the activities of the UNICEF and UNFPA by practitioners or were commissioned as an official history (Salas 1976; Sadik 2002; Black 1987, 1996). Can we explain the actions and operations of health IOs through the lens of traditional IR theories? In some ways we can. **Liberal internationalist** ideals were fundamental to the creation of the WHO, UNICEF and UNFPA (see Box 5.1). In the aftermath of WWII there were new pressures for advancing international cooperation for the greater good. Direct actions of the new agencies would provide relief to millions. The same sentiment drove the creation of UNAIDS in 1996. The UN funds and programmes were based on voluntary contributions for the public good. Beyond this, the basis of the new agencies and programmes would be informed by **functionalist** arguments on the need for specialist technical experts stripped of politics to best meet the mandate of the new IOs, such as doctors dominating within the WHO.

Of course, from the instantiation of these IOs, power politics would cloud decision-making, especially once the Cold War began in earnest. **Realist** and **neorealist** theories can explain how and why the Soviet Union and other members of the Soviet bloc left the WHO in 1949 (Siddiqi 1995: 104). Such approaches can also explain why the United States demanded the allegiance of UNICEF during this period, threatening to deny it the resources and staff needed to meet its mandate to provide emergency relief to all women and children, including in communist states (Morris 2015: 2). Morris (2015) also identifies how US foreign policy reinforced gender norms through the agency. Power politics can explain how and why states advocate for, and use, IOs to advance their own interests and ensure their security and survival.

The use of **neoliberal institutionalism** is brought to the forefront on the question of the benefits to be gained from international cooperation to meet increasingly 'global' health problems. Overall states gain from international cooperation and coordination through the WHO in relation to preventing the

Box 5.1 The United Nations Population Fund

The UNFPA grew out of concern over rapid population growth and emerging debates over the ecological limits of finite resources. It was first established as a Trust Fund under ECOSOC Resolution 1084 and UNGA Resolution 2211 in 1967. The UNFPA took its direction from the UN's Population Commission (the research advisor to ECOSOC on population). The UN has over 20 different bodies involved in population activities, but the UNFPA finances more than 90 per cent of their activities. In 1969 it was made a permanent body, but was under the administration of the UNDP. From 1973 the UNFPA was led by an Executive Director who reported to the UNDP's Executive Body; from the 1990s this Executive Board would be a joint body of both the UNDP and the UNFPA (on the UNDP see Chapter 9). The Executive Body reports directly to the UNGA.

The UNFPA was mandated to build knowledge and capacity for population and family planning; promote awareness of population problems; extend assistance to states according to their needs; and play a leading and coordinating role within the UN on population. Initially the Fund functioned by parcelling out finances to different UN bodies for population programmes, but this proved unworkable. The UNFPA now also provides project support and technical assistance directly to states. Currently it operates in over 150 states, and works with states, NGOs and other IOs to achieve its mandate.

As with UNICEF and UNAIDS, the UNFPA is dependent on voluntary contributions from member states, other IOs, foundations, NGOs, corporations and individuals. It had a budget of $979 million in 2015. The UNFPA is a highly centralised UN agency. There has been little written on the UNFPA, despite the fact that the population of a territory is a vital component of state sovereignty. Perhaps the biggest impact on its operations is when states do not honour their pledges to contribute to the fund; the states which have failed to honour their pledges include one of the largest contributors, the United States. The United States has halted financing for IOs that promote family planning that may include abortion (under Presidents Reagan, G. W. Bush and Trump). This issue, colloquially known as the 'global gag rule', best demonstrates liberal internationalist arguments about how domestic political coalitions shape states' interactions with IOs.

spread of infectious diseases. Just as with UNICEF, UNAIDS and the UNFPA, transaction costs are reduced and states benefit from information sharing through a centralised IO. With the WHO all states benefit from the speedy containment of rapidly transmitted communicable diseases. Yet there is also a high likelihood of cheating on international agreements. States that agree to share information may do so at their individual cost, leading to the prospect of defection.

The downside of alerting the WHO to an outbreak in one's territory is immediate: travel advisories lead to a loss of revenue through a drop in tourism, trade and commerce, with a significant impact on one's gross national income. Moreover, states that share their knowledge about an infectious disease with the WHO may contribute to the creation of a vaccine by a corporation, which may then sell it back to the affected state, raising questions about who gains relatively or absolutely. IR theories are useful in explaining how and why states choose to cooperate with health IOs like the WHO. However, not all actions of health IOs are best examined through state-centric approaches, and, indeed, most of the literature on global health does not do so.

IO Approaches to Explaining the WHO's Behaviour

While recognising turf battles, a lack of resources and the importance of leadership, most studies of health IOs are not theoretically based, and nor do they examine the internal material and ideational factors that direct the action of an IO. Most IO-specific theoretical approaches analyse the WHO. Both the **principal–agent model** and constructivist **organisational culture** approaches have been used to explain how and why it acts the way it does. In terms of the P–A model, scholars sought to explain why the WHO would overstep its mark in the SARS outbreak to extend travel advisories to the public, thereby engaging in IO **slack** or behaviour undesired by the principal (Cortell and Peterson 2006). The WHO has a degree of **discretion** owing to its organisational **autonomy**; staffing and voting rules allow the IO to establish its own preferences independently of its member states. Thus Cortell and Peterson argue that the two-thirds majority voting of the member states of the WHA on important questions makes it difficult to obtain shared agreement among the principals, enabling the WHO Secretariat to engage in agency slack. Yet it has not done so very often because the staff tend towards caution resulting from their shared experiences and commitment to the bureaucracy. This is akin to constructivist organisational culture perspectives, where an international professional staff creates a culture which may discourage the WHO from challenging the status quo.

WHO scholar Erin Graham (2014) further contends that the P–A model can explain the WHO's 'faithfulness' to principals' demands by examining how the internally fragmented structure of the IO increases its ability to act independently. She argues that the WHO's decentralised structure means that it is not a single agent but a collective agent. This means that actors within the WHO's regional and country offices cannot be controlled by headquarters, which in turn limits the ability of the principals to access information and control the IO (contra neoliberal institutionalism).

She argues that this explains the inability of the WHO to meet its Health for All goal via strengthening national health systems, because the country and regional offices were neither coordinated by headquarters nor effectively overseen by the WHO's member states. Headquarters staff could not act effectively because they did not have control of the budget and staffing at country level and because they lacked oversight, screening and sanctioning measures. This lack of control and effectiveness explains why member states such as the United States and Sweden limited the WHO's budget (Graham 2014: 380–381). In short, Graham argues that the WHO's fragmented structure and organisational subcultures can be invoked to explain why different units within the WHO act according to their own preferences, leading to agency slack and an inability of the WHO to meet its mandate.

Global health security scholar Adam Kamradt-Scott seeks to blend constructivist accounts of IO behaviour with ideas based on the P–A model. For example, he argues that the WHO has advanced a global health security narrative in response to disease outbreaks and that this fits some principals' interests and not those of others. He thus distinguishes between the WHO's relationship with 'proximal principals', which the WHO deems critical to its mission, and its relationship with 'distal principals', which are not (Kamradt-Scott 2015: 11). See also Box 5.2.

Constructivist organisational culture arguments have also been used to explain the WHO's behaviour. Most scholars of the WHO recognise that it has a homogeneous professional medical culture owing to the fact that most of its staff, including its Director General, are trained doctors. From this perspective the WHO takes a politically neutral, technical, biomedical approach to global health problems. This has led to accusations of being pathologically cautious and overly focused on procedure.

Commentators have argued that this affects how the WHO undertakes its mandate. For example, the shift into addressing HIV/AIDS was considered

Box 5.2 Historical Institutionalist Explanations of the WHO's Behaviour

Fragmentation is a major aspect of the WHO, influencing how budgets are determined through the regional offices and how programmes are operationalised, including semi-autonomous special programmes such as the Global Programme on HIV/AIDS. For WHO scholar Tine Hanrieder (2015), the WHO's behaviour and its ability to change are best understood through historical institutionalism. This theoretical approach, like the P–A model, recognises that there are different groups within and outside the institution that have their own interests and preferences that either favour the status quo or favour reform. However, historical institutionalism, like constructivist organisational culture, also recognises that the internal rules and norms of an organisation build up over time. These internal practices and ways of doing things become 'sticky' and difficult to change.

Hanrieder argues that it is not culture but power and local conflicts between different coalitions within and outside the fragmented WHO that explain the WHO's behaviour. Fragmentation generates a path-dependent dynamic such that the IO's actions become locked in. Over repeated efforts to reform the IO, this path dependence is reinforced. This explains why ongoing attempts to change the WHO do not fundamentally alter it, despite calls for the IO to reform or die.

difficult because the WHO had established an organisational culture that some called 'eradicationitis'. This contrasts with the rapidity with which it responded to the SARS outbreak in 2003. IO scholar Nitsan Chorev (2012), among others, goes further, arguing that the WHO has the capacity to restructure what she calls 'global ideational regimes' to accord with its organisational culture.

She examines two periods to show how: the 1970s, when developing states articulated a demand for a **New International Economic Order**; and the 1980s, when powerful member states and other IOs such as the IMF, OECD and World Bank pushed for **neoliberal economic policies** (see Chapter 9). In the 1970s the WHO responded to developing states' demands to address global inequality between states over industrialisation and unequal terms of trade with the Health for All Declaration that prioritised universal access to health. As Chorev points out, this reversed developing states' demands for economic growth first and social development second. In the 1980s the WHO responded to the broader neoliberal economic policies by embracing health policies that contributed to economic growth first and social development second. Yet the WHO never advocated for budget cuts in health care, and mobilised around a convention on tobacco control and other codes resisted by the private sector. Chorev argues that these actions constituted a strategy of strategic adaptation. The WHO chose to reframe member states' demands to accord with its preferences, which in turn changed international norms on health.

Competition over Providing Global Health: Philanthropists, Hybrid IOs and Activists

Over the last few decades there has been an influx of actors and resources in the field of global health at the transnational, international and global levels. Of course, the health IOs discussed here compete with each other and with other IOs in terms of shaping international practice. Powerful IOs such as the WTO were effectively creating binding rules regarding the trade of health services and health products, including pharmaceuticals, that directly impinge on the ability of the WHO to meets its mandate. However, health, like other international issues, is not dominated exclusively by IOs. Overwhelmingly this has led scholars to view international health cooperation in terms of global health governance.

In health the activities of foundations have been fundamental. The Rockefeller Foundation was vital to advancing work on international health and identifying the need for the WHO. The Rockefeller Foundation's mandate is to promote the well-being of humanity throughout the world. It provides grants for researching new ways to think about problems plaguing humanity, funds practical research in testing new initiatives, and uses its position, knowledge and networks to advance new ideas globally. In 1935 it developed a vaccine for yellow fever in its laboratory in New York, and it has since trained over 360 scientists in 26 states. It has approximately $4 billion in endowment.

The work of the Ford Foundation was instrumental in drawing attention to population as a problem needing an international response, facilitating the entry of the UNFPA into the field. The Ford Foundation has a similar mandate to advance human welfare. It provides grants directly to individuals, as well as institutions, to examine how to address social problems. It has a board of 17 trustees to oversee its work, is headquartered in New York, with 10 regional offices, and has an endowment of over $12 billion (Ford Foundation 2017). The Bill and Melinda Gates Foundation (see also Chapter 9) is also a major influence in health governance. Their mandate is to improve people's health and well-being. The foundation provides grants that focus on addressing hunger and poverty; using science and technology to save lives in developing countries; and improving education. It has helped establish and invested in partnerships to achieve these aims. It has over 1,300 staff and an endowment of $44 billion. The Bill and Melinda Gates Foundation has contributed to the rise of hybrid IOs comprised of state and non-state members that seek to address specific diseases, for example UNAIDS (see pages 92–94) and the Global Alliance for Vaccines and Immunization (GAVI), which also receives funding from the Rockefeller Foundation among others.

GAVI is a public–private partnership or collaboration involving the WHO, World Bank, UNICEF, bilateral aid organisations, developing states, research institutes, NGOs and vaccine manufacturers, which was established in 1999 with the crucial backing of the Bill and Melinda Gates Foundation. Its mandate is to provide vaccines and their delivery to people in the poorest countries, facilitate vaccine research and development, and provide support for developing states through assisting them to strengthen their health-care systems.

It functions to provide secure funding for vaccination programmes, to ensure that vaccines are affordable, to facilitate routine immunisation and vaccination campaigns, and to help strengthen vaccine delivery (GAVI 2014: 4). Structurally, GAVI is governed by its Board, which is made up of its alliance members as well as unaffiliated experts. The Board delegates operational decisions to an Executive Committee. GAVI's CEO manages the small secretariat. In its first phase (2000–2006) GAVI had a budget of $1.67 billion.

Another hybrid IO is the Global Fund to Fight HIV/AIDS, Tuberculosis and Malaria (GFATM), which was created in 2002. Its mandate is to attract, manage and disburse additional resources. It is a public–private partnership that seeks to provide a sustainable and significant contribution to the reduction of infections, illness and death from HIV/AIDS, tuberculosis (TB) and malaria. It functions as a financing instrument to raise money to invest in national health systems in developing states. Decision-making is determined by the Board, which is structurally unusual because it includes one NGO from a developing country, one NGO from a developed country, one representative of someone living with the diseases, nine regional seats, six national seats for major donors, one private-sector seat, one private-foundation seat and four non-voting advisory seats allocated to the WHO, the World Bank, UNAIDS and a Swiss national. They have equal voting powers to facilitate more democratic decision-making. The GFATM is located in Geneva, and has a secretariat with approximately 650 staff. By 2015 it had raised over $33 billion (GFATM 2015).

As this book has identified in Chapter 2, many IOs emerge through a process of emanation from others (such as the UNDP), while some may be ushered in by the work of NGOs (such as the ILO). The actions of the NGO Save the Children helped pave the way for UNICEF, as well as providing the basis for the League of Nations' and United Nations' Declarations on the Rights of the Child. It was also the first to articulate the idea that children had a special claim to be protected from the scourge of war and begin programmes to rehabilitate children after atrocities.

The mandate of Save the Children, which was founded in 1919, is to inspire breakthroughs in how the world treats children, in order to make an immediate and lasting change in their lives. It functions as a humanitarian emergency organisation as well as being an advocate for children to promote their survival, learning and protection. Save the Children International is now an umbrella NGO comprised of 28 national NGOs that operates in 120 states. In 2016 it spent $1.24 million on its operations (Save the Children 2017b).

Another NGO working directly in health is Médecins Sans Frontières (MSF) or Doctors without Borders (on the International Committee of the Red Cross see Chapter 3). MSF was established in 1971. Its mandate is to provide medical assistance to victims. This includes situations of conflict, natural disasters and epidemics as well as health-care exclusion. It functions to

- provide basic health care,
- carry out vaccination campaigns,
- fight epidemics,
- operate nutrition centres,
- provide mental-health care,
- perform surgery,
- rehabilitate and run hospitals and clinics (MSF 2017).

It was established as a private association and is comprised of medical professionals who prioritise medical ethics, neutrality and impartiality. MSF International is now comprised of 24 national and regional associations that link into five operational directorates with a central office in Geneva. The operational directorates undertake humanitarian assistance programmes. It has missions in over 80 developing states, and employs over 30,000 staff. Approximately 90 per cent of its funds are raised by donation. In 2014 it had a budget of €1.28 billion (MSF 2014).

There are thousands more NGOs operating at multiple scales (local, national, regional and international) to address ill-health. States as well as health IOs depend on these organisations to tackle health problems. Health, as with other topics covered in other chapters, is increasingly seen through the lens of global governance, and Chapter 11 examines the benefits and pitfalls of doing so for IO scholars.

Chapter Summary

Health is a ubiquitous concern for humanity. We all want to be well. Yet the chances for being healthy vary significantly across the globe. Over time, international health regulations for protecting and securing health have emerged, as have IOs to work towards this aim. States invest IOs with the authority to act on issues of international and global health. The WHO remains the lead organisation for responding to global health concerns, although other UN agencies (and the World Bank) play their parts as shaped by their mandates. IOs like UNICEF and the UNFPA often work together, although turf wars do occur. Much of the literature on global health focuses on the problems within the WHO and how best to improve its operations. Considerable theoretical work has been undertaken to examine whether the problem lies with the principal or the agent, whether reform is possible, and whether this problem results from rational action or organisational culture. How the WHO will interact with NGOs, hybrid IOs and philanthropists as it responds to old, resurgent and new health concerns remains to be seen.

Guiding Questions

1. What are the different ways in which health is viewed as a problem?
2. What are the benefits and costs of international health cooperation?
3. Can we consider the culture of a health IO as affecting its ability to meet its mandate?
4. Is discussion of health IOs redundant, given the shift towards hybrid IOs?

5. Does the recognition of the security impact of major outbreaks of disease and bioterrorism increase the likelihood of effective international health cooperation?

Further References

Internet Resources

Global Health Hub: Provides original commentary and information from academic research on health for practitioners, www.globalhealthhub.org/

The Lancet Global Health Blog: The blog of the prestigious health journal covering all health issues, http://globalhealth.thelancet.com/

SciDevNet: News and analysis of science and development aspects of health, www.scidev.net/global/health/

Further Reading

Black, M., 1996, *Children First: The Story of UNICEF: Past and Present*, Oxford, Oxford University Press.

Chorev, N., 2012, *The World Health Organization between North and South*, Ithaca, NY, Cornell University Press.

Davies, S. E., 2010, *Global Politics of Health*, Cambridge, Cambridge University Press.

Fidler, D., 1999, *International Law and Infectious Diseases*, Oxford, Clarendon Press.

Hanrieder, T., 2015, *International Organization in Time: Fragmentation and Reform*, Oxford, Oxford University Press.

Knight, L., 2008, *UNAIDS: The First Ten Years, 1996–2006*, Geneva, Joint United Nations Programme on HIV/AIDS.

Lee, K., 2009, *The World Health Organization*, London and New York, Routledge.

Weindling, P., 1995, *International Health Organisations and Movements, 1918–1939*, Cambridge, Cambridge University Press.

6 Providing Financial Governance

Introduction

In 2007 the world became embroiled in the **Great Recession**, the deepest and most significant financial crisis since the **Great Depression** of the 1930s. **Financial liberalisation** has increased the number and the severity of financial crises since the late 1980s and they are now 'problems without passports' since most states liberalised financial markets in the 1990s. The 2007 crisis spread from the United States to the advanced states in Western Europe, but most damagingly hit Iceland, Belarus and Hungary. The 'PIIGS', or Portugal, Ireland, Italy, Spain and Greece, then suffered a major **debt crisis** from 2009 that threatened the **Eurozone** and raised the spectre of abandoning the euro as a viable currency.

This chapter will examine

- the main IO tasked with governing global finance, namely the International Monetary Fund (IMF), and the informal multilateralism of the Group of Seven (G7);
- the rise of the Group of Twenty (G20), the Bank of International Settlements (BIS) and the Financial Stability Board (FSB);
- the main problems these IOs are now seeking to solve, from ensuring the financial health of states in a stable international monetary system of fixed exchange rates up to the 1970s to maintaining the health of the global, volatile, **laissez-faire** system from the 1990s onwards;
- the drivers of financial IO behaviour, as analytically unpacked using both IR and IO-focused theoretical approaches.
- competitors to traditional IOs where transnational private regulators attempt to self-govern the financial sector, including credit risk agencies, the G30 and transnational regulatory networks.

The Mandate, Function and Structure of International Finance IOs

Since the 1997 Asian Financial Crisis (Box 6.1) debate has focused on reinvigorating the global financial architecture to mitigate financial crises and their spread. In outlining the activities of the main IOs and institutions governing global finance, their mandate, function and structure are detailed.

The International Monetary Fund (IMF)

The most important IO governing the international monetary system is the IMF (or the Fund). Outside the UN's responses to war, no other IO has received as much vitriol as the IMF, not even the World Bank and the WTO, although together they advance **globalisation**. The IMF is largely a technical financial institution, currently staffed by 2,600 economists, and became a household name only in the 1980s when it began to increase the number of conditions to its agreements (loans). The IMF's policy of directing states towards increasingly

Box 6.1 The IMF and the Asian Financial Crisis (AFC)

East and Southeast Asia experienced one of the longest periods of high economic growth in history, the so-called 'Asian Miracle'. In the 1990s, Asia was attracting nearly half of all capital flows to developing states, with no concern over its stability. Yet financial volatility is a reality where institutions are weak or just becoming established, as is the case in many emerging markets. IMF surveillance of economic conditions ignored the high volume of short-term inflows of capital into these countries. This was problematic because such inflows are the 'most volatile and footloose form of foreign capital' (Eichengreen 2008).

The crisis first hit when short-term investors realised that economic conditions in Thailand were no longer favourable. Investors began to speculate on the value of the Thai bhat. Thailand used its foreign reserves to uphold the value of the bhat against speculative attacks throughout 1997. Fears regarding other Asian economies fuelled a rapid outflow of foreign capital in Malaysia, the Philippines and Indonesia, leading to a drastic depreciation of their currencies and a sharp contraction of GDP. The AFC then affected Taiwan, Hong Kong and South Korea, spreading, albeit with less effect, to Argentina, Mexico, Brazil and the New York Stock Exchange. Caught by surprise, the IMF proposed large bail-out packages with harsh austerity conditions to Thailand, South Korea and Indonesia.

IMF prescriptions are now recognised as having contributed to a deepening of the crisis. Malaysia was the only state to impose capital controls to stop the outflow of capital, which went against IMF recommendations. It was the only economy that was relatively protected. Thailand, Indonesia and South Korea all experienced severe economic contractions and high rates of unemployment, toppling their governments. The IMF was roundly condemned for its response to the AFC, with many critics holding the view that the Fund was protecting investors from industrialised states rather than defending the interests of its borrower member states.

detailed economic reforms called the **Washington Consensus** meant that the Fund's programmes encountered mass opposition (Peet 2003).

Debates continue to rage over the necessity and effectiveness of the IMF and its **conditionality**, especially over its role in the AFC (see Box 6.1) and its prescriptions for Africa, as well as for Eastern European states transitioning post-communism (Woods 2006a). Despite this, membership in the IMF (it had 189 members as of 2018) became nearly universal in the 1990s with the collapse of communism. How and why did it shift from being a reputable technical institution to being an infamous leviathan?

The IMF in the International Monetary System

The IMF was designed to be the lynchpin of the international monetary system. Accordingly the Fund has significant **authority** and **autonomy** to make technical economic decisions (Best 2005). The IMF was central to the post-WWII international economic order along with the stillborn International Trade Organization (later the GATT and the WTO) and the World Bank. The post-WWII order established a system described by political scientist John Ruggie (1982) as **embedded liberalism**. This was based on three components: an adherence to (**Keynesian**) economic liberalism; **multilateralism**; and the rule of law.

At Bretton Woods, in New Hampshire, 44 WWII Allies meeting at the UN's Monetary and Financial Conference established an international monetary **regime** (known as Bretton Woods) that consisted of two components. First, currencies would have fixed exchange rates and be 'pegged' to the US dollar. The US dollar was the main currency for international trade. In turn, the US dollar was valued at 35 dollars per ounce of gold. This meant that the United States would exchange its dollars for gold with whoever was holding them. Fixing exchange rates to gold would prevent the fluctuations in money markets that had occurred in the inter-war period. Second, strict controls were put in place to limit the flow of capital between states. This would make the international monetary system inflexible but stable. A stable monetary system would enable trade to flourish while supporting states' efforts to promote full employment.

The Mandate of the IMF

The IMF was mandated to assist states in international monetary cooperation, to promote exchange rate stability, and to provide members with short-term arrangements (loans) if they were beset by **balance-of-payments** problems. The IMF is a service IO. International monetary cooperation is conducted among member states, but it is then implemented by IMF staff under its Managing Director. Originally, the IMF sought to monitor states' exchange rates and approve small adjustments to a currency's exchange value. In terms of its function, the IMF never really met its original objective of maintaining pegged but adjustable exchange rates between Western Europe and the United States. The United States demanded that its Western European allies not seek IMF assistance in return for the 1947 Marshall Plan to rebuild Europe.

The Function of the IMF

Although the IMF helped determine whether and when states should adjust the valuation of their currencies, states often went ahead without Fund approval. Throughout the 1960s it became clear that the system was too rigid, and states, especially the United States, found it difficult to maintain their currency valuation in the light of government monetary policies. In 1971 US President Nixon 'delinked' the US dollar from the fixed exchange rate, stating that the United States would no longer exchange US dollars for gold. Attempts to devise a new gold standard failed. By 1973 it was clear that the de facto system of the US dollar floating against other currencies was working. Although it was more volatile than the fixed-exchange-rate system, states could intervene to buy or sell their own currencies should market swings of the value of their currency be too great. The Fund's role in adjusting exchanges rates was over.

Nonetheless, the IMF could still monitor states' exchange rates and their balance of payments. The Fund would provide arrangements (loans) to member states to ease balance-of-payments problems or those suffering a shortfall of foreign reserves. The Fund is akin to an international credit union: member states pool their resources on the basis that any one of the member states can draw on Fund resources. Should a member not be able to meet its international loan obligations, it could go to the IMF for a short-term arrangement. States could borrow foreign currency from the IMF as an international 'lender of last resort', or when private capital markets would no longer lend to them because of their deteriorating economic condition. In this way, the Fund provided states with insurance against possible economic crisis (Vreeland 2007).

The IMF created its own unit of account (currency) called Special Drawing Rights (SDRs), based on a basket of hard currencies used in international monetary markets. In December 2015, the Chinese yuan joined the basket of reserve currencies along with the US dollar, the British pound, the euro and the yen. This signals that the Chinese currency is safe and freely usable. An IMF programme is where a state can borrow foreign currency through a voluntary exchange of SDRs. This can occur between members or through an IMF designation, where financially secure states purchase SDRs from weak states (Momani 2014).

According to the IMF's Articles of Agreement, all Fund programmes aim to stabilise states' economies to enable national prosperity. In the past, four main facilities were used: the basic Stand-By Arrangements (SBA) for lending for one to two years (this remains); the Extended Fund Facility (EFF, this also remains); the Structural Adjustment Facility (SAF); and the Enhanced Structural Adjustment Facility (ESAF). The last three programmes recognise that balance-of-payments problems may require extended financing and are meant to operate for three to four years. The SAF and ESAF (which changed names in the 1990s and 2000s) required the state to adjust its economy.

By the end of the 1960s the industrialised members were using IMF arrangements less, stopping completely in 1985. Some European states would resume borrowing from the Fund after 2008. From the 1960s developing countries began to increase their use of the Fund as a result of fluctuating prices for their commodities and the 1970s oil shocks (see Chapter 9). Member states also gave the Fund surveillance powers to monitor members' economic and financial policies to ensure monetary stability.

Who Controls the Fund?

The quota held by a member state determines their vote in the Fund. The United States has the largest vote in the IMF, followed by Japan, Germany, France, the UK and China, but it has only 16.74 per cent of the vote. While seemingly paltry, this provides the United States with an effective 'veto' over decisions requiring 85 per cent of the vote, including quota reform as noted above. Organisationally the Fund's shareholder member states are all represented through the Board of Governors, which meets annually to determine the Fund's overall policy direction.

The Governors, usually the Minister for Finance or the Treasury, then delegate power to a Board of 24 Executive Directors, all of whom are representatives of member states. Voting share then determines how states are represented on the Board of Executive Directors. Up until now, member states with the five largest quotas, such as the United States, could appoint their own Executive Director who represents their interests alone. States with smaller standing in the global economy have to pool their votes and share a constituency. Thus one Executive Director would be elected to represent their diverse interests. The largest constituency represents 24 states.

Governance reforms approved in December 2015 radically depart from this practice. European shareholders have agreed to reduce their Board representation by two chairs, and members approved the removal of Executive Directors 'appointed' by the five largest members. All Executive Directors will now be elected to represent member states. It will be interesting to see whether informal norms of states working together (in coalitions and constituencies) will shape future elections of Executive Directors. Even if this radical shake-up does alter entrenched norms about how and with whom to vote, traditionally voting in the IMF is rare, with decisions made by consensus. Yet it is clear which way powerful member states vote.

How Effective Is the IMF?

How effective has the IMF been in supporting states with balance-of-payments problems? While this is not a contentious question, it gets to the heart of the controversy over the IMF. Fund programmes were initially to stabilise states' economies, allowing them to stave off economic crisis and revert to focusing on economic growth. In reality, states that turned to the IMF for help with their balance of payments or high levels of debt found they became dependent on the Fund. SBAs became universal in the 1960s, with developing states everywhere needing help.

By 1965, all states in Latin America had had an arrangement with the Fund. On average, developing states were using the Fund repeatedly for five-year periods. Some states, such as Haiti, Panama, Peru and the Philippines, were in IMF arrangements for decades. Between 1951 and 2000 a quarter of the world was in an IMF arrangement (Vreeland 2007). This is despite the purpose of the IMF programmes being solely for short-term financing in times of economic crisis.

The IMF then began to extend financing to restructure developing states' economies. This occurred after the Latin American **debt crisis** of the 1980s. The IMF then devised ever more detailed policy prescriptions or 'conditions' for an IMF arrangement to structurally adjust borrowers' economies (the **Washington Consensus**). The IMF had thus shifted to become a global crisis manager (Momani 2014). The problem was that there was no evidence that the programmes were working. In the 2000s, the Fund responded by establishing 'prior actions' that states were required to undertake *before* an arrangement would be approved.

Critics argued that these Structural Adjustment Programmes (SAPs) were not working. On the political right, critics argued that the IMF was propping up developing states that were making poor policy choices. Those on the left argued that **conditionality** was hurting the poorest and most marginalised of developing societies where cuts to state expenditure were being felt the most (Vreeland 2007). The IMF argued that its programmes were generally successful, but failed when developing states were not implementing them correctly or abandoned them. All of these statements were true. IMF programmes do increase economic inequality. There is also clear evidence that IMF programmes do not support economic growth. State compliance is also an issue, with borrowers nearly always being unable to meet all of the IMF's conditions (Stone 2002).

To borrow from the Fund, a state needs to be a member and must sign a Letter of Intent for an arrangement (like a contract). States agree to the conditions attached. Many states choose an IMF arrangement to signal credibility to international investors. Others do it to find ways around domestic opponents to the government's agenda (Woods 2006a). Some use the Fund as a scapegoat for 'having' to implement harsh economic policies (Vaubel 1986). Yet states will abandon an IMF programme if they are in economic freefall, including when they face mass domestic opposition, riots, civil unrest and a risk of being overthrown.

In sum, Fund programmes have had some success with aiding states' balance of payments, and succeeded marginally with improving states' budget surpluses, but have not contributed to states' economic development, while increasing inequality (Vreeland 2007). Although there was widespread agreement in the 2000s that the IMF should step back from its role in restructuring economies through **conditionality** attached to its programmes, it has not done so. How and why is discussed in the theoretical section on explaining financial IOs' behaviour.

Changing the Structure of the Fund?

Organisationally, the IMF does not have equal membership. Member contributions (or quotas of SDRs) to the Fund are assessed according to the size of a state's economy (GDP) and its degree of internationalisation. A member state's quota determines its share of the vote and the amount of financing it can access. Quotas are reviewed every five years. Until recently, quotas had not changed significantly since the Fund was founded, leading to widespread perceptions of the IMF as being the handmaiden of the United States and the G7, or those with the largest quotas.

Demands for quota reform gathered steam in the mid 2000s, with emerging economies pushing for a greater voice and representation in the IMF. The IMF was no longer perceived to be legitimate: as the primary IO for international monetary cooperation, it was still controlled by the G7, with little room for increasingly powerful states such as Brazil, China, India and Russia. Entrenching this view is the fact that the Managing Director of the IMF is, by gentleman's agreement from 1944, always a European, with an American as head of the World Bank.

Opposition to the IMF imperilled its core operations. In the 1990s financing for the Fund came from emerging and middle-income economies via IMF arrangement repayments. The IMF came under significant scrutiny during the 1997 AFC (see Box 6.1). As a technocratic IO, the IMF was used to being respected for its expertise. Yet critics began to question the credibility of the IMF's advice and its organisational structure as the crisis worsened. After the AFC, borrowers began to repay the IMF early. Increasingly powerful Asian states began stockpiling foreign reserves to avoid being at the mercy of the IMF should another financial crisis hit. Emerging states' stockpiles grew from $1.5 trillion in 1999 to $7 trillion by 2008 (Kaya 2015). In response, Asian states established the Chiang Mai Initiative, which provides participants with short-term liquidity and medium-term balance-of-payments financing to each other if needed, thus directly competing with the Fund.

The contraction of resources for the Fund was stark: from having a stockpile of 73 billion SDRs in 2003 to only 11.2 billion at the end of 2007 (Bloom 2011). New arrangements to borrow from the IMF halved between 2001 and 2007 (Joyce 2013). The IMF even began laying off staff. It seemed as though the IMF was becoming irrelevant. When the full impact of the Great Recession hit in 2008, the IMF did not have adequate resources to aid states like Hungary, Latvia and Ukraine, relying instead on a $100 billion loan from Japan (Holroyd and Momani 2012). In response to states' desperate need for short-term liquidity, the IMF established new programmes: a Flexible Credit Line (FCL) and a Precautionary Credit Line (PCL) with *no* conditions attached.

Changes to the IMF's governance were initiated also by agreement at the G20 (see pages 119–122). At the 2006 IMF annual meeting members agreed to reform quotas (and vote share), recognising that they was wildly out of alignment with the economic weight of emerging states. In 2006 the four most under-represented members, China, South Korea, Mexico and Turkey (the Singapore 4), were given an initial ad hoc quota increase with a plan for a second round of reforms. The 2008 Voice and Quota Reforms were adopted by the IMF in 2011 by amending the IMF's Articles of Agreement. Changing the Articles of Agreement requires approval by members representing over 85 per cent of the total number of votes. The quota reform essentially led to 135 states increasing their quotas, with the biggest changes for China, South Korea, India, Brazil and Mexico (IMF 2008). While the reforms were moving in the right direction, the overall effect was small, and entrenched interests prevailed.

Far-reaching changes were agreed to in 2010, including a doubling of quotas overall. This was the direct result of a massive injection of resources after the Great Recession (see page 108). This rebalanced the quotas by shifting 6 per cent from over- to under-represented members. It further ensured the protection of the quotas and votes of small member states. Votes are comprised of basic votes for all states combined with an allocation determined by their quota. Finally, it pushed the Fund towards electing members to the Board of Executive Directors (see page 121). As the then Managing Director of the IMF Dominique Strauss-Kahn stated, 'this historic agreement is the most fundamental governance overhaul in the Fund's 65-year history and the biggest ever shift of influence in favour of emerging market and developing countries to recognise their growing role in the global economy' (IMF 2010).

These changes make Brazil, Russia, India and China members of the top 10 shareholders of the IMF along with the United States, Japan, France, Germany, Italy and the UK. This reflects their standing in the global economy by GDP (World Bank 2015). Moreover, the changes gave emerging and developing countries collectively 44.8 per cent of the vote compared with the 41.2 per cent of the G7 (IMF 2013). The changes were approved by IMF members in 2010, but the US Congress blocked the reforms for five years, agreeing to the changes only in December 2015.

The Group of Seven (G7)

Outside the IMF, states also choose to cooperate on financial issues through informal **multilateralism**. States frequently establish different 'groups' to advance common interests. This means that informal multilateralism may compete with formal IOs, but such groups may also direct IOs' activities. The two most well-known groups are the G7 (for a while including Russia, the G8) and the G20, but others also exist (on the G77, see Chapter 9). Both the G7 and the G20 have steered global financial decision-making, including shaping the role of the IMF.

The G7 is extremely influential in the international monetary system. It was established in 1961 as a means of ensuring agreement among a small group of states for accessing capital for financing payment imbalances and to provide liquidity in emergency situations (Baker 2008). Originally it began as informal discussions on international monetary and financial affairs. These meetings furthered understanding of balance-of-payments problems and were supported by the OECD (see Chapter 9), the BIS (see Box 6.2) and the IMF. However, the actual work was undertaken by the deputies of the states' finance ministers in preparation for the meetings.

Box 6.2 The Bank of International Settlements (BIS) and the Basel Accords on Banking Supervision

The Bank of International Settlements (BIS) was established in 1930 to serve central banks in their pursuit of monetary and financial stability. It promotes cooperation by acting as a trustee or agent with regard to international financial settlements. The BIS, which is currently comprised of 60 central banks, is therefore both a bank for its members (central banks) and a discussion forum for sharing financial information with public and private financial actors.

The BIS, which is based in Switzerland, has just over 600 staff and a number of committees. In 1974 it created the Basel Committee on Banking Supervision, which, in turn, created the Basel Accords on Banking Supervision. These agreements seek to create a sound international banking system and to reduce competitive inequality among international commercial banks. There have now been three Basel Capital Accords. The first, in 1988, sought to classify bank assets into types, such as by differentiating short-term from long-term loans.

After the AFC it was realised that short-term loans could affect the stability of the entire global financial system. Basel attempted to establish minimum capital requirements for banks to offset risky investments. Private banks from industrialised states were successful in 2004 in having their proposal for the Basel Accords II taken up. This retained a bank-by-bank approach rather than examining the risk of the entire banking industry.

After the Great Recession, the Basel Accords III were endorsed by the G20, coming into effect in 2012. Basel III requires higher minimum capital standards for commercial banks, and strengthens the framework for regulating the complex financial transactions that were at the heart of the 2007 crisis. Despite the importance of regulation for the stability of the international economic system both Basel II and Basel III have fallen far short of their goals, which can be attributed to the influence of the private sector, and coalitions of firms and national regulators, in shaping rules for international banks.

These meetings became a permanent fixture from 1975, beginning the G7 process. It was ad hoc, informal, incremental, evolutionary and, over time, institutionalised. From 1986 the meetings of central bank governors and finance ministers were brought into line with the G7 leaders' summits. It is recognised that G7 leaders take their cue from their finance ministers when it comes to setting agendas in international financial governance. The G7 emerged to meet the needs of states in their increasing **interdependence**. This meant that the G7 finance ministers' and central bank governors' meetings became the dominant forum for setting international monetary and exchange rate policy (Baker 2006). At each summit, a communiqué is released as to what the G7 has agreed to undertake, sometimes with additional reports and action plans (and a group photo!).

The G7 was a principal vehicle for US initiatives and ideas, particularly in its first two decades. In the past, the G7 has played a powerful coordinating role in the global financial system. In 1985 the G7 helped negotiate the depreciation of the US dollar against the German deutschmark and the Japanese yen (the Plaza accord). The members of the G7 agreed to coordinate their exchange rates to avert a recession by devaluing the US dollar. This demonstrated the power of informal multilateralism. However, the G7 failed to respond to the recession and the oil shocks of the early 1970s. Moreover, coordination among the members of the G7 on financial arrangements and exchange rates declined as international capital mobility accelerated from the early 1990s. The G7 came under increasing criticism for not being able to address global financial problems, particularly recurrent financial crisis in the 1990s (see Box 6.3 on the G7's response to the AFC), and for being illegitimate because emerging economies were not represented.

The Group of 20 (G20)

The AFC not only rocked the IMF and led to the creation of the FSB, but also precipitated the formation of the G20, where major advanced and emerging economies sought to stabilise global financial markets. The initiative was an outreach from the G7 to emerging economies begun by US President Clinton in 1997, which accelerated as the AFC unfolded. Meetings of the G20 finance ministers and central bank governors were established in 1999. The G20 became a leaders' summit in 2008 owing to the severity of the Great Recession. In 2009 it was agreed that the G20 should be the main body for steering the global economy.

The G20 frames itself as representative for managing the global economy. Member states represent approximately 90 per cent of global gross national

Box 6.3 The Financial Stability Forum (FSF)/Board

After the AFC, the G7 central governors and finance ministers agreed to create the Financial Stability Forum (FSF) in 1999. It aimed to achieve systemic financial stability through establishing common rules and standards for all emerging markets. The FSF was comprised of meetings of senior national financial authorities, including central banks, supervisory authorities and treasury departments from the developed world; committees of central bank experts; and international regulatory and supervisory groupings. In the aftermath of the Great Recession the Forum was enlarged to become the Financial Stability Board (FSB) in April 2009. This institutionalised governance of the international financial system.

The IMF was given the job of coordinating the FSB, which is based in Basel, Switzerland. The FSB has been provided with a full-time Secretary General and an enlarged Secretariat (currently 33 staff). Membership of the FSB was extended to all members of the G20. The FSB attempts to strengthen financial systems and stabilise international financial markets. It does so through information exchange and coordination among states; by assessing vulnerabilities in the international financial system; and by enacting (with the IMF) an Early Warning System to assess whether states' economies can withstand external financial shocks. It has established 12 standards and codes on the basis of which financial actors are to be assessed. These are known as the Reports on Observances of Standards and Codes (ROSC) and include directives on transparency, corporate governance, securities, insurance and payment systems. The FSB also reviews international standard-setting bodies. After 2009 the FSB enacted over 60 recommendations.

product, 80 per cent of world trade and two-thirds of the world's population. It represents large economies (constituting 90 per cent of the world economy); populous states (such as China, Indonesia and Mexico); and states from all regions. It brings together 'systemically' important industrialised and developing economies (and the EU) to discuss key issues in the global economy.

The G20 remains an informal network. There is no condition of membership; there are no voting rules; and there has been no allocation of voting shares on the basis of economic criteria. The G20 operates in the same way as the G7 with a 'troika' of past, current and future chairs which rotate around the membership annually. There are deputies' meetings and meetings of central bank governors and finance ministers, as well as summit meetings of G20 leaders. The G20 agenda for discussion has expanded since 1999 to cover a range of issues, including terrorism, development and climate change among others. Other actors have jumped on the G20 bandwagon, with associated groups meeting alongside states with the Business B20, Labour L20, Civil Society C20, Youth Y20 and Academia and Think Tanks, Think20.

It is a forum body rather than having power to monitor and enforce decisions. The leaders' summits were initially hailed as the new steering mechanism for the global economy. Some even saw it as the vehicle for a new Bretton Woods-type agreement (Helleiner 2010). This did not eventuate. Work on developing technical expertise (such as the FSB) and the monitoring of states' behaviour (IMF) were already being done elsewhere. Many of the initiatives agreed to at the G20 leaders' summits in London and Pittsburgh in 2009 were already in train through the institutional regulatory bodies such as the BIS (Box 6.2).

The G20 leaders direct the IMF, while reinforcing the legitimacy of existing financial IOs. Members of the G20 have jump-started the IMF. They gave it more resources and an expanded mandate, and ensured that its governance would be reformed. The G20 agreed to give the IMF its largest ever contribution of 250 billion SDRs to provide liquidity in the international financial system in 2009. The G20 members also agreed to expand IMF funding to over 500 SDRs through the New Agreement to Borrow, *tripling* the IMF's lending capacity. Additionally, 277 billion SDRs were added to the IMF's capital structure.

Aided by the FSB, the IMF's role in surveillance has been refocused to cover all of its members, including the United States, through its Financial Sector Assessment Programs (FSAPs). This gives the Fund the power to 'name and shame' members that were not in compliance with sound macro-economic policies. The creation of FSAPs enacted by the G20 gives the Fund power to undertake surveillance without Executive Board approval, thus depoliticising the process and giving the IMF even more **autonomy**. The G20 also gave the IMF a mechanism of multilateral surveillance.

Final changes pushed through by the G20 included the 2010 IMF governance reforms discussed above, which states accepted partly in return for financial support from emerging economies to address the Great Recession. The end result is an IMF that is bigger than ever before, and an IO that is again at the forefront of global financial governance (Momani 2014).

While the G20 demonstrated a capacity to react quickly to the Great Recession, it is unclear whether it can regulate and coordinate the international financial system and ensure lasting IMF reform. Nonetheless, the G20 has the capacity to be the main driver of change in governing global finance. It is an improvement over the G7 in terms of the representation of states in steering the global economy.

The Problem: From Balance of Payments to Systemic Financial Instability

The shift away from the embedded liberalism of the post-WWII order began in the 1970s. It was replaced with a 'competitive liberalism' (McNamara 1998) based on an adherence to neoclassical economic ideas, whereby advanced industrialised states began to experiment with financial sector reform, including the removal of direct capital controls, the removal of taxes on the movement of capital, and the deregulation of financial activity within national finance markets. With flexible exchange rates, foreign currencies as well as stocks and bonds began to be traded freely. A consensus began to emerge around the self-regulation of finance among the private sector and industrialised states. This was increasingly reflected as a new orthodoxy within both the OECD and the IMF.

While many attribute the drive for financial liberalisation to the increasingly **neoliberal** economic policies of the UK under Prime Minister Thatcher and the United States under President Reagan, IOs played an important role in pushing for financial liberalisation and increasing capital mobility. For example, political scientist Rawi Abdelal states that

While the Europeans – and particularly the British, Germans, and Dutch – supported liberal rules for capital movements, three policy makers in the EU, OECD, and IMF played central roles in crafting the informal and formal rules of those organizations. Jacques Delors of the EC, Henri Chavranski of the OECD, and Michel Camdessus of the IMF took part in proposing new liberal rules for the members of their organizations. By all accounts, a consensus in favor of the codification of the norm of capital mobility would have been inconceivable in the EC without Delors, or in the OECD without Chavranski. Camdessus nearly forged such a consensus on the IMF Executive Board. Delors, Chavranski, and Camdessus share a great deal in common, but one attribute stands out: each of them is French (Abdelal 2006: 6).

As French leaders of the EC, OECD and IMF were advocating for liberalisation, technocrats in the IMF and the World Bank were at the forefront of devising policies for liberalisation that the UK and United States would later endorse.

Financial Liberalisation and Private Finance

In the 1990s financial liberalisation spread to developing countries, and both long- and short-term capital flows across borders expanded exponentially. In the 1990s there was a huge increase in the variety and volume of financial instruments and of the actors trading them, and the speed at which they were being traded exploded: government-issued bonds, foreign exchange, derivatives, futures, swaps. These were bought and sold by market funds, hedge funds and pension funds. For example, pre-financial crisis hedge funds had combined assets of $1.6 trillion, a five-fold increase between 1999 and 2007 (Chwieroth 2010). Meanwhile, *daily* foreign exchange (forex) trading increased from $850 billion in 1986 to $3.2 trillion in 2007 (Copelovitch 2010).

The forex market facilitates cross-border trade and investment through converting currency. Previously this was for buyers and sellers of foreign goods and services who needed foreign currencies to settle their transactions. Most sales nowadays are speculative financial transactions, and the global forex trade is now 10 times world GDP. This can negatively affect the 'real' economy (producing goods and services) because it provides economic incentives to gamble on financial instruments, while diverting funds from long-term productive investments. Finance capital brings volatility in interest and exchange rates, and can undermine states' abilities to institute policies which may seem to be protectionist, such as advocating full employment or reducing inequality. There are significant costs of financial crises, including high unemployment, increasing poverty and wiping out of savings.

The Great Recession

The Great Recession demonstrated how financial markets were driving economic growth and how globally interconnected financial markets had become. It also revealed how finance can affect the real economy. In the United States people lost their jobs when a number of big investment banks collapsed. The government had to bail out the banks with a $700 billion rescue package at the taxpayer's expense. In the UK, Northern Rock bank was nationalised in January 2007 after the largest bank run in over 100 years. The bail-out packages by industrialised governments bought up bad debts to keep the financial industry afloat while seeking to restore confidence in the market. Owing to the structural importance of finance in the international political economy, it was argued that these investment banks were 'too big to fail', since there would be catastrophic effects if they did. The financial crisis then crossed over from the virtual economy to the productive economy, where even sound productive businesses were worried about accessing credit, while unemployment remained high.

Causes of Financial Crises

Financial crises often result from an economic **bubble** bursting, and can occur in any market, such as the US 'sub-prime' housing market in 2007. They may also occur as a result of unsustainable levels of **sovereign state** debt or the devaluation of a currency by the government. In major financial crises like the AFC, banking crises (on whether banks are sound) and currency crises (where a currency faces speculative attack) occur simultaneously (Copelovitch 2010). That the 2007 crisis came from an advanced state with the most sophisticated financial market in the world revealed inherent weaknesses in the United States' ability to regulate new and highly technical financial instruments.

For instance, the sub-prime crisis was based on US investment banks' packaging debt from poor mortgage owners and selling it as a 'mortgage-backed security' (a security is anything that can be traded like a stock or bond) to banks and institutional investors everywhere. These were given strong ratings by private credit-rating agencies, such as Moody's, Standard and Poor's, and Fitch, which signalled to the market that, despite their high risk, they were a relatively safe investment. The Great Recession occurred because US, British, mainland-European and Asian Banks purchased US securities that credit-rating agencies had given strong ratings. Some bankers faced prosecution for not providing investors and regulators with information about the quality of the product. Previous incidents point to the inability of banks to monitor their traders. In 1995, one rogue banker, Nick Leeson, brought down the 233-year-old Barings Bank through trading on the future of the Nikkei Index. In January of 2010, rogue trader Jérôme Kerviel lost Société Générale, France's second-largest bank, $7.14 billion.

The new form and content of capital mobility challenges traditional conceptions of state sovereignty, including the power of the state to resist market pressures (Strange 1996; Weiss 1998). The impact of financial liberalisation means that the state has less control over the flow of capital into and outside of its borders. Financial liberalisation creates opportunities for accelerated economic growth and development but it also increases the potential for economic and political destabilisation. Financial crises have doubled in frequency in comparison with the 1945–1973 period, their frequency now being akin to the situation in the 1920s and 1930s (Joyce 2013). Owing to the speed and inter-connectedness of financial markets, it is now not uncommon for stock markets to have their biggest falls since the Great Depression in a single day.

Explaining Financial IOs' Behaviour

How can we analyse the actions of states in creating and using the IMF and the G7 and G20? Do IR theories explain states' decisions to cooperate on financial governance? Are IO-specific theories useful for accounting for the IMF's actions?

IR Theoretical Explanations of Finance IOs' Behaviour

International financial and monetary affairs have long been dominated by the United States. The creation of the IMF, the role of the G7 and even the shift to the G20 have been driven by the **hegemon**. Realist explanations are persuasive. The United States has long seen finance IOs and informal multilateralism as means to advance its interests. The US dollar remains the main international currency. The United States advocated a stable liberal international economic order, pressing for its vision of the IMF to come to fruition. The IMF has long been the centre of the international monetary system because the United States has been able to advance its interests through the IO. The United States managed exchange rates through the G7 until it was no longer in its interests to do so, and reached out to rising powers through the G20 when faced with rising costs for maintaining the international economic order.

While these efforts were clearly in the United States' interests, international economic stability is also a **'public good'** that enables all states to engage in international trade while preventing competitive currency devaluations of the kind that had precipitated the Great Depression. Financial IOs and informal groupings thus ensured international economic stability for all states and their peoples, as understood by adherents to the tenets of liberalism. Technical IOs such as the IMF, but also the BIS, FSB and OECD, are important for helping to construct and maintain the liberal order, helping states to become ever more integrated into the global economy. For neofunctionalists, the increasing number of technical IOs working on international finance furthers the prospect of **integration**.

Realist and liberal explanations are not mutually exclusive: Finance IOs advance liberal economic ideas and policies while also meeting US interests as per realist theoretical arguments. The confluence of US interests and the rest of the world participating in the international monetary system was captured by **hegemonic stability theory.** This advanced the idea that the economic system would be strong only with a hegemon to uphold it. In contrast, constructivists argue that the identity of the hegemon is important for explaining the international monetary system (Ruggie 1993).

For **neorealists** and **neoliberal institutionalists,** states derive clear benefits from cooperating to achieve international monetary stability, although the type of forum needed to achieve this stability may depend on whether the situation requires short- or long-term collaboration and coordination. Finance also has a security element: for example, the OECD has helped devise rules on tax havens and measures against money laundering in response to concerns about corruption and the funding of global terrorism.

The operations and impact of the IMF can be explained by the power of the United States and the rest of the G5 (France, Germany, Japan and the UK). The United States, as the largest shareholder in the Fund, has been able to both formally and informally shape how decisions are made (Stone 2011). Shareholder member states can only vote on policies and programmes that are submitted to the Board by the IMF's Managing Director, leaving the Fund **discretion** to determine what it wants to have approved. Although voting in the Fund is consensual, it is recognised that the interests of the powerful member states shape what policies and programmes go to the Board for approval. Even after the Great Recession when member states agreed to give the IMF the ability to monitor and assess US efforts to meet sound macro-economic policies to ensure financial stability, they agreed not to make these public.

Power-based analyses of the IMF have demonstrated that the United States and to a lesser extent the other members of the G5 are able to get preferential treatment for their allies in accessing IMF arrangements. Voting alignment with the United States, on issues of importance to the United States within the United Nations Security Council and the UNGA, does increase the likelihood of receiving an arrangement from the IMF (with more favourable conditions). Moreover, states receiving bilateral foreign aid from the United States are likely to suffer less if they do not meet IMF conditions than those not receiving foreign aid. US allies were recipients of the IMF's no-conditions-attached Flexible Credit Line during the Great Recession. Arguably then, the IMF remains significant in the international monetary system because it benefits the United States.

IO Approaches to Explaining the IMF's Behaviour

A rationalist P–A model approach can identify what drives US interests in the IMF. While powerful states are concerned about international monetary stability, US support for the IMF is underpinned by the interests of US 'money-centre' banks, or banks that focus primarily on international lending. Put simply, US money-centre banks support politicians running for Congress, who in turn advocate for the United States to provide resources to the IMF. This means that the United States supports the IMF, and the IMF provides arrangements for borrower states where the money-centre banks may be the most exposed. Here the delegation chain runs from the voter to the US Congress to the IMF Board. The amount of exposure of US money-centre banks in IMF borrower economies does influence the likelihood of a loan and the size of the programme (Oatley and Yackee 2004).

The IMF's institutional design influences how power plays out, for example in how voting rights were reallocated. It is also important for how decisions are made. The IMF has a weak Executive Board but strong management. This allows the United States to informally govern, or go around formal procedures, to negotiate directly with the Fund's Managing Director to get what it wants. *Both* powerful member states' interests and the interests of IMF staff explain the size of loans and the degree to which IMF conditions are imposed on borrowers. When the members of the G5 have strong preferences as a collective principal, they are able to have their preferences realised. When there is disagreement among member states, IMF staff have greater autonomy for determining loan conditions (Copelovich 2010).

In contrast to **P–A model** explanations is the argument that the key factor determining the size of an IMF loan, the number of conditions and the severity of punishment for non-compliance is actually the degree of ideological affinity with the IMF's economic beliefs. When the borrower state is on the same page as the IMF on what needs to be done to reform the economy, the IMF is more lenient, because it accepts the state's intention to follow through on its commitment (Nelson 2014).

Constructivist **organisational culture** approaches trace how and why the IMF advocates specific economic policies. Owing to its technical economic expertise and its relative financial autonomy, the IMF was able to determine how to address balance-of-payments problems. Its technical solution was to focus on domestic credit creation, given the difficulty of accessing economic data from developing states. This ultimately led the IMF to focus more on domestic economic policy-making, leading the Fund on a path of increasing intervention in borrower states. When the model did not work, the IMF expanded it to include more variables and more policy conditions to stabilise member states' economies. **Conditionality** was increasingly applied on the basis of technical decisions, with the solutions fitting an organisational adherence to neoliberal economics, thus establishing **Washington Consensus** policies (Barnett and Finnemore 2004).

The average number of conditions per loan went from fewer than 10 in the 1980s to more than 30 in the late 1990s. An extreme example of conditionality was Indonesia needing emergency loans from the IMF after the AFC – it was offered loans with 100 conditions attached! At the beginning of the 2000s member states demanded the Fund scale back its conditionality, but management reforms stalled because of an entrenched cultural adherence to conditional lending measures (Momani 2005).

The IMF's organisational culture has changed over time, diverging from the original rules and policies governing it. The shift has led to a focus on neoliberal economics instead of its previous use of Keynesian economics that supported government intervention in the market (Babb 2003). The IMF's organisational culture reflects its staff's neoclassical economist training in US universities. This is most evident in the IMF's promotion of capital account liberalisation, or allowing money to flow freely. Staff took up the idea that capital mobility is best for economic growth; this is the exact opposite of what the IMF's founders intended. Capital account liberalisation was neither in the IO's mandate nor driven by the United States. Fund staff were its primary advocates. The IMF lobbied hard for member states to change the IMF's Articles of Agreement to make capital mobility fundamental to the rules of the IO. It failed because the AFC hit, revealing how damaging capital mobility could be and how wrong IMF advice was. In the aftermath the Fund had to retrench from arguing that capital mobility was appropriate in all circumstances, although this view remains embedded in the IO.

Competitors in Global Financial Governance: Corporations and Transnational Regulatory Networks

With financial liberalisation came an increase in the number of private financial actors operating at the international level. They were also allowed to create their own global regulatory standards. This section identifies the role of corporations like credit-rating agencies; private clubs like the G30, which influence banking standards; and transnational regulatory networks. Increasingly decisions are being made not at the national level or by IOs but elsewhere.

Unlike in areas such as war, health and the environment, civil society activists are generally not involved in global financial governance. This is because the field is highly technical. Banks and credit-rating agencies play an important role in shaping the rules for global governance. They can do this through their market behaviour, or by operating together through private clubs like the G30. Credit-rating agencies, for example, provide market analysis for corporations and states on their financial health and provide (for a fee) a credit rating.

The G30 actively shapes global regulations. The G30 is a transnational policy community comprised of financial experts from the public and private sectors, where membership is based on position and prestige in the financial policy-making process. The Basel II Accords in 2004 on banking supervision were heavily influenced by the G30. Individuals moved between public and private positions within the transnational policy community while creating shared ideas on financial standards. This does not adequately represent the public interest because it reinforces the power of the private sector in a field where democratic decision-making is absent.

Credit-rating agencies also have power. A credit rating signals to prospective investors whether the corporation, bank or state is financially sound and worth investing in. The top two credit-rating agencies, Moody's and Standard and Poor's, provide ratings to over 120 **sovereign states**. Thus, private-sector credit-rating agencies have the authority to rate financial actors and states' credit soundness despite their reliance on the very same actors to buy their services. It becomes problematic when such ratings are incorporated into states' financial regulations, not only accepting market actors' determinations but making them law. While states have begun to re-regulate financial practices that contributed to the Great Recession, they continue to follow pre-existing regulatory models.

Transnational regulatory networks are evident in the financial areas of accounting, through the International Standards Accounting Board (ISAB); securities, through the International Organization of Securities Commissions (IOSCO); and insurance, through the International Association of Insurance Supervisors (IAIS). These highly technocratic public–private networks shape international markets. Financial regulation in the 1990s was driven by the private sector, with state support in transnational regulatory networks for credit-rating systems, banking supervision, accounting, securities regulation and insurance.

Chapter Summary

Both formal IOs and informal multilateralism have been important means through which states seek to manage their international monetary affairs. The IMF has been challenged regarding how it seeks to help states. Its efforts in the AFC contributed to further economic devastation. Over time its arrangements have had some success with aiding states' balance of payments, but have not contributed to states' economic development, while increasing inequality. In contrast, the informal groupings of the G7 and the G20 have been promoted by the United States to maintain the international economic order. The extent to which they can do so remains unknown. IR theories can explain why states choose to cooperate on international monetary affairs: power politics is evident, yet a working international system is also a public good and may further international integration. IO-specific theories too provide insight into how the Fund operates: arrangements are decided when there is agreement of the G5, or by Fund staff without agreement. The culture of the Fund is also critical to how it seeks to interpret its mandate, as efforts to have members endorse capital mobility attest. Meanwhile, private and transnational regulatory networks increasingly determine the rules of the financial services industries.

Guiding Questions

1. What is the IMF?
2. What does the G7 do?
3. Is the G20 important for financial governance?
4. In what ways are less well-known IOs like the BIS and FSB important?
5. Are transnational regulatory networks worth examining for their role in financial governance?

Further References

Internet Resources

IMF World Economic Outlook and Global Financial Stability Reports: Find the latest global and by country economic data here: www.imf.org/external/pubind.htm

Project Syndicate: The world's best economists often blog here: www.project-syndicate.org

The Multilateralist: David Boscoe's blog covering global governance for *Foreign Policy*: https://foreignpolicy.com/category/the-multilateralist/

Centre for International Governance Innovation: Find the latest books and research papers on global financial governance here: www.cigionline.org

Further Reading

Abdelal, R., 2007, *Capital Rules: The Construction of Global Finance*, Cambridge, MA, Harvard University Press.

Boughton, J., 2001, *Silent Revolution: The International Monetary Fund 1979–1989*, Washington, D.C., International Monetary Fund.

Copelovitch, M., 2010, *The International Monetary Fund in the Global Economy: Banks, Bonds and Bailouts*, Cambridge, Cambridge University Press.

Helleiner, E., S. Pagliari and H. Zimmerman (eds.), 2010, *Global Finance in Crisis: The Politics of International Regulatory Change*, London, Routledge.

Joyce, J. P., 2013, *The IMF and the Global Financial Crisis: Phoenix Rising?*, Cambridge, Cambridge University Press.

Moschella, M., and C. Weaver (eds.), 2013, *Handbook of Global Economic Governance*, London and New York, Routledge.

Peet, R., 2003, *Unholy Trinity: The IMF, World Bank and WTO*, London and New York, Zed Books.

7 Promoting International Trade

Introduction

In Chapter 1 we identified trade between states as one of the predominant factors advancing international cooperation and **globalisation**. Scholars point to the international trade **regime** as one of the most successful areas of inter-state cooperation in history. However, IOs devoted to promoting trade are in fact relatively new and surprisingly scarce: bilateralism and informal **multilateralism** were the main methods for securing international agreement between states for most of the twentieth century. The General Agreement on Tariffs and Trade (GATT) is the foremost example of informal multilateralism (see Chapter 2).

It was the primary mode for establishing the international rules for trade, and has been accompanied by waves of **regionalism** as groups of states attempted to create trading blocs to advance **free trade** (see Chapter 8). The World Trade Organization (WTO), which was created in 1995, is a newcomer compared with many of the IOs examined throughout this book. Although it was designed to be the centrepiece of the international trade regime, since 2001 international trade negotiations in the WTO have been deadlocked, raising questions as to its viability. Despite the quagmire in which the WTO is stuck, international trade remains a vital component of international economic growth even after a precipitous drop in trade flows after the 2009 **Great Recession**, when it was feared that states would resort to **protectionism** to defend their economies.

This chapter examines

- the emergence of the GATT and the international trade **regime**;
- the WTO's mandate, function and structure;
- the bilateral free-trade agreements (FTAs) to which states have increasingly turned since the early 2000s, rather than multilateral efforts to secure their trade preferences, of which there are over 300 in existence to date (World Bank 2010).
- the impact of global trade agreements through the WTO that are deeper regarding the elimination of all forms of **tariffs** and **non-tariff barriers** (NTBs) to trade as well as more extensive in terms of the issues now covered (goods, services and intellectual property);
- the competing trade rules which have proliferated as states seek bilateral and regional trade agreements to advance their interests, such as the North American Free Trade Agreement (NAFTA), promoting regional free-trade areas (for example the Free Trade Area of the Americas) and trans-regional agreements such as the Trans-Pacific Partnership (TPP).

Informal Multilateralism of the GATT and the Mandate, Function and Structure of the WTO

This chapter introduces students to the WTO in order to examine why it behaves the way it does and whether it can remain the central vehicle for advancing and defending free trade. The global trade **regime** aims to eliminate all impediments to trade, yet there are intractable divisions within and between major trading states, rising powers and developing states over governing trade. At the heart of the discussion is the question of whether all states agree that the benefits of free trade outweigh the negative consequences such as increasing inequality and accelerating environmental deterioration. When global trade negotiations become gridlocked, states use a variety of multilateral processes to advance their trade preferences, including bilateral, regional and plurilateral trade agreements. Nonetheless, the WTO is mandated with more than advancing multilateral trade negotiations: it has the power to monitor and enforce trade rules through its Dispute Settlement Body (DSB). This gives the WTO teeth, which most IOs lack.

The GATT and the Creation of the International Trade Regime

As with the IMF discussed in Chapter 6, the germ of an idea for creating a world trade body originated in the final days of WWII. The International Trade Organisation (ITO) envisaged as the third pillar of an international order based on **embedded liberalism** as agreed upon at the Bretton Woods conference never materialised. The US President never even took the idea to Congress for ratification owing to a strongly held belief that a trade agreement would encroach upon the **sovereignty** of the United States (Narlikar 2005). Since the United States is the largest trading state, any multilateral trade agreement needed to include the United States if it were to succeed.

As an interim measure, states agreed to negotiate through what became known as the General Agreement on Tariffs and Trade (GATT). The GATT was essentially a process for negotiating **trade liberalisation** through establishing an agreement or contract among the parties. The General Agreement establishing the rules for international trade was endorsed in 1947, forming the basis for the current global trade regime. It would take nearly 50 years for the idea of an international trade body to come to fruition.

Three factors underpinned the push to multilateralise international trade. The first was the liberal economic idea that free trade between states is mutually advantageous and therefore improves people's welfare, on the basis of **comparative advantage** (see Box 7.1). This challenged the statist arguments put forward by **mercantilists** and **economic nationalists** that states should protect their interests and power by ensuring that they benefit more than their competitors in any agreement (this is similar to the view held by neorealists). Economic nationalist sentiments underpinned states' **beggar-thy-neighbour** policies, including the raising of tariffs on imports to protect their own producers that

Box 7.1 The Theory of Comparative Advantage

The theory of comparative advantage was outlined in 1817 by the classical economic liberal David Ricardo. The premise is simple: within a system of free trade, each state should devote its resources (labour) to producing those goods and services that it can produce the most efficiently. The theory is built on the idea that 'pursuit of individual advantage is admirably connected with the universal good of the whole' (Ricardo, reproduced in Crane and Amawi 1997: 75). Ricardo argued that trading partners such as England and Portugal should specialise in the products they make the most efficiently: England should produce more cloth than wine, while Portugal should focus on producing more wine than cloth. They can then trade those goods for those that they do not have a comparative advantage in, thus leading to greater benefits for all. The theory has been refined to take more factors such as land and capital into account. However, it has been criticised for not reflecting the political terms of trade between states: Matthew Watson identifies how, in the English–Portuguese case, a flooding of the market with cheap English cloth could not be met by Portugal increasing its output of wine, leading it to plunder its colonies for gold mined by slaves to pay for English imports (Watson 2017: 455). The importance of the political terms of trade has recently led to calls not for free trade but for fair trade.

contributed to the **Great Depression**. The second was the recognition in the aftermath of WWII that economic growth was being driven by an increase in international trade, not just the manufacture of goods, and that liberalising trade would therefore facilitate greater economic growth (O'Brien and Williams 2007). Third, the United States as the **hegemon** was an advocate of multilateralism, with the willingness to create, and resources to expend on creating, international rules for trade (Ruggie 1992).

With the aim of eliminating trade barriers, 23 states became GATT contracting parties in 1947; 13 of them were advanced economies then representing 80 per cent of world trade. Put simply, states agreed to go beyond traditional forms of bilateral trade agreements to adhere to common principles for reducing trade barriers multilaterally.

There are three central guiding principles of the GATT identified in the **most-favoured nation** (MFN) treatment (WTO 1994a: Article I). The first is non-discrimination. The second is the idea that states will agree to treat all contracting parties the same as their most-favoured trading partner. In this way, all GATT contracting parties benefit. Third, a state may agree to reduce tariffs on the goods it imports from its trading partner, thus allowing imports to compete with domestic goods. It is called the 'most-favoured-nation' treatment because it gives all contracting parties the same favour.

The GATT exemplifies John Ruggie's (1992) three principles of multilateralism: it is indivisible (the agreement itself constitutes a good from which all states benefit); it is non-discriminatory to all parties; and it is 'diffusely' reciprocal, meaning that all members are expected to benefit from the arrangement overall and over time (Ruggie 1992; Keohane 1986).

Neoliberal institutionalists, neorealists, constructivists, Marxists and post-structuralists have all sought to explain and understand the motivations and actions of actors in pursuing multilateral trade agreements. One point of discussion particularly between neoliberal institutionalists and neorealists is that contracting parties to the GATT can effectively **free-ride**: states can benefit from others reducing tariffs, while offering none in return. Trade concessions operate on the principal-supplier principle: this means that principal or main suppliers and consumers of a specific product negotiate tariff reductions. They then offer the result (concession) to all of the GATT contracting parties (Narlikar 2005). In the early decades of the GATT, the United States offered the most tariff concessions, while Europe remained protectionist as it rebuilt after WWII (Winham 2005).

The enacting of tariff reductions took the form of informal negotiation 'rounds', where the GATT contracting parties would meet periodically to eliminate tariffs on specific goods. Because the GATT is not an IO, the rounds took place in different places over time: Annecy (1949), Torquay (1951), Geneva (1956), the Dillon round (1960–1961), the Kennedy round (1963–1967), the Tokyo round (1973–1979) and the Uruguay round (1986–1993). As can be seen from the durations of the rounds, the trade negotiations would become more protracted as the contracting parties agreed to deeper levels of tariff reductions.

The early trade rounds were to identify common ground for negotiation and to institutionalise the process of trade negotiations. It was not until the Kennedy round that dramatic tariff reductions were agreed upon, with an average tariff reduction of 35 per cent. The Kennedy round was also important for members of the European Community to negotiate as a single bloc (as a forerunner to the EU, which is a major trading entity, discussed in Chapter 8). This round was also where states agreed to making more explicit GATT Article VI on **anti-dumping duties**, which would begin the move to establish arbitration procedures for trade disputes (Winham 2005).

Up until the Uruguay round, the GATT focused primarily on reducing tariffs for manufactured goods, as this was the primary concern for the major traders (Gilpin 2001: 218). As a result, tariffs that had made up on average over 40 per cent of the import value of goods in 1947 were reduced to 3 per cent by 2000. This is a dramatic reduction in the tariffs over time. Trade barriers had largely been eliminated from the international trade of industrial goods. The reduction of tariff barriers was considered to be a strong causal factor in the growth of international trade (O'Brien and Williams 2007).

Yet the GATT excluded agriculture and textiles, where developing states had an export advantage. The GATT even enabled developed states to use quotas to *restrict* agricultural goods from entering their market, to use subsidies to protect their own producers, and to enact other NTBs. Some agreements even explicitly allowed for the protection of industrialised markets, such as the EU's Common Agricultural Policy from 1962, and the Multi-Fibre Arrangement (1974–1994), which limited the entry of textiles and clothing into developed states' markets.

The mammoth Uruguay round not only focused on reducing tariffs and tackling the rise of NTBs that had emerged in the 1970s, but also established 28 separate accords between contracting parties, thus extending trade to agriculture, intellectual property rights, foreign investment, services and textiles (Gilpin 2001). Importantly, it also instantiated the WTO in response to the increasingly unwieldy nature of negotiations for global trade rule-making.

By this stage, the GATT had increased in membership from its original 23 to 123. Numerically there were now more developing states than developed ones in the GATT, with many developing countries shifting from protectionist stances to embrace free trade during this round (Ford 2003). Increasingly powerful states like India began to argue in favour of free trade rather than the ineffectual **Generalised System of Preferences** that had been instantiated in the GATT in 1971 in response to the push for a **New International Economic Order** (NIEO) by the G77 through UNCTAD (see Box 7.2; on the G77 and the NIEO see Chapter 9). After Uruguay, the process for trade negotiations continued under the auspices of the WTO, with the Doha round commencing in November 2001. Over 15 years later, Doha is effectively dead, for the reasons discussed below.

The Mandate, Function and Structure of the WTO

The WTO came into being in January 1995, having been established as part of the Uruguay round negotiations, with 128 members. Its mandate is to provide a

Box 7.2 The United Nations Conference on Trade and Development (UNCTAD)

Beginning in 1964, UNCTAD was created to be a single one-off conference for developing member states in the UN to discuss how to establish a common international trade and development policy. Owing to the numerical superiority of developing states in the UN in the 1960s, they were able to push for UNCTAD to become a standing body in which to articulate their ideas for a **New International Economic Order** (NIEO; see Chapter 9). The basis for the NIEO was to recast relations between newly independent states and the former imperial powers, in order to devise a more level trading field that would acknowledge the specific hurdles developing states face in seeking to develop.

UNCTAD's mandate is to provide a forum where developing states can articulate their economic problems and needs. It functions include the following: to identify principles of international trade; to coordinate UN agencies in relation to international trade; to further international trade; and to be a forum for states to harmonise their trade, development and commercial policies. It can do so by collecting data, undertaking research analysis and providing policy advice for developing states.

All UN members are members of UNCTAD. Originally it was an organ of the UNGA, which used regular contributions from the UNGA budget. UNCTAD is located in Geneva, with offices in New York and Addis Ababa. It is now part of the UN Secretariat under the UN Secretary General. It reports to the UNGA and ECOSOC. UNCTAD has its own Secretary General and a staff of approximately 470 in five divisions: Africa, Least-Developed Countries and Special Programmes; Technology and Logistics; International Trade in Goods, Services and Commodities; Investment and Enterprises; and Globalisation and Development Strategies. In 2017 it had a regular budget of $69 million, with an additional $40 million from extrabudgetary technical assistance funds.

UNCTAD is widely regarded as not meeting its aims. Although it was able to push through some changes to the GATT, such as introducing the **Generalised System of Preferences** in 1971 that gave exceptions to developing countries with regard to the most-favoured-nation principle, these were not enough to give developing countries the concessions they needed in order to tackle the momentous challenges they faced. In the light of the shift towards financial and trade liberalisation in the 1990s, UNCTAD reversed its position and began to advocate for **globalisation,** with some caveats. UNCTAD remains an organisation committed to research into the impact of international trade and development. It remains of value to states in the **Global South,** as it helps them integrate into the international trade system through accession to the WTO.

common institutional framework for the conduct of trade relations among its members, in accordance with GATT agreements (WTO 1994a: Article II, point 1).

The WTO was given six functions:

1. administer and implement WTO trade agreements;
2. provide a forum for trade negotiations for member states;
3. manage trade disputes through the Dispute Settlement Body (DSB);
4. monitor national trade policies through the Trade Policy Review Mechanism (TPRM);
5. supply technical assistance and training for developing states;
6. cooperate with IOs such as the IMF and World Bank (WTO 2017).

Despite the number of functions it was given, it has only a small secretariat, of 640 staff, under the Director-General, currently Roberto Azevêdo. As with the UN, the WTO is both a **forum IO** like the UNSC and a **service IO** like the IMF and the World Bank. As noted above, it has been given functions akin to those of service IOs that member states expect to be enacted. For example, function 4 in the above list is to review member states' trade policies, which is similar to the IMF's surveillance of its members' economic policies. Indeed, the WTO was specifically created to provide functions that the GATT could not.

Yet the secretariat is small because the WTO was arranged as a continuation of the GATT's forum practices. The WTO is very different from the originally envisaged ITO, which was structurally the same as the IMF (see Chapter 6) and the World Bank (see Chapter 9) with executive boards and management overseeing their operations (Narlikar 2005). This has fundamental differences for how we theorise its behaviour, as discussed in the theory section.

Decisions within the WTO are made by all of the members (states and **customs unions;** on the latter see Chapter 9). Trade agreements are not delegated to the WTO secretariat to undertake on behalf of member states; rather the 164 current members of the WTO constitute the rule-making body. It is frequently described as a member-driven IO. This has led commentators to claim that it is a democratic organisation (*The Economist* 2001). In contrast with the one dollar, one vote approach of the IMF and the World Bank, every member has a vote, and agreements are arrived at by consensus; although contributions to the WTO budget are determined by one's share of international trade. There are provisions for majority voting along one country, one vote lines should consensus not be achieved, but this procedure has never been used.

The WTO is a forum IO or a talking shop. As a member-driven IO, the WTO determines agreement through negotiation by members at the regular ministerial conference. The agreements reached are then enacted by the WTO's General Council – also comprised of all members, almost all of whom have permanent missions to the WTO in Geneva. The General Council may meet at different times as the DSB (to determine whether a dispute triggers a panel hearing of jurors from the Appellate Body) or as the TPRM to monitor states' adherence to their WTO obligations.

To reiterate, all WTO members constitute these different components of the decision-making structure of the WTO, with no delegation to management. Even the three delegated councils that report to the General Council, on Goods, Services and Intellectual Property, are comprised of all members. Additionally there are five committees that deal with specific issues such as trade and the environment; trade and development; regional trade agreements; balance-of-payment restrictions; and budget, finance and administration. An additional Trade Negotiation Committee was established, with representatives from the five committees and various working parties, to identify how to move the Doha Development Agenda (DDA) forward, with negotiation groups on areas of contention, including on market access, trade rules and trade facilitation.

This is not a hierarchical bureaucracy that operates independently of its members to provide a service to states. Instead, there are various levels at which members negotiate within councils, committees and working groups, which feed up to the General Council and then up to the ministerial conference. By 2001 it was estimated that there were approximately 1,200 formal and informal meetings per year for WTO members (Hoekman and Kostecki 2001).

To gain a consensus agreement, members present at WTO meetings must not object; states or groups of states can stymie agreements by objecting. This also means that the WTO cannot force a contract onto an unwilling member. Of course, this does not mean that there are not onerous obligations on states that now want to accede to membership of this increasingly global body (Allee and Scalera 2012; Pelc 2011).

While the WTO may appear democratic at first blush, in actuality decisions have been made in a highly non-democratic manner, leading many to challenge the process of how global trade rules are made. Members meet at ministerial conferences every two years to negotiate trade agreements. Yet decisions are made prior to the ministerial meetings in so-called Green Room meetings. These are invitation-only meetings of the Director General and the major traders. This means that WTO rules are created by a small group of rich members (sometimes including India and Brazil). These are then presented to the rest to accept. Smaller and developing countries are therefore disadvantaged: they do not have access to the discussion on what the trade rules should look like; they have considerably less technical capacity to negotiate during the ministerial meetings where the rules are presented; and they have difficulty implementing trade rules once they are agreed upon (Wilkinson 2014).

For this reason many concerns of developing countries have not been addressed. This structural inequality began under the GATT. It led rising powers such as India to demand not only the inclusion of developing country concerns into the Uruguay round negotiations but also that the next round be made a 'development' round. The subsequent round was therefore designated as the Doha Development Agenda to focus on issues of concern to the majority of WTO members. Protracted disagreements between various coalitions of states have impeded any new major multilateral trade agreement since the emergence of this purportedly powerful IO.

The Impact of the WTO

The initial fear of, and vitriol levelled at, the WTO by civil society groups all over the world through the **anti-globalisation movement** (see Chapter 2) was based on two factors: first, that this IO now had the capacity to determine trade rules with global impact; and second, that those trade rules can now be enforced. WTO trade rules shape our everyday existence, with trade liberalisation necessarily creating winner and losers (see Box 7.3).

How are you affected? Trade rules determine whether and how you have access to goods and services. They impact on whether industries that provide jobs in your area are globally competitive enough to stay in business or whether that income moves offshore. They affect whether you can legally stream music or television from overseas; the cost you will pay for the latest smartphone (see Box 7.4); whether you have access to financial advice from a foreign bank; or how much life-saving medicine costs.

Most of these effects result from the 'new issues' that advanced states put on the agenda during Uruguay: a General Agreement on Trade in Services (GATS),

Box 7.3 Is Globalisation Good?

Within the international political economy of trade it is recognised that states play a two-level game (Putnam 1988). States negotiate trade agreements internationally on the basis that liberalising trade leads to welfare benefits overall. However, the process of trade liberalisation necessarily creates winners and losers domestically. Exporters benefit from the lowering of trade barriers giving them access to new markets while importers face competition from foreign imports. Labour unions face pressure for workers to be more efficient in order to lower the costs of producing goods and services compared with cheap labour from states with little or no welfare protection. Consumers overwhelmingly benefit from the availability of cheap goods.

WTO rules now exert greater influence over what states can prioritise in terms of national policy. For example, many highlight how the Trade-Related Aspects of Intellectual Property Rights (TRIPs) agreement supports the more stringent interpretation of copyright favoured by the United States in comparison with many states' national regulations. This has had negative impacts, for example on whether developing countries can produce generic drugs in their battle to fight the HIV/AIDS pandemic (Love 2007).

The agreement on Trade-Related Investment Measures (TRIMs) also limits the capacity of developing states to regulate foreign investment within their borders. The upshot is that developing states are now more constrained in their efforts to develop than the advanced industrial states were, which may exacerbate inequality between states (Wade 2003). Others point out that trade liberalisation is also increasing global inequality between the super-rich and the rest (Wilkinson 2014). WTO rules also constrain advanced states in terms of whether regulations to protect human rights or the environment constitute a legitimate barrier to trade or whether they can be used to disguise protectionist measures (Jaspers and Falkner 2013). Meanwhile greater production, trade and consumption leads to greater overall environmental deterioration, which is unsustainable.

TRIPs and TRIMs. Agreeing to WTO membership also means changing domestic laws to meet WTO rules, which had not been the case under the GATT. The level of intrusion into the everyday lives of people from Berlin to Brasilia to Beijing and Boston raises fundamental concerns over state sovereignty or the ability of governments to determine national policy for their own citizens.

Box 7.4 Global Supply Chains

How goods are produced influences not just trade patterns but how we live. In the early twentieth century, Henry Ford created the Model T Ford car on an assembly-line, creating mass manufacturing. This made automobiles affordable for a majority of Americans. Fordist mass-production techniques would then be adopted worldwide. By the end of the twentieth century, post-Fordist production techniques would focus on smaller-volume manufacturing for specialised markets. Lower trade barriers, cheap labour and government incentives would then enable manufacturers to source the components required for producing a single good across multiple borders. This created global supply chains linking the producers in different states of the various components of a product to assemblers in another state to suppliers that ship the product to consumers in different markets worldwide. The globalisation of production has been facilitated by free trade. Any increase in tariffs in major producing or supplying states would necessarily impact the global supply of goods and the price we pay for that good as consumers.

Enforcing WTO Rules

The WTO was given powers that few IOs have: the ability to monitor and enforce its rules. Monitoring is embodied through the TPRM to review whether members are following the rules agreed to within the WTO. The WTO was also given enforcement provisions to uphold trade rules: it has judicial powers to resolve trade disputes. While this had begun under the GATT, the full realisation of arbitral powers was given to the WTO through the Dispute Settlement Understanding agreed to during the Uruguay round. The resultant DSB gives the WTO real enforcement power.

If there is a claim that a state is not meeting its obligations under the WTO, an automatic dispute settlement procedure is triggered. Unlike the GATT, the WTO's DSB is not dependent on consensus of the parties for arbitration to proceed. Trading states engaged in a dispute may have their case reviewed, and, if a state is found to be non-compliant, sanctions ensue. The injured exporting state is able to retaliate against protectionist practices by an importing state across whichever good they choose, enabling them to punish states that violate the agreement 'where it hurts them most' (Narlikar 2005).

Over 400 claims were initiated in the DSB's first 15 years, compared with 452 disputes in the 46-year history of the GATT (Shaffer and Meléndez-Ortiz 2013). This is an effective enforcement of global trade rules: 95 per cent of rulings by the DSB are complied with by states (Goldstein and Steinberg 2008). The major claimants are the United States, the EU and rising powers like Brazil, Mexico and India. Over 40 per cent of claims have been against the United States and the EU, which is unsurprising as they are the largest markets. Although the DSB was designed to arbitrate for all members equally, it does favour major traders in its procedures and rulings (Brutger and Morse 2015).

Importantly, the DSB's rulings on whether cross-border trade has been impeded often conflict with domestic laws that seek to protect human rights and the environment (Jaspers and Falkner 2013). Despite the often ambiguous nature of international trade agreements, once a claim has gone to the DSB the adjudication process may lead to an interpretation of the agreement that cements WTO practice. Some fear that trade negotiation may be substituted by adjudication as a means of determining international trade rules, which could challenge the longer-term sustainability of the WTO's agreements (Narlikar 2005).

The Problem: Expanding and Deepening Trade Liberalisation

The famous liberal trade economist Fred C. Bergsten argued that there is a 'bicycle theory' of trade liberalisation: like riding a bicycle, if trade policy does not continue to greater openness for the general interest, then it will topple over in the face of pressure for protectionism (Bergsten 1988: 137). Thus forward momentum prevents the slide backwards into protectionism that was witnessed during the Great Depression. Since the WTO was created, there has been limited success in the ministerial meetings in Geneva (1998), the infamous 'Battle' of Seattle (1999, see Chapter 2), Cancún (2003), Hong Kong (2005), Geneva (2009 and 2011), Bali (2013) and Nairobi (2015). Although the DDA was meant to be completed in 2005, trade talks have lurched from ministerial meeting to meeting with little to show.

Why has this been the case? The number of members, the structure of the WTO negotiations and the issues on the table all matter. First, the WTO began with 128 members, compared with only 23 original contracting parties of the GATT. Some argue that the consensus-based voting style of the WTO makes it near impossible to reach agreement on the myriad issues on the table (Gallagher and Stoler 2009). States need to have not only common interests, but also common preferences for how to enact those interests. For rationalists, this is a classic problem for how to achieve international cooperation otherwise known as the 'breadth–depth trade-off' (Gilligan 2004; Downs *et al.* 1998).

For cooperation to be effective, how many members are preferable? Larger numbers may make the agreement globally legitimate, but may lead to a lowest common denominator in terms of what members can actually agree on. Agreements with a smaller number of parties may lead to more advanced, deeper agreements, as was seen under the GATT with regard to manufactured goods, but developed states continued to restrict imports on the following: agricultural products, automobiles, consumer electronics, steel and textiles (Gilpin 2001). Taking on board more members as trade negotiations deepen should lead to equilibria among the parties (Downs *et al.* 1998).

However, the complexity of the issues raises difficulties in coordinating members' preferences. In order to actually reach an agreement during the Uruguay round, states agreed to a 'Single Undertaking'. Previously GATT contracting parties had established a number of **plurilateral agreements** under the GATT umbrella which had enabled parties to 'pick 'n' mix' the agreements they wanted. As a means of concluding the drawn-out Uruguay negotiations the round introduced the Single Undertaking procedure. This was an 'all or nothing' agreement to commit contracting parties to all 28 agreements of the round, including the creation of the WTO and the DSB.

The DDA continues this practice. Trade experts Peter Gallagher and Andrew Stoler (2009) argue that this created an impossible hindrance to negotiations: it prevents flexibility for members to opt in and out of certain measures that enabled the GATT to move forwards even if states could not immediately agree to specific measures. The size in terms of the number of players and the structure of the negotiations contribute to making negotiations within the WTO increasingly untenable.

Issues also matter. The Single Undertaking brought old issues that had previously been ignored, like agriculture, and new issues, such as trade in services, intellectual property rights and investment measures, to the table. This only meant that members would agree to discuss liberalising them during the next round, not that there was common agreement on any of these issues. Trade talks stalled in 2003 in Cancún when developing states walked out on what they saw was an unfair agreement on market access for agricultural products after the EU and the United States had agreed to limited liberalisation measures.

Developed states ignored the push by developing states to address cotton as a key concern while advancing the **Singapore Issues**, which developing states opposed.

Little progress was made two years later in Hong Kong, and no further agreement was reached in 2006 before talks officially collapsed in 2008. A breakthrough was near in 2009 in Geneva, but this also failed. Since then, there have been ongoing attempts to resurrect the meetings, with various limited concessions being given by the EU and the United States, both of which blame each other and developing countries for not getting an agreement. In 2013 in Bali the first agreement since the WTO was created was achieved: members accepted an Agreement on Trade Facilitation alongside minor concessions for developing states on agriculture. Yet this did little to address either the highly asymmetric power imbalance or the discontent of states about negotiating through the WTO.

Explaining the WTO's Behaviour

Which theories best explain how the WTO acts? IR theories are concerned with the motivations of states. Considering the member-driven nature of the WTO, IR theories might seem to apply best. Yet IO-specific theories have increasingly been used to shed light on interactions between principals and the WTO, with limited research having been done on the organisational culture of the IO.

IR Theoretical Explanations of the WTO's Behaviour

Within the WTO the central **unit of analysis** remains the state (including the EU, which is a **supranational** unit that is also a major trader). Three approaches are pertinent: functionalism, neoliberal institutionalism and neorealism. Constructivist and critical approaches to the WTO are also discussed below. **Functionalist** arguments favour the operations of the WTO because it provides greater predictability and stability in smoothing international trade relations. Clearly states can cooperate through the WTO, binding states together through their common interests. They can also peacefully resolve their disputes without resorting to harmful trade wars. However, functionalism cannot explain much of the horse-trading within WTO negotiations: politics has not been stripped from bargaining because members' interests remain at the forefront at all times. Thus, while there is a high level of technical decision-making owing to the deeply specialised nature of trade discussions, it certainly is not apolitical, and trade specialists assist rather than undertake negotiations.

Arguably, however, the functionalist focus on cooperation leading to peace is not completely ruled out: certain trade decisions, such as the prospect of returning to high levels of protectionism after the 2008 **Great Recession**, were arguably lessened because of the high degrees of interdependence between trading states and the strength of the WTO's arbitration procedures. The WTO's monitoring and enforcement mechanisms do strengthen adherence to trade rules.

Owing to the member-driven nature of the WTO, IR theories, particularly neoliberal institutionalism and neorealism, dominate explanations of states' (and the EU's) behaviour in trade negotiations. Trade is a game with states negotiating to best reflect their interests and preferences according to their power in the international trading system. For **neoliberal institutionalists** the WTO and its rules make trade more stable and predictable, which reduces the prospect of states cheating on their agreements, and enables trade to flourish.

States have been demonstrably able to cooperate over the last 80 years to realise their trading interests. Neoliberal institutionalists point out that iterative trade negotiations have led to positive-sum gains for all in the form of wealth maximisation. Indeed, states that have not benefited from globalisation tend to be outside the global trade regime and have protectionist policies. The focus for neoliberal institutionalists is therefore to examine each negotiation round in terms of the expected pay-off for states and how this ranks with states' preferences.

They aim to identify when and how states might engage in free-riding or defect from the agreement, and the WTO assists the negotiation by providing information and securing compliance through its monitoring and enforcement powers. The WTO even has the effect of committing states to refrain from using trade to coerce other states to achieve their interests, thus enhancing cooperation (Carnegie 2015). However, even neoliberal institutionalists caution that there may be unintended effects from the WTO's spread of information and tight, unforgiving, binding rules for domestic support of international trade agreements (Goldstein and Martin 2000).

Neorealists are quick to point out that states do not necessarily become bound by past practices, but may use a variety of strategies to get other states to do what they want. Powerful states always have a choice: they may choose to engage in forum-shopping to achieve their interests, such as shifting to other regional trade agreements outside the WTO, or they may choose to 'go it alone' rather than engage in multilateralism (Gruber 2001). The rise of preferential trade agreements (PTAs) is evidence of powerful trading states choosing alternative methods to achieve their interests (Mansfield and Milner 2012). The relative gains of any trade agreement are fundamental to whether and how an agreement is reached and enforced (Grieco 1990).

Therefore we can understand the negotiation process of trade rounds that take both rules followed by neoliberal institutionalists and power as recognised by neorealists into account. Thus, all states agree to the rule of consensus voting in trade negotiations that improve states' economic conditions overall. This enables all states to negotiate a trade agreement because rules help generate information about each other's preferences. This makes it possible to create trade agreements that favour powerful states, while still being acceptable for all negotiating states. The process makes the agreement legitimate for all states. However, states tend to engage in power politics to conclude trade rounds by invoking their market power. This further skews the outcome in favour of powerful states, which undermines the economic outcomes for all and weakens the legitimacy of the negotiation process (Steinberg 2002). Thus in the history of the trade rounds consensus-based negotiations repeatedly give way to power struggles.

Yet deadlock set in at Cancún in 2003 precisely because the members of the 'Quad' (comprised of the United States, the EU, Canada and Japan) were unprepared for developing states not to cave in as they usually did (Narlikar and Van Houten 2010); on breaking WTO deadlocks see Odell 2009). Coalitions have been the predominant means through which states achieve their interests, with different coalitions seeking different outcomes over time. The major traders, or the Quad, have dominated the trade agenda for decades. The members of the Cairns Group, a group of developed and developing agricultural traders, have tried to advance their preference for the free trade of agriculture. The Like Minded Group of developing states emerged in 1996 to oppose any new negotiating round until the Uruguay round agreement had been implemented.

Over time there has been a G20, G33, G90 and G110 for advancing different issues and collective bargaining. The changing power dynamic resulting from the rise of India, Brazil and China has meant that the DDA is effectively dead despite the fact that rising powers are in favour of trade liberalisation (Hopewell 2016). The key concern for constructivists has been to understand how free trade is socially constructed, how states' trading cultures are established, and how the WTO fixes meaning as to what should be liberalised and how (Lang 2011; Mortensen 2012).

Meanwhile, Marxists and critical theorists contest the very legitimacy of the GATT/WTO, based as it is on the restructuring of the global economy to meet the interests of the global capitalist class (Rughaven 1990). This has been primarily forged by Western states under US hegemony advancing the neoliberal project (Chorev 2005). The interests of a global elite have been served within the WTO because of the highly asymmetric power differentials between the **Global North** and the **Global South** within WTO negotiations. Not only have Western states had the power and resources to conduct non-transparent rule-making through Green Room pre-meeting discussions compared with developing member states, but also this has been done with the involvement of Western members' business representatives.

Business interests have been accommodated by including business advisors as part of powerful states' national trade delegations. Developing states have frequently been unable to challenge the rule-making of Western states and have had fewer resources to negotiate a better deal. For Marxists this has ushered in a new period of corporate globalisation where monopoly capital not only controls global markets but helps write the rules as well. Evidence of such power is the increasing profits of the top global companies compared with workers' wages and the ongoing immiseration of the bottom billion (Fukuda 2010). For other critical theorists, the symbolic power of the WTO is evident in how it legitimates a vision of the world constructed through trade policy that reinforces certain interests and practices over others (Eagleton-Pierce 2012).

IO Approaches to Explaining the WTO's Behaviour

Is IR theory better placed than IO theories to explain the ways in which the WTO behaves? On the surface it would seem so, with considerable discussion taken up with how states negotiate. However, despite the member-driven nature of the WTO there are **P–A model** analyses of the WTO. IR scholar Manfred Elsig (2010) has used the P–A model to argue that, despite the functionalist reasons for delegating to the WTO secretariat, members have been increasingly reluctant to do so, thus limiting the role of the secretariat as an agent.

Political scientists Andrew Cortell and Susan Peterson (2006) argue that the combination of difficulty in gaining agreement among the principal members with a (small) staff of independent professionals provides space for the IO to establish its own preferences. This in turn could lead to **agency slack**. Here they refer to the DSB's Appellate Body of jurists appointed for their professional expertise and given discretion to arbitrate on trade disputes. Yet they ultimately find that agency slack by jurists is rare because of the potential consequences such actions would have on their mission and reputation (Cortell and Peterson 2006: 257). Yet IR scholars Manfred Elsig and Mark Pollack have used the P–A model to argue that principals have been influential in the process of appointing jurists. Indeed, they tend to appoint jurists whose nationality, judicial philosophy and views on specific issues align with their own. This in turn shapes the behaviour of the agent (Elsig and Pollack 2014: 393).

Perhaps because of the limited powers of the secretariat, there does not seem to be a constructivist analysis of the **organisational culture** of the WTO. Hypothetically, the WTO's small secretariat has little autonomy and independence, which could limit organisational culture as an intervening variable in shaping the WTO's behaviour. Although the Director-General has substantial leeway to promote the WTO and act as a mediator during meetings (Deese 2008), the secretariat of the WTO is limited in serving the administrative needs of its members (Blackhurst 2014).

Yet the expertise of the civil servants of the GATT/WTO does help frame issues and identify interests, thus influencing trade decisions. While this may be the case, the secretariat remains on a 'short leash'. Of course, the WTO has a unique organisational culture, which is informal, non-transparent and 'club'-like. One possible methodological reason why there is little account of the impact of the WTO's organisational culture is that it is difficult for scholars to penetrate (Hopewell 2016).

Competition over Freeing International Trade? Overlapping Preferential Trade Agreements

As the WTO seemingly arose to become the most powerful IO in international relations, at the same time there was also a dramatic shift towards bilateral free-trade agreements and trans-regional trade agreements (Mega-FTAs), compared with pre-existing regional trade blocs. These are all preferential trade agreements (PTAs) in the sense that they give preferential access to members of the agreements' markets (Mansfield and Milner 2012). Since the late 1990s there has been a rapid proliferation of PTAs with over 300 bilateral free-trade agreements signed (with another 200 under negotiation). This has led many to describe international trade as the 'noodle bowl' of PTAs (Ravenhill 2009).

While expressly allowed under the GATT/WTO, there has been a push within the WTO to fast-track its transparency mechanism to review whether or not all of these PTAs systemically challenge global trade rules (Low 2010). This is because PTAs contravene the principle of non-discrimination (by not giving favoured treatment to third parties) and are therefore trade-distorting. States' preference for bilateral PTAs is understandable: they avoid difficult domestic decisions over who benefits from free trade by tailoring what is in or out of each agreement to suit parties' interests. They also enable the major traders, such as the **hegemon**, to push their preferences through a web of PTAs that have been rejected multilaterally.

PTAs are also in some respects direct competitors to the WTO in terms of where states put their energy and resources. However, bilateral PTAs and regional trade blocs are certainly not new. Regional trade blocs have emerged in different periods, often in response to whether trade negotiations were progressing at the international level. Regional PTAs may take the form of **customs unions** (the Common Market of the South or MERCOSUR), **free-trade areas** (NAFTA) and **common markets** (such as the EU) (see Chapter 8). Despite no common conception of what constitutes a 'region', states have chosen to cooperate and coordinate economic policy based on **regionalism** in waves since WWII (Fawcett and Hurrell 1995). The first wave was from the 1950s to 1970s as states engaged in copy-cat regionalism, fearing competing discriminatory trade blocs in the light of the EEC, most of which failed. The next wave took place from the 1980s onwards, with the creation of the Asia Pacific Economic Community (APEC, 1989), MERCOSUR (1991), NAFTA (1994), the Common Market for Eastern and Southern Africa (COMESA, 1994) and the South African Development Community (SADC, 1992) among others. These remain regional economic agreements rather than IOs, and have varying degrees of commitments by their members to coordinate their trade policies (rather than attempting to further integrate their economies, see Chapter 8).

From the 2000s onwards, states have attempted to move beyond the confines of these agreements by promoting the Free Trade Agreement of the Americas (FTAA) and the Free Trade Area of the Asia Pacific (FTAAP). States' preferences for PTAs have morphed into combining them into larger mega-FTAs such as the prospective Transpacific Partnership, the Transatlantic Trade and Investment Partnership and the Regional Comprehensive Economic Partnership (RCEP). It is unclear, however, whether these 'many-lateralisms' (Brummer 2014: 79) provide a stepping stone for states to adhere to global trade rules through the WTO or whether the proliferation of PTAs fundamentally undermines the global system.

Chapter Summary

States create IOs for a number of reasons. The international trade regime emerged without one. Over time it solidified into a series of negotiating rounds through the GATT. Opposition to the international trade regime emerged just as the WTO was brought into being. Not only did the WTO seek to create a common forum for WTO negotiations but also it sought to provide states with a dispute-settlement body to arbitrate over trade disagreements. The WTO now oversees negotiations across a range of issue areas from manufacturing to agriculture, services and investment. The deepening of eliminating trade barriers as well as extending the removal of tariffs across more sectors of states' economies has advanced globalisation. It has also created domestic winners and losers. The changing balance of power between states also affects the willingness of states to negotiate within the WTO. Neorealist and neoliberal variants of institutionalism provide insights into the costs and benefits to states in negotiating within the WTO. Cultural accounts of how trade negotiations work also shed light on the capacity of the Secretariat to influence how the WTO operates. Meanwhile, deadlock at the global level helps propel regional, bilateral and plurilateral agreements as alternative means to further trade liberalisation.

Guiding Questions

1. What do states gain from being a member of the WTO?
2. Why have WTO negotiations been deadlocked since 2001?
3. Which theories best explain the WTO's behaviour?
4. Are there alternatives to the WTO?
5. What impact does the WTO have on you?

Further References

Internet Resources

GATT General Agreement 1947: www.wto.org/english/docs_e/legal_e/gatt47_01_e.htm
WTO Agreement: www.wto.org/english/docs_e/legal_e/final_e.htm

Professor Dani Rodrik's weblog on economics, trade and globalisation: http://rodrik.typepad.com/

European Centre for International Political Economy blog: http://ecipe.org/blog/

The World Bank's Global Preferential Trade Agreements Database: http://wits.world bank.org/gptad/database_landing.aspx

Further Reading

Croome, J., 1995, *Reshaping the World Trading System: A History of the Uruguay Round*, Geneva, WTO.

Deese, D., 2008, *World Trade Politics: Power, Principles and Leadership*, London and New York, Routledge.

Gallagher, P., 2005, *The First Ten Years of the WTO: 1995–2005*, Geneva, WTO.

Hoekman, B., and M. Kostecki, 2001, *The Political Economy of the World Trading System: The WTO and Beyond*, second edition, Oxford, Oxford University Press.

Hopewell, K., 2016, *Breaking the WTO: How Emerging Powers Disrupted the Neoliberal Project*, Stanford, CA, Stanford University Press.

Narlikar, A., 2005, *The World Trade Organization: A Very Short Introduction*, Oxford, Oxford University Press.

Taylor, I., and K. Smith, 2007, *United Nations Conference on Trade and Development*, London and New York, Routledge.

Wade, R., 2003, 'What Strategies Are Viable for Developing Countries Today? The World Trade Organization and the Shrinking of "Development Space"', *Review of International Political Economy* **10** (4): 621–644.

Wilkinson, R., and J. Scott, 2013, *Trade, Poverty, Development: Getting Beyond the WTO's Doha Deadlock*, London and New York, Routledge.

8 Creating Regional IOs

Introduction

In a domestic election on 23 June 2016 Britain momentously voted to exit the EU. It is the first member state to choose to exit the Union, undermining over 40 years of integration with Western European states. The EU has long been upheld as the most advanced regional experiment in history. By creating a **supranational** organisation, its member states agreed to forgo sovereign prerogatives in exchange for greater economic and social **integration**. The EU has long been held up as a model to which other regional IOs should aspire. In comparison, regional IOs elsewhere do not have the same degree of integration, density of overlapping **institutions** and powers. While the Organization of

American States (OAS) has a long tradition and ASEAN has taken on more issues over time, neither has the ability to control activities within its remit and command obedience as the EU does (on the African Union see Chapter 3). There is a wide variation of regional projects globally, raising questions as to how best to examine the phenomena.

This chapter examines

- the mandate, function and structure of the EU, ASEAN and the OAS, with a box on regional security arrangements;
- why states would choose to aggregate their sovereignty, with varying degrees of intensity, through regional cooperation across economic, social and security areas;
- what theories best explain the behaviour of regional IOs established by states;
- the competition faced by regional IOs for their member states' attention, such as Britain's decision to exit the EU with greater focus on **bilateral** and **plurilateral** governance compared with **multilateralism**.

The Mandate, Function and Structure of the EU, ASEAN and the OAS

Regional **cooperation** requires states to specifically choose to coordinate their policies to achieve conformity. States make a political decision to increase regional cooperation, which is called **regionalism**. Regional cooperation may be determined on the basis of increasing **regionalisation** or social and economic interactions across borders. Geographical proximity and contiguity is important for regionalisation in order to enhance cross-border flows of goods, services, investment and labour. Regionalism requires this and social cohesion. This refers to the extent to which there are social, political, historical or cultural reasons for realising common interests (Hurrell 1995). Accepting that there are common interests across a region may also contribute to perceptions of a regional identity (of Europe compared with the Americas, for example).

States may have a variety of reasons for advocating regionalism. They may do so for **functional** reasons, such as smoothing relations between states in non-political areas. Or it may be desirable for security or economic reasons. In the 1950s it was a clear strategy of the **hegemon** to promote regional security arrangements during the Cold War: NATO and the ECSC (see Chapter 3) in

Europe, and the failed Southeast Asia Treaty Organisation in the Asia Pacific, which ceased operating in 1977.

Most regional IOs were created for economic purposes. States can choose the extent to which they want to create common rules and remove barriers to economic exchange. There are steps to increasing economic integration: from a basic **free-trade** area, to a **customs union**, to a **common market**, to a full-blown **economic and monetary union** (EMU). There are now 284 regional trade agreements (RTAs) in force, with nearly 500 notifications of RTAs lodged with the WTO (WTO 2018). The EU is the most advanced economic and monetary union, although its members have increasingly negotiated opt-outs and derogations concerning their level of integration, particularly the UK. On 29 March 2017 Britain triggered Article 50 of the Treaty of the European Union to withdraw: treaty provisions allow two years for Britain to extricate itself from the Union (Box 8.1).

The Mandate, Function and Structure of the EU

The EU is the most politically and economically integrated region in the world. It has over 500 million citizens. If taken as a single bloc, it is the second-largest economy by GDP in the world (as of August 2017). It has its own administrative structure and legal system. The 1951 Paris Treaty started the ball rolling. It created the European Coal and Steel Community (ECSC). This brought six Western European states together to regulate the use of coal and steel between former enemies France and Germany (see Chapter 2). The ECSC structure would be the antecedent for EU. It had a Higher Authority over members' coal and steel industries, with the power to make and enforce decisions on its members. This was intended to overcome attempts by the member states to exert control and impede its activities to ensure greater efficiency and cooperation. Important decisions would be approved by the six-member Special Council of Ministers, comprised of member states' government ministers. A Common Assembly of 78 members from members' national parliaments was given supervisory powers. A Court of Justice made up of seven members would settle disputes. While the ECSC was ground-breaking in terms of the powers given to it, it did not advance integration through **spillover** as had been hoped (see Chapter 2).

In 1957 members signed the Treaty of Rome establishing the European Atomic Energy Community (Euratom) and the European Economic Community (EEC). Euratom was designed to create a common market for atomic energy. The Treaty of Rome included an agreement for a common agricultural policy and agreement to establish a common external **tariff** for all goods entering the

Box 8.1 Britain's Decision to Exit the EU (Brexit)

Why did the UK choose to exit the EU? EU scholars might not be that surprised. Britain showed no interest in the ECSC, favouring a broader European free-trade area over the six-member customs union created by the Treaty of Rome. When the European Economic Community (EEC) proved dynamic, Britain controversially reversed its long-held reservation about European integration and asked to become a member. Such a decision would prove contentious for decades to come, with sceptics of integration in both the Conservative and Labour political parties. After having been rebuffed twice, Britain ratified its membership in 1973.

Britain was unhappy with the accession agreement, and immediately demanded a renegotiation backed by a domestic referendum. The EEC acquiesced, and, in 1975, Britain held its first ever referendum. Voters chose to stay in the EEC, but dissatisfaction remained. During the 1980s Britain would champion the Single European Act for a common market but remained committed to limiting the power of the EU over national sovereignty, including opting out of the Schengen agreement. Britain stridently opposed the advancement towards an Economic and Monetary Union, winning an opt-out from the Maastricht Treaty. Meanwhile public distaste for European rules and court rulings, combined with a rapid influx of labour migrants from accession states after 2004, fuelled the rise of the UK Independence Party (UKIP) and popular demands to exit.

After the **Great Recession** Britain resisted broadening and deepening the EU's powers in its efforts to address the Eurozone crisis. Britain wanted to carve out a place within the EU without being beholden to the Eurozone and the idea of an ever-closer union. In 2013 Prime Minister David Cameron sought a 'new settlement' for the UK requiring speedy changes to the EU treaty, followed by an in–out domestic referendum. Although many principles for accepting Britain's position were agreed upon, treaty changes within the timeframe were impossible, and there was little movement on restricting labour migration. In 2016 voters narrowly opted to end membership of the EU.

Negotiations have settled on the amount the UK must pay to exit the EU, what happens to British citizens in Europe and vice versa, and the Northern Ireland border. Vigorous debates continue as to whether there will be a 'soft' exit with Britain remaining in the single market until 2019 – including the free movement of people – or a 'hard' version with immediate withdrawal. Negotiations may extend beyond 2019 if all members agree. If not, the UK parliament must then enact the Great Repeal bill, turning EU legislation into British legislation and formally ending its engagement with the EU.

community, with an aspiration to create a single market allowing the free movement of goods, services, capital and people. The EEC's structures would emulate the ECSC's in terms of having a Commission, a Council of Ministers, a Parliamentary Assembly and a Court of Justice.

Throughout the 1960s and into the 1970s there were concerns that the European project was stalling, and 'eurosclerosis' or paralysis had set in. In 1965, the ECSC, Euratom and the EEC were merged. Membership of the EEC (later also known as the European Community) would expand to include the UK, Denmark and Ireland in 1973, with more members joining during the 1980s and 1990s. In 1985 some members established the Schengen agreement to remove border controls. The biggest EU membership increase took place in 2004, with 10 states acceding. At the time of writing there are 28 members of the EU; 22 are part of the Schengen area.

In 1986 the Single European Act was passed, whereby EEC members agreed to, among other things, a timetable for completing the common market. It entered into force in 1993, making the EC the biggest single market in the world. In 1992 the Maastricht Treaty replaced the EEC with the European Union. It vastly expanded the powers of the Union: outlining the conditions for the creation of an economic and monetary union; establishing a Common Foreign and Security Policy (CFSP); giving the EU 'competence' or authority over justice and home affairs; and giving the European Parliament co-legislative powers with the European Council (see page 160). In 2002, 12 members abolished their national currencies and adopted the euro. Of the 28 EU members, 19 are now part of the **Eurozone** and use a single currency. The European Central Bank was created to manage its interest rates and the money supply.

All EU treaties were incorporated into the Treaty on European Union and the Treaty on the Functioning of the European Union. The subsequent 1997 Treaty of Amsterdam, 2001 Treaty of Nice and 2007 Treaty of Lisbon would deepen the integration of EU members and expand the powers of EU organs. The Treaty of Lisbon aimed to create a constitution of the EU, but this was rejected in referendums in France and the Netherlands. Once mention of the constitution had been removed, most aspects of the treaty were accepted. These amendments aimed to modify the previous treaties to make the EU more effective.

According to the Treaty of the European Union, the EU's mandate is to create an ever-closer union (Article 1). It has six functions (Article 2):

1. promote peace, its values and the well-being of its peoples;
2. provide freedom, security and justice as well as the free movement of people;

3. create an internal market balancing economic growth, price stability, aspirations for full employment and social progress, environmental protection
   and scientific advances;
4. establish an economic and monetary union with the euro as its currency;
5. advocate its values and interests internationally;
6. pursue the objectives of the Union by means appropriate to its
   competences.

The EU is a constellation of forum and service IOs covering all aspects of
members' activities. The EU generates and enforces rules throughout the Union.
How the EU meets its mandate depends on the specific organ in question.
Structurally, the EU is made up of five primary organs and underpinned by
the treaties outlined above and by European legislation. Together the EU's
policies and laws are called the *acquis communautaire*. The different organs of
the EU are important because they give different degrees of power to the
organisation compared with member states.

1. The European Commission, like the ECSC and EEC organs before it, is a
   quasi-executive organ of the EU with the capacity to initiate legislation and
   draft the budget.

   The European Commission is supranational in being able to not just
   propose legislation but also verify its application. It also has authority over
   competition within the single market (including scuttling corporate mergers),
   and it negotiates international trade agreements on behalf of the EU, such as
   in the WTO, for example. The Commission is comprised of 28 Commissioners
   nominated by their head of government for five-year terms. They hold
   specific portfolios such as transport and energy as per national politics. The
   Commission has a President and Vice-President; the latter holds the foreign
   affairs portfolio. They are elected by the European Parliament on the proposals of the European Council.

   Decisions are by majority, but are generally consensus-based. Although it
   can initiate policies and legislation, only one-fifth of its work is self-
   generated. Its policy and legislative decisions must be approved by other
   EU organs. The commission is supported by approximately 33,000 permanent
   civil servants, who are appointed through a meritocratic examination process
   (Kenealy *et al.* 2015). This supranational body is increasingly vying for power
   with the European Council and the Parliament.
2. The Council of Ministers may then legislate on the Commission's
   submission.

The Council of Ministers has 10 configurations, such as member states' ministers of agriculture meeting, compared with ministers of energy, or the environment.

They make decisions by a double-majority voting system. This requires 55 per cent of member states and 65 per cent of the populations they represent to vote affirmatively, although consensus is generally sought. Much of the negotiation is done in the prelude to Council meetings by the Committee of Permanent Representatives (COREPER). While the ministers are backed by a staff of fewer than 3,000, the COREPER has over 140 working groups and committees that determine the basis for Council approval.

3. The European Parliament, with members directly elected by the people of the EU, approves the members of the Commission, approves the budget, and has some co-legislative powers with the Council of Ministers.

The European Parliament is the only directly elected multinational parliament with power in the world. The 751 members of this parliament align according to political party. The Parliament has more than 20 standing committees, organised by portfolio. The Parliament is independent from the EU executive organs, meaning that elections do not change the composition of the Commission or the Councils. This Parliament independently exercises its role in legislating, budgeting and ratifying international treaties. Over time it has acquired more power.

4. The European Council comprised of members' heads of government determines the overall direction of the EU.

The European Council (of heads of state) decides on matters that are beyond the remit of the Council of Ministers and the Commission, as well as instigating new directions for the EU, such as enlargement, and acting on climate change. It also elects governors to the European Central Bank.

5. The European Court of Justice (ECJ) interprets the treaties and legislation and enforces the EU's legal authority.

It has 28 judges from the member states, who are appointed for six-year renewable terms, with nine Advocates General who write advisory opinions. A lower General Court addresses cases in the first instance. The ECJ is the arbiter of disputes between the EU institutions, its member states and its citizens. In 1964 the Court ruled that EU law prevails over domestic law, but enforcement of the rulings remains with states.

The EU began as an economic project. However, it always sought integration as a means to promote the well-being of its citizens and peace. It is therefore as much a political as an economic project. Yet the EU suffered setbacks in 2009, with citizens rejecting an EU constitution on the basis that it suffers a **democratic deficit**. There remains considerable debate over the extent to which the EU acts to further **neoliberal economic policies** or whether it is able to ameliorate the effects of **globalisation**. Over the last decade the EU has had to grapple with the mass refugee flux arising from the Arab Spring and the war in Syria; Greece's default on its loans and the Eurozone **debt crisis** following the **Great Recession** (see Chapter 6); and Britain's decision to exit the Union (see Box 8.1). Nonetheless, it remains the most advanced regional project in history, one that may remain unique.

The Mandate, Function and Structure of ASEAN

For a considerable time scholars argued that the EU was the model to which other regional IOs should aspire. ASEAN has often been compared unfavourably. Yet there is no doubt that a less legalistic, less bureaucratic and more informal and consensual approach to regionalism has created stability in the region. ASEAN is now recognised as the most successful regional organisation in the developing world. Beginning in 1967, the Association of Southeast Asian Nations was established by the ASEAN (or Bangkok) Declaration signed by Indonesia, Malaysia, the Philippines, Singapore and Thailand. They would be joined by Brunei Darussalam, Vietnam, Laos, Myanmar and Cambodia.

The ASEAN Declaration mandated the creation of a new organisation to facilitate regional cooperation. It gave the organisation a wide remit, with six functions, including

1. accelerate economic growth, social progress and cultural development;
2. promote regional peace and stability;
3. collaborate on economic, social, cultural, technical, scientific and administrative issues;
4. work together on agriculture, trade, commodities, transport, communications and improving the welfare of citizens;
5. advance Southeast Asian studies;
6. collaborate through regional and international organisations with similar aims and purposes and explore further means for closer cooperation (ASEAN 1967).

The organisation was therefore given broad economic, social and security areas for cooperation. How ASEAN members would cooperate would be spelt out in the Treaty of Amity and Cooperation (TAC) in Southeast Asia in 1976. This includes the following fundamental principles for interactions between states: the mutual respect of states' **sovereignty**, including territorial integrity; the right of states to be free of external interference; the principle of **non-interference**; the peaceful settlement of disputes, renouncing the threat of the use of force; and effective cooperation among the members.

Functionally, ASEAN operates as a forum IO for member states to come together to agree on how to achieve its mandate in accordance with these principles. Given the high level of distrust between the members in the 1960s, the decision of the members to promote peaceful cooperation is impressive. In the period of decolonisation, Singapore broke from the emergent Malaysia, while the latter had engaged in confrontation with Indonesia. Wider Cold War threats heightened tensions, including the US containment strategy in Asia against the Soviet Union and China, and the war in Vietnam (which had spilled over into Cambodia and Laos).

The single most important function of ASEAN was to promote confidence-building and trust within the region. ASEAN has been credited with ensuring regional peace and stability (Nesadurai 2008). It did so gradually, through providing a forum for states to meet. Structurally, ASEAN is comprised of biannual summit meetings of the heads of state. This is the primary decision-making body of the organisation where policy is determined and the Secretary General is appointed. The first summit was held in 1976.

Over time, ASEAN members would create ritualised practices for interacting known as the 'ASEAN Way': informal, non-confrontational, consensus-driven deliberations at the level of intergovernmental cooperation. Considerable work towards building confidence has been undertaken through 'two-track' diplomacy or unofficial dialogue between diplomats, business and think tanks, which feeds back into summit meetings.

ASEAN members eschew formal organisations, choosing not to invest power in the ASEAN Secretariat, which was created in 1977. The Secretariat, located in Jakarta with approximately 99 staff, is mandated to coordinate ASEAN organs to make them more efficient and effective. It also seeks to establish and maintain collaborations with stakeholders in accordance with the ASEAN Charter. The Secretariat is overseen by the Secretary General, who is appointed for a five-year term and is selected by rotation among the member states. The Secretary General also facilitates and monitors ASEAN agreements.

In 2007 ASEAN members ratified the ASEAN Charter (ASEAN 2015), which updates the Bangkok Declaration and ASEAN's guiding principles. It also significantly extended the organisation's structure and remit. It gave legal personality to the organisation, increased the Secretariat's powers, and committed members to the rule of law, democracy, human rights and good governance. Structurally, the Charter formalised a Coordinating Council of member states' foreign ministers, who meet at least biannually to prepare for the summit meetings, organise the implementation of ASEAN agreements, and coordinate with the community councils, including taking their reports to the summit.

ASEAN now has three pillars through which it seeks to meet its mandate: a political and security community; an economic community; and a socio-cultural community. Each of the three community councils has sector-specific ministerial bodies to implement ASEAN agreements. In this way ASEAN remains very much an intergovernmental body.

ASEAN's Achievements

While understandably limited in its early years, ASEAN would emerge as the key organisation for facilitating regionalism. In 1992 it agreed to establish an ASEAN Free Trade Area (AFTA) by 2005. Agreement on the AFTA included a common effective preferential tariff scheme (CEPT), reducing tariffs on manufacturing and processed (and later all) agricultural commodities to 0–5 per cent. ASEAN intended to create a single regional market under pressure from foreign investors. By the mid 1990s it was clear that rules for meeting these goals needed to be established in order for AFTA to be realised. Creating rules worked: the first phase for the CEPT was met by 2002; the original six members have now met their targets, and newer members are making substantive progress.

Nonetheless, business groups outside ASEAN continue to push for greater regional integration. This prompted the ASEAN Economic Community (AEC) initiative, which is to be implemented by 2020. The AEC seeks to liberalise trade, services, investment and labour within the region. The push for the AEC, which was launched in 2007, gives greater power to the ASEAN Secretariat to interpret, monitor and enforce AEC targets, as well as creating arbitration bodies to deal with economic disputes. It is unclear whether this will occur as scheduled.

While much of the work of ASEAN has been focused on economic cooperation, ASEAN has played a vital role in political and security issues. Indeed, ASEAN has become a hub for other regional 'spokes', which enables ASEAN to help shape regional diplomacy. This originated from its Post Ministerial Conferences, begun in 1978, enabling ASEAN to interact with external actors. ASEAN has been the locus for economic, security and political cooperation between East Asia through the ASEAN Plus Three (APT), including China, Japan and South

Korea, and the ASEAN Plus Six involving Australia, China, India, Japan, South Korea and New Zealand.

APT launched the Chiang Mai initiative in 2001 to pool currency reserves as a strong regional alternative to the IMF in case of another financial crisis (see Chapter 6). It also launched the East Asian Summit in 2005 to grapple with transboundary and international issues such as avian flu, energy and food security, and other non-traditional security concerns. Meanwhile, the ASEAN Plus Six grouping seeks to solidify gains from the free-trade agreements of its members by establishing the Regional Comprehensive Economic Partnership (RCEP), which was launched in 2012.

Militarily, ASEAN has contributed to peaceful relations through the ASEAN Regional Forum (ARF), which was established in 1994. The ARF now has 27 participants, including Australia, China, the EU, India, Japan, New Zealand, North Korea, Russia and the United States. The ARF embodies **cooperative security** and comprehensive security, in mitigating tensions within the region. In other words, it views regional security as more than just military threats. Moreover, 35 states have now signed ASEAN's Treaty of Amity and Cooperation, signalling wider acceptance of the ASEAN approach to regional security.

Over time ASEAN has faced challenges over its position on Myanmar's military dictatorship, its backing of Indonesia's control over East Timor prior to East Timor's independence in 2002, its attempts to grapple with border disputes, and territorial tensions in the South China Sea. It has also been caught flat-footed with regard to significant regional threats such as the environmental hazard from haze spreading across the region from burning forest fires in Indonesia, and the SARS outbreak and avian flu, which dramatically affected the people and economies of Southeast Asia.

Of course, ASEAN has also drawn criticism on account of its overly economic focus, and its track II diplomacy, or backchannel diplomacy, has not allowed much of a role for NGOs and civil society. Even the ASEAN Peoples Forum established in 2005, the ASEAN Intergovernmental Commission on Human Rights established in 2009 and the Declaration of Human Rights in 2012 have done little to assuage concerns that these remain merely symbolic gestures from authoritarian-leaning states.

The Mandate, Function and Structure of the OAS

The OAS is one of the oldest regional organisations, with antecedents reaching back to the first International Conference of American States in 1889. The OAS was established at the ninth conference in 1948, along with the American Declaration of the Rights and Duties of Man. The OAS Charter was adopted in 1951. The OAS is now comprised of all 35 states of the Americas, and has an additional 69 observers, including the EU. The OAS mandate is to promote peace and justice, solidarity and collaboration, while defending members' sovereignty, territory and independence (OAS 1993, Article I).

It has manifold functions, including to:

1. strengthen the peace and security;
2. promote and consolidate representative democracy;
3. ensure the pacific settlement of disputes;
4. provide for common action in response to aggression (collective security);
5. seek solutions to political, juridical and economic problems;
6. cooperate to advance economic social and cultural development;
7. eradicate extreme poverty;
8. limit conventional weapons (OAS 1993: Article 2).

As with the other regional IOs examined here, the OAS is both a forum IO and a service IO. It seeks to address four main areas: democracy, human rights, security and development. Like the EU, its activities are undertaken by a variety of organs according to its structure. The OAS has seven main organs.

1. The General Assembly, which is the main decision-making body of the OAS, with each state having one vote.

    States meet annually in locations determined by rotation. Decisions are made by consensus or majority vote, except regarding issues such as the budget that require two-thirds majority voting. The General Assembly appoints the Secretary General, and determines the mechanisms, policies and actions of the OAS.
2. The Permanent Council, which is comprised of all members and undertakes work entrusted to it by the General Assembly. Members' ambassadors sit in the Council, with the aim of ensuring peaceful relations between states and assisting with the peaceful settlement of disputes. It also oversees the other organs of the OAS, prepares work for the General Assembly, maintains relations with other IOs such as the UN, and ensures the operation of the Secretariat when the General Assembly is not in session. Decisions require a two-thirds majority, but consensus is the norm.
3. The Meeting of Consultation of Ministers of Foreign Ministers.

Once a proposal for such a meeting has been accepted by a majority vote in the Permanent Council, members' foreign ministers may meet as the Organ of Consultation to address issues requiring urgent attention, including an armed attack on a member state. Together with the Permanent Council, this comprises the **collective security** apparatus of the OAS.

4. The Inter-American Council for Integral Development (CIDI), which is comprised of members' ministerial representatives and reports to the General Assembly.

   CIDI, like the UN's Economic and Social Council (see Chapter 9), promotes development, poverty alleviation, human rights and social and cultural activities. It has a number of subsidiary bodies to implement technical cooperation and development programmes such as the Inter-American Agency for Cooperation and Development (IACD).

5. The General Secretariat, which is led by the Secretary General, who has a five-year term and is appointed on the basis of wide geographical representation. After the Cold War, the Secretary General, like the UNSG, was given the power to bring matters that threaten peace and security to the General Assembly or Permanent Council.

   The General Secretariat is a permanent body based in Washington, D.C., with secretariats for strengthening democracy, integral development, multidimensional security, administration and finance, legal affairs, access to rights and equity, and hemispheric affairs. The General Secretariat prepares the budget and oversees the operations of the OAS organs.

6. The Inter-American Juridical Committee, which is comprised of 11 jurists with four-year terms elected by the General Assembly. It provides advice to the OAS on judicial matters, and promotes the development of international law and the harmonisation of members' legislation.

7. The Inter-American Commission on Human Rights, which is an independent organ made up of seven members elected from the General Assembly who serve in an individual capacity. This Commission, which was brought into force in 1960, seeks to promote and protect human rights in the Americas. It can do so by receiving petitions to act on human rights abuses, by monitoring human rights abuses in member states, and by focusing on priority 'themed' areas. The Commission relies on states to enact its recommendations.

The OAS Charter also recognises specialised IOs that were in existence prior to the OAS, such as the Pan American Health Organization (PAHO, see Chapter 5), and other autonomous entities such as the Inter-American Court of Human Rights.

The Achievements of the OAS

The OAS was the first regional IO to identify its role in securing the peaceful settlement of disputes as per Article VIII of the UN Charter (see Chapter 3). It was able to use fact-finding, diplomacy, mediation, verification and observation missions, as well as **peacekeeping**, to resolve 40 disputes in its first 20 years (Vaky and Muñoz 1993). Later it was able to prevent conflict between Costa Rica and Nicaragua, and between Honduras and El Salvador.

During the **Cold War** period the OAS was used as an instrument of US foreign policy, including isolating communist Cuba and supporting dictatorships in its efforts to contain communism; and, in contravention to the OAS Charter, the OAS intervened in Guatemala (1954), the Dominican Republic (1965), Grenada (1983) and Panama (1989). Only after the civil war in the Dominican Republic did the OAS enter with an inter-American peace force (Herz 2011). The OAS has had no success in stemming the ongoing civil war in Colombia.

After the Cold War, the OAS was revitalised. From the 1990s onwards heads of state met at summits approximately every four years to discuss common policy concerns. Apart from US operations in Haiti, the OAS has not intervened in the Americas since 1990, and the OAS is no longer dominated by the United States. The OAS was central to resolving disputes between El Salvador and Honduras (2006), and between Guatemala and Belize (2008). It has worked to resolve tensions between Honduras and Nicaragua, and between Ecuador and Colombia. However, its first intervention into Haiti to challenge the 1991 coup d'état was considered ineffective, leading to a joint OAS/UN mission thereafter. It has also undertaken joint efforts with the UN in El Salvador and Nicaragua. Unlike the UN, the OAS is not focused on peace operations, but it has undertaken peace-building activities in relation to disarmament, truth and reconciliation, and electoral monitoring. Since 1990 it has undertaken almost 100 electoral missions in 20 states.

The OAS increasingly shifted its understanding of security to one of **cooperative security**, including confidence-building in the region. This is because of the nature of the transnational issues it grapples with: drug and weapons trafficking, transboundary environmental problems, migration, refugees, crime, money laundering and terrorism. In 1991 the Cartagena Declaration prohibiting weapons of mass destruction covering Latin America was issued.

The OAS has a strong focus on strengthening democracy within the region. It assists member states by providing information, technical assistance, electoral monitoring and procedures for intervening when members' democracy is at risk.

Indeed, in 1997 the OAS Charter was amended to allow for the suspension of a member state if its government is forcibly overthrown. This relaxes the IO's non-intervention norm. However, its scorecard for upholding democracy is mixed, and its efforts are considered weak.

The OAS also focused on ensuring human rights and engaging with civil society and NGOs. Over 300 NGOs are now recognised by the OAS. The reinvigoration of the IO has an economic element as well. Recognising that it had done little to achieve its economic development mandate, and as most states began to advocate for trade liberalisation in the 1990s, it promoted the Free Trade Area of the Americas (FTAA). Given its broad remit, it is unsurprising that the IO is under-resourced on trade and development. Much of the work on trade liberalisation occurred outside the OAS, although the push for the FTAA lost steam in the mid 2000s.

The Problem: Aggregating Sovereignty to Advance States' Goals

At the beginning of this chapter we asked why states choose to cooperate regionally. As with other forms of cooperation, regionalism can both strengthen and undermine state sovereignty. It can strengthen sovereignty because it can create more avenues for states to achieve their interests and preferences, such as wealth creation and protection, through cooperative security. Moreover, states generally retain control of the decision-making structure of regional organisations (the EU Commission is the exception). Regional cooperation can also undermine sovereignty because decisions are no longer the sole prerogative of a single government but must be accepted by all members of the regional IO, thus limiting the means through which states can act. So why would states choose regionalism over other forms of cooperation?

Regionalism has gone in and out of favour over time. Waves of regionalism have been triggered by different factors. In the 1950s and 1960s there were fears that Europe was creating a regional economic bloc that would be closed to other states. This prompted a push for other groups in Africa, the Americas and Asia to establish their own economic blocs to compete (the Soviet economic bloc was already closed).

Regionalism was therefore seen through a zero-sum lens: states were either benefiting from being in an agreement or they were losing. This is curious: why would states compete in regional blocs when the purpose is to create greater cooperation or even integration between members? The entry into a regional agreement is essentially to give preference to those within the regional bloc. This, by its nature, means that states outside the bloc do not receive the same gains. Thus members inside a regional security arrangement are protected against attack from the outside, and economically a common external tariff is applied to goods entering the bloc from non-members.

In terms of security, the main fears lie with NATO and EU expansion towards Russia, isolating the latter and challenging its dominance in its own region. Of course, NATO is a collective defence pact, meaning that it was created to defend states against the Soviet Union. In other regions, security arrangements have attempted to grapple with regional-level tensions and disputes (ASEAN, the AU and the OAS) rather than being the primary means through which all breaches of the peace are adjudicated (which remains the UN).

Advocates of economic regionalism argue that it is one of the means towards **globalisation**. Eliminating tariff barriers within a bloc is still eliminating rules and barriers between states. This can sit within, or be nested inside, a multilateral system like the GATT/WTO (see Chapter 6). Scholars would try to untangle whether regionalism is a stumbling block or a building block to globalisation in a truly multilateral system (Bhagwati 1991). Of course, the devil is in the detail. Some regional economic agreements may be trade-diverting because they interfere with how the market allocates resources. For example, having a common external tariff may enable a regional member to prevent extra-regionally produced goods from entering the market at a competitive price.

If a regional trade agreement is trade-distorting then it may undermine the overall welfare gains to states. An alternative to closed regionalism is an open regional agreement, like the Asia Pacific Economic Cooperation (APEC), a forum created in 1989 by Japan and Australia, which covers 21 Pacific Rim countries from Canada to Chile to China. It encourages cooperation and the removal of barriers to trade but without discriminating against external partners.

Economically there are a myriad of reasons why states may choose regionalism. It may be a means to bargain with trading partners or transnational corporations. It may be a means for demonstrating the credibility of domestic economic reforms by tying them to a regional agreement. It may be a means to satisfy domestic constituencies. Or it may be easier to achieve than a larger multilateral agreement. Regionalism might also be preferred because it can enable deeper levels of integration between states by enabling companies to benefit from economies of scale, and to facilitate regional production networks.

There is evidence that regional agreements do lead to greater investment and do not significantly divert trade.

By the 1970s many of the first-wave regional agreements had failed. The 'new' regionalism, beginning in the 1980s, is not focused on competing blocs but is intended as a means to grapple with **globalisation**. New regional projects were established, including, among others, the North American Free Trade Agreement (NAFTA) of Canada, the United States and Mexico; the Common Market of the South (MERCOSUR, made up of Argentina, Brazil, Uruguay, Paraguay, Venezuela and Bolivia); and the Andean Community (Colombia, Bolivia, Ecuador, Peru and Venezuela).

The combined effect of the end of the Cold War, the EU's consolidation into a single market, deadlock in the WTO and the rise of neoliberal economic ideas led to a rapid increase in the number of regional agreements. New regionalism therefore addresses not only the removal of barriers to the free flow of goods, services, capital and labour but also unbounded problems like transnational conflict, the fast spread of infections, transboundary environmental pollution and climate change, terrorism, money laundering, weapons, migration and refugees (Hettne 2005). The dramatic rise of intra-state conflicts in the 1990s and the overstretching of the UN would also give regional IOs permission to respond to regional conflicts (see Box 8.2).

Explaining Regional IOs' Behaviour

With such divergent regional experiences, can we theorise the behaviour of regional IOs? Given the amorphous nature of regionalism, theorising how and why states choose varying degrees of cooperation and integration within regions may seem impossible. Not only do the regions have differing relations between neighbours with divergent histories, cultures and patterns of inter-actions, but also the aims and structures of regional IOs are heterogeneous. Nevertheless, there are both IR and IO-specific theories that have been used to explain and understand how regional projects have emerged in the way they have.

The primary starting point is the **functionalist** argument that states can cooperate on non-political issues in order to smooth relations between states (see Chapter 2). The basis for functionalism was the European project, but other regional IOs have also started from a low base in order to facilitate cooperation

Box 8.2 Regional Security IOs

Regional security arrangements are not new. However, since the end of the Cold War there has been an increasing shift towards using regional IOs for securing peace. The rise of **peace enforcement** in states in order to ensure regional and international stability has led the UN to promote regional efforts to address local conflicts (see Chapter 3).

Regional IOs responded: NATO and the EU in Europe, the OAS in the Americas, the ARF in Southeast Asia, the Shanghai Cooperation Organisation (SCO) in Central Asia; as did sub-regional IOs: the South African Development Community (SADC) and the Economic Community of West African States (ECOWAS) among others in Africa.

Both the SADC and ECOWAS are interesting in terms of how they moved from being primarily economic organisations promoting economic integration to engaging in peace enforcement, although the latter initially did not have a security mandate. Contemporary peace-enforcement actions generally take place under the mandate of an IO, although they may be under the control of a 'lead' state willing to direct the operation.

---

in economic, social and cultural areas, which may have spilled over into political ones. Regional IOs as different as the EU, the AU and ECOWAS have incorporated into their charters their intention to advance regional integration, while ASEAN promotes 'ever-closer' regional cooperation. Like the EU, some of the other regional IOs see their role as promoting regional cooperation as a means to further peace and stability. Outside the EU, many regional IOs have highly aspirational goals that have not progressed their economic let alone security agendas.

As discussed in Chapter 2, the **neo-functionalist** agenda advanced by political scientist Ernst Haas argued that individual loyalties could be transferred from the state to either a federal or a supranational IO that was cognisant of the politics of its decision-making. Yet events within the EU, specifically the rise of the state-centric European Council and the European Monetary System, revealed how states, not IOs or transnational coalitions, were driving the EU agenda. States within the AU, ASEAN and the OAS have retained a tight grip on decision-making. Nonetheless, a modified version of neo-functionalism is still being used in relation to the EU. This revised version argues that the EU's ability to construct, interpret and enforce rules makes it a major interlocutor for transnational coalitions and that this interaction leads to further integration (Sandholtz and Stone Sweet 1998).

IR Approaches to Regional IOs

Traditional IR theories have had to deal with European integration. At the end of the Cold War, the realist John Mearsheimer (1990) famously argued that the end of the bipolar system would make Europe more violent than it had been for the previous 45 years. He argued that European states would revert to utility-maximising behaviour to advance their own self-interest. The panoply of EU institutions would not mitigate the effects of anarchy; indeed, they held out a 'false promise' that international cooperation could overcome concerns of military capabilities and relative gains. His provocative thesis remains unproven.

Realists expected the EU to balance the United States as the second of two main superpowers after the Cold War. Evidence of disagreement between the two became evident over the 2003 war in Iraq. Others argued that the EU would lose ground to new powers such as China and India. Yet the EU is not demonstrably doing that either. It maintains its relationship with the United States despite the 2003 Iraq invasion and the later unpredictability of the US Trump Administration. It engages with China over trade and investment, while enlarging in 2004, recovering from the Great Recession and Eurozone crisis, and responding to a mass influx of refugees. It remains a substantial power as a bloc.

With regard to its global military role, realists argue that the EU's advance of normative ideals globally is based on its material capabilities. Geopolitical stability and credibility explain why the EU intervenes in conflicts like Bosnia, Kosovo and the Congo, rather than the reason for intervention being because it is the right thing to do.

Another line of inquiry holds that the effects of anarchy could be tempered by certain conditions, including modern nationalism, geography, strategic beliefs and military technology. This could make the prospect of war less likely under anarchy, as might be the case for Western Europe. Neoclassical realism would go further and introduce unit-level variables (domestic politics) into the mix to argue that interest groups and elite perceptions, among other factors, could mediate the pressures of anarchy. Yet this is not a characteristic of realism alone, and lies at the heart of liberal approaches to explanations of regional IOs' behaviour.

Liberal intergovernmentalism is also state-centric, viewing states as utility-maximising actors. However, liberal intergovernmentalism, most prominently articulated by political scientist Andrew Moravcsik (1993), argued that states drove regionalism on the basis of their interests and preferences, rather than regionalism arising from the structure of the international system as per realists or from transnational coalitions and the institutions as per neofunctionalists. What makes the approach liberal is the recognition that it is political negotiations at the domestic level that determine states' preferences at the regional IO level.

Liberal intergovernmentalism is predicated on states taking national-level preferences to the regional bargaining table to negotiate with other states. Power politics plays a part in the deals states make with one another. The reason why states decide to pool their sovereignty at the regional level is in order to realise the gains of cooperation. Why do they then choose to give power to supranational organisations? Arguably this is because it makes the commitments states make to each other credible by locking in those agreements in treaties that bind them to each other. Liberal integovernmentalism remains a baseline theory for EU studies, although the extent to which it is transferable to other regions with less democratic states remains unclear.

IO-Specific Theories

IO-specific theories in some ways build on IR theories. The P–A model is a **rationalist** explanation of states' behaviour in delegating to regional organisations. The P–A model has been extensively applied to the EU. Member states pool their sovereignty, acting as a principal to EU agents such as the European Commission, the European Court of Justice (see Chapter 4) and the European Central Bank. They do so not only to credibly commit themselves to international cooperation but also to receive the benefits of lower transaction costs and the expertise of their agents. States delegate to these agents the task of monitoring their compliance and efficiently implementing rules agreed upon by the principals. Principals determine the scope of the activities of the agent, and oversee their implementation. They can sanction agents should they not meet their end of the contract. Variation of agent autonomy derives from the decisions negotiated by states in creating the agent.

In contrast, constructivist approaches focus on the three aspects of regionalism: how ideas and discourse create the need for regional IOs; how interactions between states within regional IOs create common understandings about the need for further integration; and how integration affects community-building within states through processes of socialisation (or support at the national level for a regional project). Again significant work has been done by constructivists on the EU and ASEAN in terms of building trust and cooperation between states towards creating a community. Owing to the fact that few of the regional IOs have significant secretariats with autonomous decision-making, there is less constructivist organisational culture analysis of regional IOs.

Within the EU one might expect there to be an organisational culture that shapes decision-making. Within the European Commission, EU scholar Liesbet Hooghe (2005) assessed whether adherence to the internal rules of the Commission, which are based on supranationalism, autonomy and impartiality, shapes staff preferences in favour of the EU over national identity. The effect was marginal. Studies on the European Council of Ministers working groups also revealed limited identification of staff with their supranational role (Beyers 2005). However, an examination of the COREPER does show staff adherence to norm-guided rules that influence decision-making (Lewis 2005).

Competition for Advancing States' Goals: Bilateral, Plurilateral and Multilateral Agreements

Is there any real alternative to regional organisations? In Chapter 2 we noted that there is never a real need to create IOs, yet states continue to do so. Decisions to create regional IOs are political ones, tied to states' interests and willingness to bind themselves to rules and a central organisation that can enforce them. From the end of WWII the European project has been a drive towards greater integration. This fundamentally means a move to eliminate barriers between states, and to create an ever-closer union. Although the end goal is a political community as well as an economic one, there has been considerable discussion as to whether states and their polities view this as highly desirable. It remains a work in progress.

While other regional IOs also advocate regional integration, there has been significantly less institutionalisation of rules in other regions. In other words, many regional IOs do not undermine, or usurp authority from, their sovereign state members. Yet we continue to see aspirational plans to move towards creating larger free-trade areas, the strengthening of regional IOs such as ASEAN and the OAS, and the increasing use of regional IOs for security.

The dense network of regional economic agreements, and the shift towards plurilateral or extra-regional trade agreements, can be seen as another building block towards global economic agreements. Given the deadlock of the WTO (see Chapter 7), this might be another means to achieve the same aims. Do extra-regional agreements undermine regional IOs? As with other questions, the specifics of the agreements will determine the extent to which they include a role for regional IOs. Regional IOs often have a high level of technical expertise, yet many remain relatively limited in their autonomy compared with their sovereign member states or larger multilateral bodies.

Regional IOs do not replace multilateralism at a larger scale, but they do provide alternative means through which cooperation may be achieved. Some things may be best achieved globally (for example, responding to climate change), while other issues are best dealt with regionally (such as territorial disputes). Certainly the appetite for regional security responses has enabled regional IOs to take up the peace-enforcement mantle when the UN proved overwhelmed. At this point in time it is unlikely that a greater aggregation of political power, such as the creation of a world parliament, would occur at the global level rather than regionally.

Chapter Summary

This chapter questioned why states would choose to engage in regional cooperation. Regional IOs have been created in two waves, in the 1950s and 1960s and again after the 1980s. Regional IOs vary significantly in form and function. Yet they occupy an important place in international relations. While most IOs have been created for economic reasons, there has been an increase in the use of regional IOs for security purposes over the last two decades. This applies even for regional bodies that do not have a security function! The chapter examined the different mandates, function and structure of the three largest and most successful regional IOs: the EU, ASEAN and the OAS. How each of the three operates is influenced by regional specificities.

The 'problem' regional IOs attempt to solve is the need to provide a degree of cooperation and integration sought by their member states in order to achieve their interests. Ideas and discourse do play a role in shaping what the regional IOs look like, but there is less organisational culture analysis here owing to the limited nature of many regional organisations. Alternatives to regional IOs exist in the form of weaker regional and plurilateral arrangements or, of course, the universal multilateralism found in the UN and WTO. Some see regional IOs as a path to greater international cooperation and multilateralism; others do not. What do you think?

Guiding Questions

1. Why do states choose regional integration?
2. What are the strengths and weaknesses of the EU model?
3. Should ASEAN remain an economically focused regional organisation?
4. Is the OAS qualitatively different from more economically focused regional IOs?
5. What theory best explains regional IOs?
6. Does regionalism impede or advance globalisation?

Further References

Online Resources

Euractiv: www.euractiv.com. A pan-European media network that provides updates on EU developments.

Centre Virtuel de la Connaissance sur l'Europe: www.cvce.eu/en/home. A repository for documents on EU integration. It was recently incorporated into the University of Luxembourg.

Institution on Comparative Regional Integration Studies: www.cris.unu.edu. The United Nations University Institute that provides research and information on regionalism.

Further Reading

Acharya, A., 2001, *Constructing a Security Community in Southeast Asia: ASEAN and the Problem of Regional Order*, London and New York, Routledge.

Ba, A. D., 2009, *(Re)Negotiating East and Southeast Asia: Region, Regionalism, and the Association of Southeast Asian Nations*, Stanford, CA, Stanford University Press.

Cini, M., and N. Pérez-Solórzano Borragán, 2016, *European Union Politics*, fifth edition, Oxford, Oxford University Press.

Dinan, D., 2014, *Origins and Evolution of the European Union*, second edition, Oxford, Oxford University Press.

Haacke, J., 2003, *ASEAN's Diplomatic and Security Culture: Origins, Development and Prospects*, London, Routledge Curzon.

Herz, M., 2011, *The Organization of American States (OAS): Global Governance Away from the Media*, London and New York, Routledge.

McNamara, K., 2015, *The Politics of Everyday Europe: Constructing Authority in the European Union*, Oxford, Oxford University Press.

Moravcsik, A., 1993, 'Preferences and Power in the European Community: A Liberal Intergovernmentalist Approach', *Journal of Common Market Studies* 31 (4): 473–524.

Pollack, M. A., 2003, *The Engines of European Integration*, Cambridge, Cambridge University Press.

Schimmelfennig, F., 2003, *The EU, NATO and the Integration of Europe*, Cambridge, Cambridge University Press.

Wiener, A., and T. Dietz, 2004, *EU Integration Theory*, Oxford, Oxford University Press.

9 Furthering Development

Introduction

Many of the IOs operating in international development have existed for a long time. The International Bank for Reconstruction and Development (IBRD, commonly known as the World Bank) was created in 1944 alongside the IMF (see Chapter 6), when the Allies during WWII met to agree on a framework for a liberal international economic order. The United Nations Development Programme (UNDP), an amalgamation of two earlier UN funds, began to provide technical assistance to developing countries in 1966. The longevity of these IOs is important, because their mandates have not changed, but the world has: in

1960 the world population was three billion; in October 2015 it surpassed seven billion. In 1945, 51 states created the UN; in 2011, South Sudan, the newest sovereign state, was admitted as the UN's 193rd member. As the world's population grows and as the sovereign state system has expanded and diversified, some problems have not changed: poverty, disease, high levels of infant and maternal mortality, lack of nutrition and access to clean drinking water, inequality and a lack of economic growth. In other ways the situation has changed dramatically with the increasing wealth of middle-income countries and rising powers.

This chapter looks at

- the mandate, function and structure of the main IOs operating in international development, including the Multilateral Development Banks (MDBs), the UN's Economic and Social Council (ECOSOC) and UNDP, and the Organisation for Economic Co-operation and Development (OECD);
- how IOs have had to adapt to new development challenges arising from the end of communism, **globalisation** and increasing demands from civil society;
- how the IR and IO-specific theories explain the actions of development IOs;
- how development IOs are increasingly competing with alternative sources of problem solving, ranging from the private sector to NGOs and philanthropists.

The Mandate, Function and Structure of International Development IOs

IOs have been at the forefront of debates over what constitutes development and how best to achieve it. The activities of the main IOs governing global development are detailed, as are their mandate, function and structure.

The Multilateral Development Banks

In many ways the World Bank is emblematic of the official way to do multilateral development. Its practices have been emulated by the regional multilateral development banks (MDBs), notably the African Development Bank (AfDB), Asian Development Bank (ADB) and Inter-American Development Bank (IDB). These were all created from the late 1950s to the 1960s. In addition, the European Bank for Reconstruction and Development (EBRD) was created in 1991 with the break-up of the Soviet Union.

The World Bank and the MDBs' Mandate and Function

The World Bank is mandated to provide loans to states for economic growth and development, particularly where funding from the private sector is unavailable. States may not be creditworthy as a result of financial crisis, debt or war. The World Bank functions as a bank. All the MDBs follow the model of lending to **sovereign states**, although they are increasingly lending to the private sector in developing countries (except the World Bank). The World Bank Group includes the International Finance Corporation, which lends and invests in private-sector companies and projects, and the Multilateral Investment Guarantee Agency, which provides political insurance to the private sector. Most of the MDBs also have soft-loan financing facilities that aim to provide grants or loans with no interest and long maturities, called credits, to the poorest states. The World Bank's is called the International Development Association (IDA). The New Development Bank (NDB) created by the rising powers of Brazil, Russia, India, China and South Africa in July 2014 is similar in its aims, as is the new Asian Infrastructure Investment Bank (AIIB, see Chapter 1), driven by China and created by 57 members in 2015. They largely follow the World Bank's lending model, although the extent to which matters may differ in practice remains to be seen. The MDBs require their loans to be repaid (using the US dollar). As the nature of development expanded (see pages 190–193), the World Bank followed the IMF in increasing the number of loan **conditions** it attached in order for its loans to be repaid.

The World Bank is important for three reasons. First, because it is considered pre-eminent in the field of international development owing to its global reach, its **technical expertise** accumulated from lending since 1947 and its resources. It has lent on average $20 billion per annum since the late 1990s. The policies determined by the World Bank are emulated by the other MDBs and are reinforced by the **bilateral** lending agencies of OECD member states (Box 9.1). The World Bank thus shapes what the main issues in international development are and how they should be addressed.

For example, in 1996, the then President of the World Bank James Wolfensohn (1995–2005) uttered the 'C' word: corruption. Until then, tackling corruption in international development was considered taboo. It challenged developing states' **sovereignty**, and, since the World Bank was intended to function as an apolitical economic IO, it was beyond its mandate. President Wolfensohn argued that corruption was an economic issue rather than a political one. In doing so, he helped usher in a focus on anticorruption and **good governance**, which came to dominate international development thinking.

Box 9.1 The OECD and the Development Assistance Committee (DAC)

The OECD provides macro-economic policy advice and establishes international standards for its now 34 member states. It has a mandate to promote policies that will improve the economic and social well-being of its members. The OECD is a forum IO where governments can share experiences and seek solutions to common problems (OECD 2015). It has extended its work across all policy areas from trade in services to genetic engineering and computer security. The OECD emerged out of the Organisation for European Economic Cooperation that delivered the Marshall Plan to Europe between 1948 and 1951. The OECD was created in 1961 as an IO for industrialised states to meet as equals, despite the then power asymmetry between the United States and Western Europe.

The OECD has been described as a 'rich states' club' because you must be invited in order to become a member. The OECD recognised the industrialised **Global North**'s obligations to the developing **Global South**, thus giving it a development mandate. The OECD established a Development Assistance Committee (the OECD DAC) to establish best-practice guidelines for **official development assistance** (ODA) of its 23 member states. This guides member states' bilateral aid agencies such as the UK's Department for International Development (DFID). Approximately nine-tenths of the global ODA funds flow from OECD DAC members (OECD 2011). The OECD DAC has established best practice for ODA to cover the Millennium Development Goals as well as reviewing when states meet their obligations. In 2005, 60 states and organisations signed the Paris Agreement on Aid Effectiveness that identified 12 indicators to measure progress in development and reform ODA delivery. There have now been four high-level forums on aid effectiveness. However, critics question how the OECD's aid harmonisation approach dovetails with the **neoliberal economic policy** advice it generally dispenses (Abdelal 2007).

The process was intensely political, with states, scholars and NGOs challenging the definitions and metrics for measuring whether developing states were meeting good governance goals in order to borrow from lenders like the World Bank. The World Bank itself struggled with the idea of not lending to corrupt states. The anticorruption agenda faced strong internal resistance from Bank staff and its European member state shareholders, who challenged the simplistic message of 'zero tolerance' for corruption from the subsequent

President, Paul Wolfowitz (2005–2007). They argued that it was the neediest people within corrupt states who would be hurt most by turning off the lending tap. Despite the World Bank hiring staff, establishing strategic plans and creating units on anticorruption and good governance, the organisation never truly endorsed the anticorruption agenda (Weaver 2008).

The MDBs, Debt and Conditionality

From the late 1940s onwards the MDBs sought to lend to developing states for economically sound development projects. The primary focus was on infrastructure projects such as dams, roads and power plants in the effort to spur economic growth (and allow developing states to repay their loans).

While the MDBs still lend for infrastructure, two 'oil shocks' in the 1970s had a dramatic impact on the financing and economic viability of many developing states. In 1973–1974 and again in 1978–1979 members of the Organization of the Petroleum Exporting Countries (OPEC), including Iran, Iraq, Kuwait, Saudi Arabia and Venezuela, imposed global oil embargoes to demand higher prices. The international price of oil quadrupled during these periods. This compounded the price many developing countries paid for energy. In response, developing countries borrowed heavily, both from private banks and from the MDBs, with cheap but variable interest rates. The superpowers, the United States and the USSR, encouraged this lending in order to maintain their allies during the **Cold War**, even though many developing states were led by corrupt dictators. A confluence of events then contributed to the indebtedness of many developing countries: a sharp increase in interest rates; a recession in the world economy, which led to a decline in the purchase of developing country exports; and an outflow of capital.

Recognising that there was now a need to extricate developing states from this quagmire, from the early 1980s the World Bank, and later the other MDBs, would advocate another function alongside project lending: lending for structural adjustment programmes (SAPs). SAPS were loans to assist states to restructure their economies in such a way as to rein in debt levels and spur economic growth. The primary means were loan **conditions** that included austerity measures to reduce state expenditure, facilitate international trade through commodity exports and stimulate international investment. Aiming to reduce the inefficiency associated with large state bureaucracies and state-owned enterprises, the World Bank reforms required borrowers to cut the state sector, which reduced essential state functions, but did not spur domestic growth. SAPs were part of the **Washington Consensus** of policy prescriptions favoured by the World Bank, the IMF (see Chapter 6) and the OECD (Box 9.1).

The net result was that borrowers needed more loans for basic subsistence while continuing to restructure their economies, leading to increasing levels of debt. For most developing countries, the repayment of the original debt became impossible. Even maintaining debt repayments on subsequent loans was crippling. The 1980s and 1990s are now seen as lost decades of development.

The Bank defended its record by arguing that borrowers tended to abandon SAPs before positive results could be seen. States were abandoning SAPs and IMF arrangements when faced with domestic opposition (Chapter 6). Meanwhile, the World Bank and IMF's efforts to write off debts in the 1980s and 1990s were piecemeal and limited. It was not until mass activist campaigns like Jubilee 2000 advocating for the MDBs to 'Drop the Debt' in the late 1990s that the World Bank and the IMF implemented debt-relief mechanisms. These included the Highly Indebted Poor Country Initiative, and the Multilateral Debt Relief Initiative to cancel debt to the 39 poorest states in the world.

The Structure of the World Bank and the MDBs

Much of the debate over MDBs concerns their structure, or who controls the IO. Considering the power they wield, who runs these banks has important implications. Member states created their Articles of Agreement or constitution. Member states also provide the financial base or subscriptions for the MDBs. The MDBs operate on the 'one dollar, one vote' principle, with the amount of money paid in by the member state determining their number of votes in the MDBs. States' Ministers of Finance or Treasury Ministers are the MDBs' Governors. The Governors meet only once or twice annually, delegating to their representatives on the Board of Executive Directors to oversee operations year-round. The Executive Directors approve projects and programmes presented to them by management under the leadership of the MDB's President. The President runs the daily operations of the MDB, including overseeing staff.

The United States retains over 16 per cent of the vote in the World Bank, which is not enough to wield power over determining project loans or even many policy changes. However, it is important for decisions requiring 85 per cent of the vote, such as amending the voting power of member states. In these instances, the United States has a 'veto' on major decisions. The United States also has informal power in reviewing documents before they go to the MDBs' boards for approval by the member states. Pressure from developing countries to change the structure of the World Bank has had little effect. Alterations to the voting structure in 2010 conceded little in terms of improving the vote for states whose economic fortunes have improved dramatically since 1945. For example, China has increased its vote share within the World Bank only from 2.8 per cent to its current 4.8 per cent, despite shifting from a poor state to becoming the second largest economy in the world in 2010.

Arguably states like the United States and G7 prefer to retain the unequal power they have in the World Bank. Even in the other MDBs, where regional heavyweights like Brazil and South Africa have larger votes (in the IDB and AfDB, respectively), there has been no real change in their voting weights despite their economic gains over the last few decades (Strand and Trevathan 2016). The new AIIB and the NDB are both recent entrants to international development lending, yet they mimic the mandate and function of the older MDBs. So why were they created? There are two reasons: functional and power-related.

First, there is an increased demand for international funding for infrastructure, with estimates that over one trillion US dollars is needed annually to meet developing countries' needs. The current 'old' MDBs cannot meet this demand, thus justifying the establishment of the AIIB and the NDB.

Second, the old MDBs are dominated by the United States and the G7 (as with the IMF, see Chapter 6) in terms of capital subscribed and their voting power. In contrast, the AIIB is dominated by China, while the NDB is comprised solely of Brazil, China, India, Russia and South Africa. This changes the MDB landscape for developing countries by offering an alternative funding source free of the conditionality imposed by the Western-dominated MDBs. Such alternatives are important, given the entrenched power imbalance in how the old MDBs are structured.

The AIIB and the NDB have instituted that no founding member has a veto. The United States strongly opposed the AIIB, even pressuring its allies Australia and South Korea not to join. Some argue that these new IOs undermine the liberal international economic order established by the United States and its allies in the post-WWII period (Barma *et al.* 2007), while others argue that they extend it (Voeten 2014).

The UN and Development

In contrast to the MDBs, the UN attempts to provide both a forum for and technical assistance to developing states. In the aftermath of WWII, the UN aimed to promote peace through economic growth and development, which is reminiscent of theoretical functionalist arguments. The United States desired a 'one-tent' organisation covering all aspects of international relations, thus creating both a Security Council and an Economic and Social Council (Toye and Toye 2004). Economic and social security was seen to be as important as military security for peace.

This is because the UN founders were cognisant that the Versailles peace treaty of 1919 was highly unequal. It contributed to states' using economic protectionist policies during the 1920s, which escalated into the **Great Depression** and helped militarise states for war. Today states are once again concerned about the connections between development and security: the High-Level Panel on Threats, Challenges and Change was prepared for the UN World Summit in 2005 after the 11 September 2001 terrorist attacks against the United States (Weiss 2012). While the security concerns are different, many see high levels of poverty and inequality as grounds for radicalisation.

The Mandate, Function and Structure of ECOSOC

ECOSOC's mandate is outlined in Article 1 of the UN Charter. It seeks to facilitate international cooperation for solving economic, social, cultural or humanitarian international problems. In doing so, it aims to promote and encourage human rights and fundamental freedoms for all irrespective of race, sex, language or religion (United Nations 1948a: Article 1, Section 3).

As provided for in the UN Charter, ECOSOC has the following four functions:

1. prepare reports and recommendations to the UNGA on economic, social, cultural, educational and health issues;
2. make recommendations for promoting human rights and fundamental freedoms;
3. draft conventions for submission to the General Assembly;
4. organise international conferences (United Nations 1948a: Chapter X, Article 62; see also Chapter IX).

ECOSOC is a forum IO where states can advocate for policy recommendations, prepare draft conventions, provide coherence to the UN system, and interact with NGOs (Rosenthal 2007). Early on it dropped efforts to promote full employment, while turning towards sustainable development from the 1980s.

Structurally, ECOSOC is comprised of 54 member states elected from the UNGA according to regional representation. It is ambiguously both a principal organ, like the UNSC, but also subordinate to the authority of the UNGA.

Moreover, it can only provide recommendations, not enforceable resolutions. The contrast between ECOSOC and the UNSC is stark: the UNSC is a principal organ of the UN with a two-tiered membership of permanent and non-permanent members. Its permanent members require unanimity to make decisions, and it has enforceable powers (Chapter 3).

In its initial decades ECOSOC was small and indecisive in its operations. It had a considerable mandate, but there was no agreement as to how to carry it out. It had overlapping bodies, such as the overlap between the Council and its functional commissions, and it established regional commissions between 1947 and 1958. These exacerbated the problem of unnecessary bureaucracy, which is problematic considering that ECOSOC's purview extends to over 80 per cent of the human and financial resources of the entire UN system (Anstee 2012).

Coordination remains a significant problem, with some IOs reporting both to ECOSOC and to the UNGA, and with ECOSOC also reporting to the UNGA. It is currently comprised of 15 UN specialised agencies, which vary in their **autonomy**, including the IMF and the World Bank, which merely inform ECOSOC of their activities; nine functional commissions; and five regional commissions. It also receives reports from 10 UN funds and programmes (see Box 9.2). This organisational structure can hinder effective coordination.

UN Reform

Efforts to reform the UN's unwieldy bureaucracy were a feature of the 2005 World Summit of UN members, leading to ECOSOC being given the responsibility for following up on major UN conferences (Box 9.2). It established an Annual Ministerial Review to assess progress in the implementation of the Millennium Development Goals (MDGs) and, post-2015, the Sustainable Development Goals (SDGs) (Box 9.3). Despite this, it has changed little since the 1950s, with insiders describing ECOSOC as the UN's 'least-powerful deliberative body' that suffers from a culture where process trumps results (Weiss 2012). Moreover, as a global body ECOSOC has been a forum within which distrust between the superpowers and between the **Global North** and **Global South** has prevented the body from delivering much. In other words, states have been unable to effectively cooperate in ECOSOC for much of its existence.

The Mandate, Function and Structure of the UNDP

Central to the UN's work on development is the UN Development Programme (UNDP). The UNDP, which was established by the UNGA, is the primary

Box 9.2 The ECOSOC System

Functional Commissions
Crime Prevention and Criminal Justice
Narcotic Drugs
Population and Development
Science and Technology for Development
Social Development
Statistics
Status of Women
United Nations Forum on Forests

Regional Commissions
Economic Commission for Africa (ECA)
Economic Commission for Europe (ECE)
Economic Commission for Latin America and the Caribbean (ECLAC)
Economic and Social Commission for Asia and the Pacific (ESCAP)
Economic and Social Commission for Western Asia (ESCWA)

Specialised Agencies
International Labour Organization (ILO)
Food and Agriculture Organization of the United Nations (FAO)
United Nations Educational, Scientific and Cultural Organization (UNESCO)
World Health Organization (WHO)
World Bank (WB)
International Monetary Fund (IMF)
International Civil Aviation Organization (ICAO)
International Maritime Organization (IMO)
International Telecommunication Union (ITU)
Universal Postal Union (UPU)
World Meteorological Organization (WMO)
World Intellectual Property Organization (WIPO)
International Fund for Agricultural Development (IFAD)
United Nations Industrial Development Organization (UNIDO)
World Tourism Organization (UNWTO)

Programmes and Funds
United Nations Development Programme (UNDP)
United Nations Environment Programme (UNEP)

United Nations Population Fund (UNFPA)

United Nations Human Settlements Programme (UN-HABITAT)

Office of the United Nations High Commissioner for Refugees (UNHCR)

United Nations Children's Fund (UNICEF)

United Nations Office on Drugs and Crime (UNODC)

United Nations Relief and Works Agency for Palestine Refugees in the Near East (UNRWA)

United Nations Entity for Gender Equality and the Empowerment of Women (UN-Women)

World Food Programme (WFP)

Other Entities, Bodies and Research Institutes

Joint United Nations Programme on HIV/AIDS (UNAIDS)

United Nations International Strategy for Disaster Reduction (UNISDR)

United Nations Office for Project Services (UNOPS)

Committee for Development Policy

Committee of Experts on Public Administration

Committee on Non-Governmental Organizations

Permanent Forum on Indigenous Issues

United Nations Group of Experts on Geographical Names

United Nations Interregional Crime and Justice Research Institute (UNICRI)

United Nations Institute for Disarmament Research (UNIDIR)

United Nations Institute for Training and Research (UNITAR)

United Nations Research Institute for Social Development (UNRISD)

United Nations System Staff College (UNSSC)

United Nations University (UNU)

development organisation within the UN family, and it coordinates the UN Development Group. In the beginning the UNDP's mandate was to provide technical assistance to newly emergent and developing states as well as to help identify economically feasible development projects. It now states that its aim is to eradicate poverty, and reduce inequalities and exclusion, by helping states develop policies, skills, institutions, partnering abilities and resilience (UNDP 2017). The UNDP functions to provide grants, loans and non-concessional assistance for the following: technical assistance; capacity building (helping states learn how to develop themselves); promoting democracy; and sustainable development.

Box 9.3 Financing for Development

In 2002 the UN sponsored the summit-level International Financing for Development conference in Mexico to bring together divergent efforts to tackle international development. Fifty heads of state and over 200 ministers of foreign affairs, trade and finance attended. The resultant Monterrey Consensus sought to eradicate poverty, achieve economic growth and promote sustainable development. The aim was to do so through recognising developed and developing states' financial responsibilities across the key areas of aid, trade, debt and technology. This was reiterated at the Doha Declaration in 2008.

In 2015, states met again in Addis Ababa to assess progress in meeting the Monterrey Consensus and the Doha Declaration (United Nations 2015a). Unlike other high-level UN summits, the Monterrey Conference did not establish a new IO to operationalise the agreement. Rather, both the UNGA and ECOSOC were given roles for coordination and follow-up. Since 2003, ECOSOC has held an annual special high-level meeting of the Council with the World Bank, IMF, WTO and UNCTAD in order to address issues of cooperation, coherence and coordination in development financing (United Nations 2015b).

Unlike the World Bank and the MDBs, which are located in major capital cities and send out 'missions' to their borrowers, the UNDP is structured as a network, with offices in over 177 states and territories. The UNDP's resident representatives in the country offices now coordinate all of the development work within host states for the entire UN. Its network also extends to over 90 entities created by the UNDP through a process of **emanation** (see Box 9.2).

How Do the UNDP and the MDBs Compare?

Clearly there are major organisational differences between the MDBs and the UNDP. Three stand out. The first is that their structure is different: hierarchical versus horizontal. The second concerns how they promote international development: while the MDBs also provide technical assistance, it is predicated on states then asking for a loan to implement a project or programme designed by the MDBs. In comparison, the UNDP provides the technical assistance for borrowers to do it themselves.

Their funding sources are also distinct. The World Bank's lending is about $20 billion annually, with funding derived from trading on international capital markets and repayments and interest from previous loans. Its soft-loan window, IDA for poor states, lends just under half that amount. In contrast, the UNDP has an annual budget of only $5 billion, which comes from UN member states' voluntary contributions and other IOs and NGOs. Core contributions that are not 'tied' to specific activities represent only one-fifth of the UNDP's budget and come from only 15 states. Member states can thus determine whether their donations should be directed to the core budget of the UNDP, giving it more **autonomy** and control over how to spend it, or non-core resources, where member states determine how it can be spent.

The third difference is that the values, or **organisational culture**, of the UNDP differ from those of the World Bank. The organisation is highly thought of in developing states, where the UNDP is seen as a partner in their development efforts, because it respects their **sovereignty** and encourages learning. In contrast, the World Bank is considered to be highly knowledgeable but also arrogant on account of its specialised knowledge. The view is that the Bank has elite economists who have been trained at the top universities in the United States and UK, who seek to implement untested theoretical economic models in developing states with a research department at the Bank that affirms its operations. Both are respected as having knowledgeable and passionate staff, but the World Bank is a donor-driven bank, while the UNDP is considered to be a partner to developing states (Murphy 2004). The differences between the development IOs include their opinions on how best to solve the question of international development.

The Problem: International Development as an Expanding Concept

Central to our discussion of IOs as problem solvers is the critical issue of identifying what it is they are attempting to solve. This may seem straightforward, but the concept of development has changed over time and continues to evolve. In the post-WWII period it was assumed that '**underdeveloped**' states had low savings rates and that both international investment through the MDBs and bilateral ODA were needed to spur economic growth. The World Bank and the UN agencies differ in their ways of operating, but they worked to achieve the same aim.

The MDBs have focused on spurring economic growth to facilitate development. This was underpinned by modernisation theory or the view that the provision of capital and technology could help borrower states 'take off' from traditional agrarian states to a higher stage of modern industrial development. Development economics shifted from **Keynesian** liberalism with a focus on state-led development to the neoliberalism of the Washington Consensus in the 1980s; reducing the role of the state and letting markets take over. While this Washington Consensus prevailed, alternative development approaches were being articulated within the UN (Box 9.4). However, the national accounting indicators for economic growth have remained the same over time: measuring states' Gross Domestic Product (GDP), or domestic economic production.

The ability of the MDBs to marshal resources to lend to developing states has consistently outstripped the resources being provided by industrialised states through the UNDP. As a result, **conditionality** drove the development agenda. Yet it should also be recognised that the World Bank's resources were not the only reason for it being the central development agency. IOs can be powerful drivers of change in their own right owing to their **rational–legal authority** and **technical expertise**. The locus of change may lie within the IO, in its management, staff and organisational culture. In the late 1960s the World Bank was able to reconceptualise international development (what it is that states and the international community should do) to include poverty alleviation as a result of its charismatic President Robert S. McNamara. The incorporation of the consideration of poverty as a component of development continued within the Bank even during the height of SAP lending.

Owing to the UNDP's lack of influence compared with the MDBs, its efforts to promote normative ideals about solidarity with borrowers and development that promoted human rights were overlooked. Some argue that the UNDP has been ahead of the curve in realising how these and other factors contribute to development. For example, they advanced ideas now being recognised as integral to development: the need to incorporate the environment into development; the need to prioritise poverty and equality; the need to recognise the role of women in other societies and their inclusion in formulating development plans.

By the 1990s it was recognised that the UN needed reform after losing influence to the World Bank, the IMF and, in trade, the WTO (see Chapter 7). After the lost decade of development (see page 183) there was a renewed interest in addressing poverty and inequality, with many states in worse condition than before the 1980s. In 1990, the UNDP released the first of its Human Development Reports (HDRs) that sought to provide a more comprehensive understanding of development. It argued that World Bank and IMF SAPs undermined social

Box 9.4 The UN, the Economic Commission for Latin America (ECLA) and Dependency Theory

Alternative approaches to development emerged within the UN, particularly in the Secretary General's office, the Department for Economic Affairs (DEA) and the Economic Commission for Latin America (ECLA). ECLA is a regional commission under ECOSOC charged with undertaking economic reports and surveys of Latin America.

Despite its focus on being politically impartial, there was room for intellectual freedom within the UN. Within the Secretary General's office economists began to provide alternatives to the increasingly dominant wisdom of the benefits of **free trade**. Argentine economist Raúl Prebisch used ECLA as a platform for disseminating the radical idea that there was a long-term downward trend in commodity prices compared with industrial goods, and that this would lead to unequal trade between developed and developing states. This later became known as the 'Prebisch–Singer thesis' as the idea was proposed by Prebisch at the same time as by the economist Hans Singer.

The thesis challenged the assumption of mainstream economics that all states were equal, that equal trade and monetary rules should apply, and that the process of economic development was the same for all states. Prebisch argued that northern industrialised states were the 'core' of the world economy, compared with a 'periphery' of less developed states that were dependent on the core. The continuation of the global liberal economy would enable the North to continue to advance to a new industrial epoch while the South would be left further behind.

Dependency theory would take these structural ideas and provide political and social reasons for developing states' inability to develop. ECLA thus challenged the economic thinking of Keynesian liberalism and provided the theoretical proposals for a **New International Economic Order** (NIEO) in the 1970s. Although they were popular, dependency theory and neo-Marxist development approaches could not account for the rapid rise of several northeast Asian states (Japan, Hong Kong, Singapore, Taiwan and South Korea), radically undermining its explanatory power.

safety nets in developing states and that this contributed to impoverishment (UNDP 1990).

The reports established a framework for integrating different development concerns including human rights. The UNDP, invoking Amartya Sen's concept of human capability, argued that development should enhance human capabilities and choices in being able to undertake activities that people value rather than see the poor as passive recipients of development aid. Thus development policies should focus on enhancing people's ability to survive and thrive through improved nutrition, better health, literacy, training and protecting their rights.

The UNDP provided alternative metrics, developed by Mahbub ul Haq, to viewing development as GDP: the Human Development Index (HDI) and the subsequent Multi-dimensional Poverty Index (MDI). The HDI established indicators for life expectancy, literacy and income, among other things, for measuring a long and healthy life, having knowledge and a decent standard of living (UNDP 2015a). Attempting to identify indicators from philosophical reasoning is not without complications. However, the indices are incredibly powerful.

For example, they demonstrate that states with high GDP are not necessarily states where people have the highest quality of life. The world's largest economy, the United States, ranks fifth in terms of human development, with Norway consistently ranking first. Singapore, Ireland and Iceland all rank ahead of the UK (UNDP 2015b). The UNDP's 1994 HDR would also outline the conception of human security, emphasising security of the person, in contrast to standard IR theories that focus on the state (Chapter 3). This is particularly important given the UNDP's development efforts in post-conflict states. The focus on human needs would help pave the way for the Millennium Development Goals and the subsequent Sustainable Development Goals (Box 9.5).

In sum, the concept of development has expanded beyond providing capital and technology for states' economies to 'take off'. In the 1990s and 2000s the MDBs, UN agencies, the IMF and the OECD, among others, all had to grapple with an expanding concept, as debt, poverty, good governance, gender, democracy and issues such as HIV/AIDS came to the fore. Development was not only an increase in states' GDP but increasingly seen as a human right (Chapter 4). The next section uses IR and IO-specific theories to explain development IOs' actions in grappling with shifting ideas about what they should be doing in the international political system.

Explaining Development IOs' Behaviour

Development encompasses a wide area in IR, and the IOs created to respond to this area vary significantly in terms of their autonomy. As a result, different

Box 9.5 The UN and the Millennium Development Goals (MDGs) and Sustainable Development Goals (SDGs)

The Millennium Development Goals (MDGs), building on targets established by the OECD DAC, the UN's Decades of Development and various UN summits, were ambitiously adopted at the UN Millennium Summit in 2000. With eight targets and 15 indicators, the MDGs were an attempt to create an overarching scoreboard for how states were progressing in terms of meeting the minimum requirements for eradicating poverty and improving people's lives. The eight MDG targets were to reduce extreme poverty and hunger; achieve universal primary education; promote gender equality and empower women; reduce child mortality; improve maternal health; combat HIV/AIDS and other diseases; ensure sustainable development; and establish a global partnership for development.

In 2015, UN member states set their post-2015 agenda, building and adapting the MDGs to create 17 Sustainable Development Goals (SDGs). There is no unanimity over the utility of the goals. For some, like former World Bank economist William Easterly, this is evidence of the West's need to construct solutions, which usually fail, to problems that are better solved by the free market and the freedom of democracy (Easterly 2006). Yet many point to the normative role the MDGs have played in educating citizens and decision-makers about world poverty, and harnessing development IOs to contribute to the solution (Hulme and Scott 2010) – particularly through gathering data about where states are gaining and where they are not (United Nations 2015c: 10). Others argue that the success of the normative focus on basic needs and poverty reduction in the MDGs overlooks the productive changes required to lift developing states out of their predicament, specifically shifting from producing commodities to manufacturing industrial goods (Chang 2013).

theoretical approaches can be used to identify how and why states cooperate in development IOs and how and why development IOs behave the way they do.

IR Theories of Development IOs' Activities

IR theories give us the analytical framework to think through development IOs' behaviour. Both liberal and realist theories explain the structure of the international development IOs and their constraints. We can identify strong liberal internationalist sentiment for using the MDBs, OECD and UN agencies for development purposes and structuring their mandates accordingly. After the scourge of WWII, the UNGA adopted a liberal vision through the Universal Declaration of Human Rights, which was intended to promote better standards of life (United Nations 1948b). There was a functional basis, the need to address a problem, for establishing international machinery. Liberal values would infuse the development IOs in terms of the economics of the MDBs and the OECD (and the IMF and GATT) alongside the political values of the UNDP (in taking its **unit of analysis** as the individual rather than the state).

Power politics also explains the emergence of development IOs. Developed states, particularly the former imperial powers (such as Britain and France), provided development assistance as a means of facilitating relations with their former colonies through the OECD DAC. The International Bank for Reconstruction and Development (IBRD), which became the World Bank, was created primarily to ensure reconstruction after WWII, but that mandate was usurped by the Marshall Plan; it later reoriented its brief to the 'development' component of its name. As the Cold War ratcheted up, the West sought to provide resources to its allies through the MDBs and the UN while coordinating bilateral lending through the OECD DAC. As rational actors, developed states were willing to invest **authority** with relatively autonomous IOs, the MDBs, instead of providing ongoing contributions to ECOSOC and the UNDP, which had universal membership and voting rights that diluted their preferences.

Realist balance-of-power politics also explains why the UN development organs proved unable to operate effectively. The United States controlled the UNGA from 1947 to 1955, garnering two-thirds majority support. By 1960 the United States could no longer rely on using the UN as a pliant foreign-policy tool. Newly sovereign states emerged to take their place in the international system through decolonisation. This created a truly global organisation, with developing countries beginning to dominate the institution owing to the UN's one country, one vote system. In 1961 the UNGA announced its first Decade for Development, which set targets for developing countries' economic growth, development assistance and investment, and created the UNDP and UNCTAD (see Chapter 7).

Yet North–South tensions permeated most UN organs from the 1960s onwards, preventing agreement, hindering meaningful action and adding to Cold War tensions. During the 1960s developing states became more self-confident about their position in the world. They formed alliances such as the

Group of 77 (G77) and the Non-Aligned Movement (NAM), rather than choosing to ally with one or other of the superpowers. By 1970 the entire 'Third World' constituted 11 per cent of global GNP. Yet on average the developing states were more dependent on international trade than industrialised states and were less able to control the impact of fluctuations of international trade on their economies. Moreover, the gap between rich and poor within states and between states continued to widen.

Through the G77 and UNCTAD developing states called for a **New International Economic Order** (NIEO) to address historic and enduring inequalities between states. The South challenged the North's overwhelming control of resources. Developing states pushed for a generalised system of trade preferences in the GATT, in contrast to the GATT's non-discrimination rule (see Chapter 7). They sought funding through a Trust Fund within the IMF. They wanted a mechanism to stabilise wildly fluctuating commodity export prices. They asked for more financial assistance and a writing off of official debt (see Chapter 6). In response the UNGA adopted the ambitious target that industrialised states should provide 0.7 per cent of their GNP to poor states through ODA for the UN's second Decade of Development.

By the early 1980s it was clear that the NIEO had failed, as it was not in industrialised states' interests to accede to developing states' demands. Most industrialised states have never met the 0.7 per cent target, although it has been reaffirmed in various fora ever since. ODA dropped precipitously from 0.33 per cent in 1990 to the lowest level ever (0.22 per cent) in 2000 with the end of the Cold War. Indeed, developed states increasingly view private capital as the best means to address states' needs, not aid.

IO-Specific Theories of Development IOs' Behaviour

IO-specific theories provide a closer cut for analysing development IO actions. The relationship between principals and agents is insightful. In **P–A model** terms, IOs are dependent on their principals for their resources, and member states retain oversight of their activities. Although concerns with effectiveness and efficiency had always been part of member state oversight, once the Cold War ended donor states were increasingly critical of where their funding was going. Concerns over development IOs' performance led to a focus on results-based management, or the establishment of indicators against which IOs would be measured for their 'outputs'. Funding for development dried up, and development IOs increasingly had to defend their actions in terms of their effectiveness and efficiency. Indeed, the UNDP lost 35 per cent of its core untied funding between 1992 and 1997. For the UNDP such a drop in resources created a need for private-sector partners, which challenged its traditional focus on helping states build their own development abilities.

The UNDP's 1994 organisational restructure was a response to its own financial crisis. It replaced its Governing Council with a 36-member Executive Board drawn from the regional groups of ECOSOC (and answerable to it). The UN, including the UNDP, has been under constant pressure to reform ever since its inception. In part this is because the UNDP has faced financial constraints throughout its history. This has led to reform fatigue (Santiso 2002).

The MDBs were also under scrutiny from their donor member states. In the 1990s all of the MDBs established task forces to review their lending operations to evaluate whether loans were actually meeting their goals. For the World Bank, it was revealed that in 1991 staff judged that 37.5 per cent of the loans it completed were complete failures and that this was a dramatic increase in failures over the previous 10 years (Wapenhans 1992). The Bank's 'pressure to lend' culture, where staff were rewarded for the amount of money lent rather than for ensuring the quality of the projects they were delivering to borrowers, has been identified as the root of the problem

Reviews of the other MDBs were not as harsh, but all recommended major improvements. An exception was the AfDB, which was near collapse. It could not raise capital or lend to its borrowers, because both its donors and its borrower members were primarily debt-ridden African states. After a major restructure and injection of capital from industrialised states the AfDB was able to relaunch itself as the premier multilateral lender on the African continent.

Explaining the Interests and Identities of Development IOs

Recognising IOs as agents with the ability to act independently of their member states is also important for shedding light on IOs' ability to cooperate with each other. While political winds prevented inter-state cooperation during the Cold War, ECOSOC's difficulty in coordinating the agencies under its remit stems from the decentralised UN structure. ECOSOC's subsidiary bodies make token responses to calls for greater coordination within the UN while resisting any attempts to subordinate their agendas in such a way as to improve the system (Rosenthal 2007). Despite repeated reports on redressing the system, it is widely recognised that the UN system is dysfunctional. There is a waste of resources that results from duplication and competition between the different development organisational units, including the specialised agencies. This stems from the self-interest of member states and senior officials in the Secretariats (Anstee 2012). Power politics matters, but so too do the interests of the bureaucrats.

Resource demands and IOs' interests are not the only explanation of IOs' behaviour. Rationalists and constructivists together demonstrated how the World Bank can change if member states' policy prescriptions fit with the norms held by the Bank. Other constructivists have argued that the World Bank is capable of changing over time, even if the norms challenge the organisation's culture or identity (Park 2010). With regard to the UNDP, new research demonstrates that, while budgetary issues and member states' support of new initiatives are important in setting its agenda, bureaucratic culture explains how and why new policies are formulated and new initiatives are implemented.

What Member States Want from Development IOs

Of course, part of the difficulty in examining the role of IOs in solving the development problem stems from understanding what exactly member states want them to do compared with what the IO thinks it should be doing. The World Bank faced fierce criticism in the 1980s for its Washington Consensus policy prescriptions, most notably from the UN Children's Fund (UNICEF), with the publication of UNICEF's 1987 report *Adjustment with a Human Face*. It was also criticised by developing states, scholars and activists. As a result, throughout the 1990s member states pushed the World Bank and the other MDBs to increasingly adopt a broader understanding of development: focusing on health and HIV/AIDS; advocating for education for girls; incorporating environmental and social policies; and broadening the poverty-alleviation agenda (Babb 2009).

The broadening of development affected the UNDP also. During the 1994 restructure, industrialised member states advocated that it address governance and democracy concerns, leading the UNDP to incorporate these into its sustainable human development framework and its post-conflict efforts. These changes were opposed by the G77, who feared conditionality. The competing demands of the industrialised members compared with the G77 generated competing aims that UNDP senior management had to somehow reconcile (Santiso 2002).

Development IOs thus grapple with an expanding concept of development. It can be argued that the World Bank was engaged in **mission creep**, going beyond its mandate into areas in which it had no right to be or ability to act. For others, it was evidence of **antinomic delegation** – where principal member states continued to demand that the MDBs respond to broader understandings of development through creating more and more policies that needed to be addressed when lending for development projects. For the IO this represented conflicting or complex tasks that are difficult to institutionalise and implement. The net result has been for the MDBs to attempt to be all things to all actors (donors, borrowers, activists and private-sector co-financers), leading to **organised hypocrisy** and performance gaps. Other IOs have been even less successful in responding to changing conditions. For example, the UN Industrial Development Organisation (UNIDO) struggled to incorporate environmental sustainability into its **organisational culture**, which aligns with its mandate to facilitate industrial development.

Part of the reason why these IOs still operate, and are continuously being assessed for their performance, is because it is notoriously difficult to evaluate the extent to which the IO is meeting its goals and whether it is having an independent effect. After all, the development IOs considered here are just a few of the big ones involved in international development. Identifying their effect in facilitating development or contributing to poverty alleviation separately from the impacts of other actors and major events such as natural calamities and human-induced crises (war, economic shocks) is extremely difficult. Precisely because of the nature of the development problem, there is a multitude of development actors that compete with IOs to solve it.

Competition in Solving International Development Problems: The Private Sector, NGOs and Philanthropists

Development IOs identify their 'comparative advantage' relative to each other, in what they provide for states in the development arena. Other actors provide both an alternative to IOs and collaborators for them. This can improve development assistance. This includes private-sector financing, including by microfinanciers, NGOs and philanthropists.

The renewed focus on international poverty alleviation with the MDGs led to a resurgence of **bilateral** OECD DAC aid commitments. Meanwhile, in the 1990s private capital finance flows to developing states were vastly outstripping ODA, peaking at $450 billion in 2007 just before the **Great Recession**, compared with approximately $100 billion in ODA. Although they were technically not in competition, the MDBs saw many development projects now being funded through private means but frequently without the same degree of oversight and environmental and social protections the MDBs had been both criticised and applauded for. Major borrowing states and rising powers now had the capacity to look for alternative sources of finance.

Much of the aid debate has focused on how and whether aid should be given to poor states. For some policy advocates, the economic market is the most effective means for solving development problems and should be allowed to operate unhindered. For others, the situation is more complex: the bottom billion people in the world are stuck in various types of poverty trap, and different solutions are required.

Micro-credit

Micro-credit is one tool used by both the public and the private sector, by IOs and NGOs. Efforts to address rural poverty using market instruments rather than aid led to the creation of an NGO called the Grameen Bank by economist Muhammad Yunus in 1976. The Grameen Bank provided small loans to poor people (with no credit rating) for self-employment and income generation. The Grameen Bank began as a research experiment backed by the Ford Foundation; by 2006 it was operating in over 40 countries, with 2,100 branches (Grameen Bank 2015). Micro-credit operations have become mainstream; indeed, in the 1990s they were undertaken by a range of NGOs as well as being included in the IMF's Poverty Reduction Strategy Papers and the World Bank and IMF's HIPC II initiative. The World Bank has backed micro-credit operations in its loans (Weber 2004). While micro-credit has been transformational for many, others criticise micro-credit operations for further immiserating the poor as they extend credit to those whose conditions may not have changed, with recipients for example using the loan just to buy food in order to survive (Gulli and Berger 1999; Leach and Sitaram 2002).

NGOs and private-sector banks are often competitors to development IOs in the provision of services to developing countries. NGOs have always operated in the development space, from religious missionaries to disaster-relief providers to long-term development operators. The three largest development NGOs operating internationally are World Vision ($2.79 billion, working in 120 states), Save the Children ($1.4 billion, operating in 120 states) and Oxfam International ($1.25 billion, operating in 98 states) (UNDP 2013). International, domestic and local NGOs are also collaborators. Development IOs often contract out their operations to NGOs and for-profit organisations where they are seen to have local expertise and operate cheaply (Cooley 2010). NGOs may be service providers or activists seeking to change the status quo.

NGOs have frequently been sources of normative change on issues like poverty alleviation and human rights, such as the Drop the Debt campaign, working with development IOs. NGOs are dependent on voluntary contributions and membership to raise funds for their efforts. As IOs are dependent on their member states, so too are NGOs reliant on their sources of income for their voluntary work, leading to recent efforts to make them more accountable in the same way (Balboa 2015).

Foundations, including the Ford Foundation and the Rockefeller Foundation, are crucial sources of financing for NGO and UN development work. The Bill and Melinda Gates Foundation is a more recent example. Bill Gates, co-founder of Microsoft, is one of the world's richest men. Together with his wife, he created the foundation to provide funds to tackle extreme poverty and poor health globally, providing over $30 billion since they began in 2000 (Bill and Melinda Gates Foundation 2015).

Chapter Summary

Multiple sources of financing for development, and development actors, are clearly necessary to help address an expanding problem. Yet they are quite different in their approaches to development, and in how they function and are structured. The MDBs operate as banks; they provide loans for development projects and programmes. These must be repaid. In comparison, the UNDP operates to provide some loans and technical assistance but is reliant on voluntary contributions. This has helped shape the development landscape. With greater resources the MDBs could offer loans linked to policy prescriptions, called the Washington Consensus. This would be backed by the OECD. Within the UN there would be challenges to the dominant economic ideas through ECLA and through the UNDP's Human Development Index. The creation of the MDGs and the SDGs from 2015 highlights the fundamental issues states still need to address if they are to develop. Development IOs work with states and non-state actors to provide financing and expertise to address these problems. Although they can be accused of mission creep, development IOs are responding to the expanding conception of development while both working with and competing against each other and other actors.

Guiding Questions

1. What do the World Bank and the other MDBs do?
2. Why is the OECD important for development?
3. What economic ideas were promoted through ECLA?
4. What obstacles does the UNDP face?
5. Are other actors such as NGOs better at financing development?

Further References

Internet Resources

Gapminder: www.gapminder.org. This interactive website uses publicly available information on states' development to compare indicators over time.

Global Economic Governance Programme at Oxford University: www.globaleconomic governance.org. Find topical papers here on the cutting edge of research on global development and finance.

Think Tanks and NGO Reports

Humphreys, C., 2015, 'Developmental Revolution or Bretton Woods Revisited?', Overseas Development Institute Working Paper 418. www.odi.org/publications/9481-develop mental-revolution-bretton-woods-revisited.

Centre for Global Development. A think tank established by former World Bank staff who sought to reform the Bank from the outside and provide independent analysis on the World Bank and the problems it seeks to address. www.cgdev.org.

Bank Information Center: An NGO that seeks to provide independent analysis of the World Bank's policies and operations. www.bankinformationcenter.org.

Further Reading

Boas, M., and D. McNeill, 2004 *Global Institutions and Development: Framing the World?*, London, Routledge.

Collier, P., 2007, *The Bottom Billion: Why the Poorest Countries Are Failing and What Can Be Done about It*, Oxford, Oxford University Press.

Easterly, W., 2001, 'The Lost Decades: Developing Countries' Stagnation in Spite of Policy Reform 1980–1998', *Journal of Economic Growth* **6** (2): 135–157.

Easterly, W., 2006, *The White Man's Burden: Why the West's Efforts to Aid the Rest Have Done So Much Ill and So Little Good*, New York, Penguin Press.

Murphy, C., 2004, *The United Nations Development Programme: A Better Way?*, Cambridge, Cambridge University Press.

Woods, N., 2006a, *The Globalizers: The IMF, the World Bank and their Borrowers*, Ithaca, NY, Cornell University Press.

10 Protecting the Environment

Introduction

As with previous chapters on human rights (Chapter 4) and health (Chapter 5), much of the current literature on addressing environmental problems at the global level deals with this issue in terms of **regimes** or **governance** rather than being specifically about a single IO. This is not surprising. The environment is affected by all aspects of human activity. As this chapter demonstrates, the impetus for creating the United Nations Environment Programme (UNEP) was to drive global decision-making on environmental issues across the entire UN family. Yet it is perceived as having been undermined from the outset because it was designated as a UN programme rather than a specialised agency with autonomy like the IMF and the World Bank (and, less so, the WHO).

The chapter examines

- how states have dealt with the environment broadly and with specific environmental issues;
- the mandate, function and structure of UNEP, the Global Environment Facility (GEF) and the UN Commission on Sustainable Development (CSD);
- the creation of secretariats for a variety of Multilateral Environmental Agreements (MEAs);
- the problem that the environment continues to deteriorate across a range of indicators, and accelerating environmental changes are now producing global consequences;
- failed efforts to create a United Nations Environment Organization (UNEO) or a World Environment Organisation (WEO) to rival the WTO in its powers (on the WTO see Chapter 7).
- the use of IR and IO-specific theories to explain how and when IOs engage with environmental problems;
- competition for addressing environmental problems with environmental NGOs (ENGOs) rivalling states in resources and influence, while there has been a mass increase in private governance arrangements for regulating industry impacts.

The Mandate, Function and Structure of the UNEP, GEF, CSD and MEA Secretariats

Continued environmental decline is occurring despite a plethora of IOs, MEAs and other arrangements to mitigate environmental damage. Even non-environment-specific IOs such as the World Bank have had a significant impact on lessening the environmental impact of development, but the debate over the Bank has focused on its ability to green itself or whether this constitutes 'greenwash'. Others question whether powerful IOs like the WTO and IMF should integrate environmental issues or whether this fundamentally undermines their ability to meet their mandates – and even whether these IOs could perform an environmental service, given their organisational cultures. Of course, the activities of IOs are still influenced by the extent to which their member states advocate for environmental change. States' intransigence in effectively responding to worsening environmental conditions is a primary reason for our present situation.

A History of Environmental Cooperation

As scientific understanding of our impact on the biosphere and civil society demands for action increased during the 1970s, states sought international cooperation. States convened large-scale UN conferences in order to ascertain the nature of the problem and how best to address it, leading to the creation of UNEP, the GEF and the CSD, as well as issue-specific MEA secretariats.

The first inter-state conference was the 1972 United Nations Conference on the Human Environment (UNCHE). This was a watershed in the development of international environmental law. It was attended by 113 states, and resulted in a 109-point action plan for states to undertake, as well as the release of the Declaration of the United Nations Conference on the Human Environment, known as the Stockholm Declaration. The Declaration is comprised of 26 principles agreed upon by states regarding how to respond to environmental issues. The meeting was dominated by representatives of the Global North, or industrialised countries, who focused on issues concerning them: transboundary conservation and pollution issues. Developing countries were keen to ensure their state sovereignty, particularly over natural resources. The Stockholm Declaration helped galvanise IOs and NGOs by drawing attention to international environmental issues. From the 1970s onwards states would seek the means to understand how to reconcile protecting the environment with economic growth. In 1987 a UN World Commission on Environment and Development released its report on how to do so. It popularised the concept of sustainable development (Box 10.1).

Subsequent milestones included the 1992 United Nations Conference on Environment and Development (UNCED, also called the Rio or Earth Summit), which would reaffirm states' commitments by producing the Rio Declaration on Environment and Development. At Rio two 'hard-law' conventions (on Biological Diversity, and the UN Framework Convention on Climate Change) were signed, and preparations for the Convention on Desertification were made. Three 'soft-law' outcomes were also produced: the Rio Declaration, further outlining the principles states agree to follow in their efforts to protect the environment; Agenda 21, a 40-chapter detailed volume on to how to

Box 10.1 Sustainable Development

Sustainable development, which attempts to reconcile environmental preservation and conservation with economic development and social justice, is relatively new. Prior to the 1960s a conservation approach dominated international environmental policy-making. Increased scientific understanding of environmental damage from rapid economic growth triggered debates over irreparable environmental change.

Sustainable development emerged as a means of overcoming divisions between the industrialised North's concern for environmental conservation and pollution prevention and the developing South's economic needs that were evident at the UNCHE. It was endorsed by states because it attempted to overcome the irreconcilable differences between protecting the environment and development.

In the 1980s the World Commission on Environment and Development was established to bridge this North–South gap, and the definition of sustainable development it produced in its 1987 report *Our Common Future* became dominant. It became the preferred means for institutionalising sustainable development because it made clear the link between poverty and environmental degradation, while recognising the importance of integrating issue areas and disciplines. It also identified how long-term environmental problems like climate change rub up against inter-generational inequities. Environmental concerns became mainstream in the 1990s once the shift from environmental protection to sustainable development had occurred; states favoured market dynamics to reconcile environmental degradation and economic growth while ignoring ecological limits to growth.

implement sustainable development; and a non-binding statement on Forest Principles (in lieu of a convention).

Rio would be followed by the World Summit on Sustainable Development (WSSD) in 2002 and the United Nations Conference on Sustainable Development (UNCSD or Rio+20) in 2012. The WSSD aimed to evaluate how much progress had been made since 1992. It generated two key documents: the Johannesburg Declaration and the Plan of Implementation. The Johannesburg Declaration is a jointly agreed upon statement that details the numerous and interconnected challenges associated with sustainable development. It includes a number of commitments to issues including the role of women and increasing democratic participation in sustainable development. The plan of implementation included a number of specific goals aimed at eradicating poverty; changing consumption and production patterns; and protecting the earth's natural resources. Specific goals centred on five areas: water, energy, health, agriculture and biodiversity. A major shift towards public–private partnerships (involving IOs, companies and NGOs) as a means to tackle environmental problems also took place here. No new substantive commitments or legally binding agreements were made at Johannesburg.

At Rio+20 states again met to review their efforts to rein in environmental destruction. There was no effort to create any new binding commitments for states to achieve, considering the difficulty they have in meeting existing targets. The conference aimed to secure a renewed commitment by states for sustainable development. It also sought to assess the implementation gaps in states' existing commitments and to address new challenges. Two themes emerged: the institutional framework for sustainable development; and how to advance a green economy and alleviate poverty. Yet states were unable to agree on policy or even what their aspirations were looking to the future. Developed states were keen to view environmental problems through the lens of a green economy, with an eye to renewable energy industries in which they lead. Developing states were concerned that this would undermine holding developed states to account for their past pledges, while making it even more difficult for developing states to develop. The final document, *The Future We Want*, merely contained vague aspirations while repackaging past commitments.

These large-scale summits have been criticised for their 'hot-air' hortatory commitments to environmental action with little to show for them. However, they have been important means through which norms about how to address environmental problems have been affirmed. While the last of the two global summits merely focused on ensuring commitment to pre-existing agreements, the UNCHE and Rio conferences did lead to the creation of UNEP, the GEF and the CSD, and of specific MEAs on climate, ozone, hazardous wastes, toxic chemicals, biodiversity, ocean pollution, regional seas, desertification, air pollution and the Antarctic.

There are now over 1,200 MEAs in action, and 1,500 bilateral environmental agreements (Mitchell 2002–2016). Many of these MEAs have their own secretariats, which are the focal point of environmental **regimes**. Here we examine the mandate, function and structure of UNEP, the GEF and the CSD and of the MEA secretariats in addressing global environmental deterioration.

Environmental IOs: UNEP and the GEF

In the wake of the Stockholm Conference, the 1972 UNGA Resolution 2997 (XXVII) established UNEP as the flagship IO to respond to global environmental problems. Its mandate is to be the leading global environmental advocate and authority. It aims to set the global environmental agenda, and promote the coherent implementation of sustainable development across the UN. UNEP states that its role is to be a catalyst, advocate, educator and facilitator in promoting sustainable development through its interactions with states, IOs, the private sector and the voluntary sector (NGOs). Some scholars argue that UNEP was purposefully designed to be a weak IO, given that it was not supported by powerful states (DeSombre 2006), while others argue that its weakness was not intended but resulted from early decisions over its location and structure (Ivanova 2007).

UNEP, which is based in Kenya, has an Executive Director with a secretariat and a decentralised structure of six regional offices with additional in-country liaison offices. The Executive Director is voted in by the UNGA on the recommendation of the UN Secretary General to serve a four-year term. The secretariat is the focal point for environmental action and coordination within the UN system and for facilitating cooperation with scientific and professional associations.

It performs five functions:

1. develop international environmental law;
2. implement agreed norms and policies, including monitoring compliance and stimulating cooperation;
3. strengthen coordination across the UN system;
4. facilitate effective cooperation and serve as a link between the scientific community and policy-makers, including as an implementing agency of the GEF (see Box 10.2);
5. provide institution-building advice to governments (UNEP 1997).

UNEP lays the groundwork for the establishment of Multilateral Environmental Agreements. It also 'hosts' various convention secretariats, which can be divided into clusters, such as the biodiversity cluster and the chemical cluster. For example, in the biodiversity cluster UNEP hosts the Convention on Biological Diversity (CBD); the Convention on the Conservation of Migratory Species of Wild Animals; and the Convention on Trade in Endangered Species of Wild Flora and Fauna (CITES). UNEP also aims to spread information, technology and

Box 10.2 The Global Environment Facility (GEF)

Established as a pilot in 1991 in the prelude to the Rio Earth Summit, the GEF is today the largest funder of projects to improve the global environment. The GEF was created by states to provide financial resources to help mitigate global environmental problems. The GEF, which is now an independent IO with 183 member states, provides grants to developing countries and countries with economies in transition to offset the impact of development projects in relation to six global environmental problems: biodiversity, climate change, international waters, land degradation, the ozone layer and persistent organic pollutants. Financing the global component of these projects links local, national and global environmental challenges while promoting sustainable livelihoods. The GEF does not implement the project.

The 1991–1994 pilot phase channelled funding to UNEP, the UNDP and the World Bank, and was administered from within the World Bank. After becoming a permanent independent IO in 1995, the GEF has broadened its partnerships to 18 IOs which implement GEF-financed projects (including UN agencies, the multilateral development banks and NGOs). The GEF is also the financing mechanism for five MEAs: the UNFCCC and the Conventions on Biodiversity, Desertification, Mercury and Persistent Organic Pollutants.

The GEF's funds are replenished every four years from 39 donor member states, akin to the International Development Association (IDA) replenishment process for the World Bank (see Chapter 9). Its financing has increased from one billion during its pilot phase to over four billion in its current replenishment phase (GEF-6 from 2014 to 2018), see GEF (2017).

The GEF, which is located in Washington, D.C., is organisationally unique. It has a small secretariat of approximately 80 staff that undertake its daily operations under the Chief Executive Officer-Chairperson, who reports to the GEF Council. The Council is its main governing body, and is comprised of 32 member state representatives. This is similar to the IMF and World Bank structures (see Chapters 6 and 9). However, the GEF Council is balanced in representation, with 16 members from developed states, 14 from developing states and two from economies in transition. Moreover, the Council is not a sitting board like that of the World Bank; it meets biannually to approve the GEF's work programme. Beyond the Council is the GEF Assembly, which is comprised of ministers from all 193 member states who meet every three to four years to review the GEF's policies and evaluate its operations. Decision-making is by consensus, and each member designates a national official to be the 'focal point' for liaising with the GEF.

Scholars argue that the GEF is one of the most open and inclusive IOs operating (Payne and Samhat 2004: 7). The GEF's structure reflects the desire of industrialised donor states to establish a funding stream outside the inefficient but equitable decision-making of the UN for specific MEAs, but pushback from developing states led to its present decision-making structure that balances North and South. Critics of the GEF point out that it endorses ecologically destructive development even though it offsets some of its negative impacts (Ervine 2007).

knowledge. It supports, facilitates and strengthens institutions for managing the environment. It can do so through its scientific advisory groups, divisions such as its Early Warning and Assessment division, and its regional and liaison offices.

UNEP also assesses environmental trends at local, national and global levels. It has undertaken global assessments for ozone, mercury, biodiversity, marine ecosystems, international waters and agricultural science and technology for development. It established the Global Resource Information Database (GRID) and the UNEP reports on global environmental trends through its Global Environmental Outlook report. A recent addition is the World Conservation Monitoring Centre on the state of the environment, which is part of the Global Earth Observation System of Systems.

Despite its broad (and vague) mandate, UNEP has meagre resources, which are based on securing voluntary funding from member states. For example, its budget for the 2016/2017 financial year is $683.6 million. This compares poorly with the on-average $20 billion budget of the World Bank (see Chapter 9), but only 7 per cent of its budget comes from regular contributions from its member states. A majority of its income comes from earmarked funds from its members, meaning that member states determine how their contribution should be spent. Moreover, UNEP is reliant on just 10 donors for 80 per cent of its overall income.

The financial constraints imposed by member states have led UNEP, like the WHO, to seek external funding assistance. In comparison, just one large conservation NGO budget dwarfs UNEP's: the Nature Conservancy had revenue of $1.11 billion in 2014, and slightly less in 2015 (TNC 2015). While its funding level is comparable to those of other UN programmes, its dependence on voluntary contributions raises questions over states' commitment to addressing environmental problems. Despite being described as small, perpetually under-resourced and peripheral within the UN, UNEP has been recognised for its ability to undertake global assessments, spread knowledge and help drive the creation of international environmental law. Owing to UNEP's marginalised status, new IOs would be created later to address environmental issues, such as the GEF (Box 10.2) and the CSD (see pages 213–215), over which UNEP would have little influence.

As a result, there was widespread recognition at Rio+20 in 2012 that institutions governing the environment were not adequately addressing environmental deterioration. It was agreed to strengthen UNEP. There had been concerted efforts over the previous two decades, by practitioners, the EU and states such as France, to bolster UNEP, with arguments that it did not have the muscle to be the primary environmental IO. As UNEP specialist Maria Ivanova notes, advocates proposed creating the United Nations Environment Organization as a specialised agency with more authority within the UN to better coordinate environmental action (Ivanova 2007).

Others argued for an alternative, a World Environment Organisation (WEO), to house all MEAs and be independent of the UN in order to centralise all international environmental decision-making (Biermann and Bauer 2005). A WEO could better rival the power of economic IOs such as the WTO, which was increasingly ruling on environmental issues in trade disputes.

The culmination of these debates at the UNCSD in 2012 was an agreement to increase the participation of all UN member states in UNEP's decision-making structure while strengthening its financial base. This led to a UNGA resolution that UNEP be granted a fixed increase in resources from the regular UN budget that would be used to cover its work programme, not just administrative costs as had previously been the case. These enhancements give UNEP more formal authority, but do not make it a UN specialised agency.

The debates did, however, lead to a reorganisation in 2013. The restructure altered UNEP's governance. The primary decision-making body is the Environment Assembly, which replaced the 58 members of the Governing Council, who used to meet annually at UNEP headquarters in Nairobi, and were elected in the UNGA every four years on a basis of equity in regional representation. The former Governing Council reported to the UNGA through the Economic and Social Council. The new Environment Assembly is constituted by all 193 UN member states, which gives it greater legitimacy but makes it unwieldy in terms of decision-making. The Environment Assembly meets biennially to set international environmental policy and shape international environmental law, including the incorporation of the environment into the UN's 2030 Agenda for Sustainable Development and the Sustainable Development Goals that were launched in 2015 (see Box 10.3).

Decisions made by the Environment Assembly are by consensus and guide the activities of the UNEP Executive Director and the secretariat. Owing to its large size, the Environment Assembly has multiple components: it is led by a president, with a bureau comprised of 10 Ministers of the Environment from all UN regions who serve for two years. In between the Environment Assembly sessions, a subsidiary organ, the Committee of Permanent Representatives, is the main governing body. It is comprised of 118 member states and it meets four times per year with a five-member bureau.

The CSD and the UN Family

UNEP is meant to catalyse environmental action as well as coordinate responses within the UN system. Efforts to ensure coordination are notoriously difficult within the UN, let alone for a programme situated outside the UN's central decision-making centres of Geneva and New York. In the aftermath of the Rio Earth summit in 1992, the UNGA agreed to establish yet another IO within the UN family, namely the Commission on Sustainable Development (CSD, UNGA Resolution 47/191).

The CSD was given an unworkable mandate: to ensure the effective implementation of Agenda 21, the 40-chapter blueprint for action for states agreed upon at Rio in 1992 that identifies efforts required at the national, regional and international levels to effectively address environmental problems. Its function was to monitor and review states' implementation of Agenda 21, including the provision of financial resources (levels of ODA). After the WSSD in 2002, the CSD was also given the task of guiding the implementation of the Johannesburg Plan of Action, another document detailing how states should meet their environmental commitments. Structurally, the CSD was established as a functional commission of ECOSOC.

While the CSD was able to highlight issues requiring attention, such as energy, sustainable production and consumption, forests and freshwater resources, ultimately it was unable to reach agreement on these and other issues. It was increasingly recognised that the CSD's performance was lacking. Many UN agencies saw it as duplicating their work, and states were unclear about the role of the CSD in navigating the sustainable development agenda, over which states fundamentally disagreed.

Box 10.3 The Sustainable Development Goals (SDGs)

The United Nations Sustainable Development Goals (SDGs) established in 2015 comprise 17 goals with 169 targets that UN member states agreed to as part of the UN's 2030 Agenda for Sustainable Development.

The goals are

1. No Poverty
2. Zero Hunger
3. Good Health and Well-being
4. Quality Education
5. Gender Equality
6. Clean Water and Sanitation
7. Affordable and Clean Energy
8. Decent Work and Economic Growth
9. Industry, Innovation and Infrastructure
10. Reduced Inequality
11. Sustainable Cities and Communities
12. Responsible Consumption and Production
13. Climate Action
14. Life below Water
15. Life on Land
16. Peace and Justice Strong Institutions
17. Partnerships to Achieve the Goal

The SDGs take over from the Millennium Development Goals (MDGs, see Chapter 9) which concluded in 2015. The SDGs identify common goals for states to meet in order to eliminate poverty, tackle environmental degradation, and ensure future prosperity. The aim is to meet the targets by 2030. The creation of the goals was more inclusive than the creation of the MDGs, which were devised within the UN; there was a widespread consultation process for creating the SDGs. In 2015 states also met in Ethiopia for the Third International Conference on Financing for Development. Along with development and finance IOs, they identified the Addis Ababa Action Agenda or the various partnerships necessary for financing the implementation of the SDGs. The SDGs are ambitious, comprehensive and universal.

Although states rarely kill off IOs, after 21 years states decided at the UNCSD in 2012 to fold the Commission. It was replaced with a new High-Level Political Forum on Sustainable Development (HLPF). The HLPF was given greater prominence within the UN, operating under both the UNGA and ECOSOC, and was mandated to provide leadership, guidance and recommendations for sustainable development. Essentially this means that heads of state will meet as part of the annual UNGA meeting every four years to review and deliberate on progress towards meeting their sustainable development commitments, while the HLPF meets annually to review and implement those commitments.

The HLPF is not a bureaucracy like the CSD. The HLPF is too new for us to review its effectiveness, especially considering how recent the Sustainable Development Goals and the UN 2030 Agenda for Sustainable Development are. However, its structure also leaves it vulnerable to the same institutional dynamics of duplication, overlap and competition between UN agencies that beset the CSD. The HLPF has been given an overwhelmingly broad mandate, with not many resources and limited authority. This means that it has to rely on its ability to guide environmental IOs in order to be effective.

MEA Secretariats

Although UNEP coordinates a range of MEAs, many of the secretariats have been reluctant to recognise its authority, particularly given the small number of member states on the pre-2013 Governing Council. This is because most MEAs have over 100 signatories. Once a treaty comes into force, a secretariat is created. UNEP may be identified as the secretariat, which in turn creates a new secretariat unit to manage the treaty, or the new unit created may be independent of UNEP. MEA secretariats operate to fulfil their mandates, namely to support the implementation and progress of the convention and any attendant protocols.

They do so through undertaking a range of functions: the collection and provision of information to the parties of the MEA; organising the meeting of the parties; analysing and circulating scientific and other input; providing technical expertise and guidance; fund raising; and, where required, monitoring treaty implementation.

Structurally they range from small secretariats of fewer than 20 staff to ones with over 500, with their work contingent upon the rotation of the meetings of the parties to the treaty. Secretariats are led by a chair, who performs many of these duties. The chair and the secretariat may be referred to interchangeably because both act in accordance with the secretariat's mandate on behalf of the chair. However, environment scholar Joanna Depledge argues that the chair and the secretariat are interconnected or locked into a mutually enforcing relationship and a symbiotic division of labour (Depledge 2007: 46). Both are important for furthering global negotiations.

Scholars have increasingly focused on whether secretariats have influence in changing states' behaviour. Leading global environmental governance scholars Frank Biermann and Bernt Siebenhüner argued that secretariats can have cognitive influence over environmental politics because they act as knowledge brokers. They have normative influence in how they facilitate negotiations amongst the members of the conference of the parties to the convention. They also have executive influence in building capacity with regard to the environmental problem (Biermann and Siebenhüner 2009: 47). More recently environmental politics scholar Sikina Jinnah has gone further to identify when secretariats can shape how states act in MEAs. She argues that secretariats can influence states when state preferences are not set and when the expertise of the secretariat cannot be easily substituted (Jinnah 2014). If these two conditions hold, then secretariats are able to shape power relations among states, shape norms, and even redistribute capabilities among states. Secretariats are also vital for managing **regime** overlap owing to their deep expertise in their issue area, contributing the vital glue needed for environmental governance (Selin 2010).

The Problem: Worsening Global Environmental Conditions

The biggest difficulty in tackling environmental problems is identifying how to do so. The biosphere has a number of inter-related sub-systems that interact in complex and overlapping ways that are not well understood by scientists, let alone policy-makers and the public. Yet we are now seeing the effects of human activity at a planetary scale, to the point where scientists now argue that we are in a new geological epoch, the **Anthropocene** (UNEP 2012). This is where human activity is leading to irreparable ecological tipping points. Across the 90 most vital global environmental goals, only four show evidence of progress. How best can we minimise our impact on natural systems while ensuring sustainable livelihoods? Is there a trade-off between poverty and development and environment protection? Do we owe a responsibility to future generations not to leave them worse off as a result of decisions we make now? There are two fundamental components to addressing these questions: normative and, for our purposes, organisational.

The normative is how we decide what is important. As students of international relations, we recognise that decision-making remains with the **sovereign state** (Conca 1995). Yet environmental problems cross state boundaries, many resources are shared, and some ecological systems constitute **global commons** that cannot be apportioned. States make normative environmental commitments through international agreements. At the Earth Summit in 1992, 178 states agreed to the Rio Declaration on Environment and Development. Of the 27 principles, four stand out: first, states have the right to 'exploit their own resources pursuant to their own environmental and developmental policies' (Principle 2, UNGA 1992). Affirming states' right to degrade their natural environment complicates efforts to address global problems such as climate change, where states' capacities to act on the problem differ, given their respective levels of economic and natural wealth. Principle 7 outlines the norm of common but differentiated responsibility, where industrialised states are recognised for the impact their development has had on the planet and their economic ability to address the resulting environmental problems. Principle 16 is one of many instruments that advance the 'Polluter Pays Principle', which specifies that the polluter should bear the costs of the pollution they engender while internalising the economic costs of doing so (current economic models do not take the environmental costs of producing goods into account). Finally, Principle 15 articulates the 'Precautionary Principle', which states that, where there are threats of serious or irreversible damage, a lack of full scientific certainty should not be a reason for delaying the taking of measures to stop environmental degradation (UNGA 1992).

While states have agreed to these principles, enacting them is another matter altogether. Tensions between coalitions of developed and developing states over common but differentiated responsibility have been a mainstay in climate-change negotiations in relation to determining 'fair' levels for reductions of emissions. Ignoring the precautionary principle, states debated whether climate change was real and human-induced, obstructing attempts to address the problem, while revealing the importance of interactions between policy-makers and scientists for creating environmental regimes. Scientific evidence of our impact on threatened ecosystems places an onus on states to act, but pressure exerted by citizens, activists, NGOs, scientists and even corporations is often needed in order to compel states to respond.

NGOs place normative pressure on states to create MEAs, to ratify such agreements into national legislation to make them legally binding, and to adhere to such laws once they have done so. This is necessary, given that states choose not to enforce compliance with MEAs through hard tools such as sanctions. Equally importantly, states continue to prioritise economic growth over protecting the biosphere, despite knowing that environmental problems are outpacing inter-state cooperation.

The second component to addressing global environmental problems is practical. How do we address environmental problems? Should states all create national environmental ministries to address environmental problems or should these issues cross-cut all other ministries regarding trade, finance, security and social welfare? If we have problems doing this at the national level, is it even possible internationally? Should, for example, the UNSC examine climate change as a security threat (Box 10.4)? How should we address over-fishing, given that fish stocks have different migratory patterns across jurisdictions? Should cooperation be tackled at the (sub)regional or global level? At the level of production or consumption?

Advocates of a World Environment Organisation argue that a single IO could provide real power and authority to address these issues at multiple levels, as a means of overcoming the overlap or 'interplay' between environmental **regimes** (Gehring and Oberthür 2008). For example, the decision to eliminate chlorofluorocarbons (CFCs) in response to ozone depletion impacted on efforts to address climate change, where CFC replacements had greenhouse effects. Political scientists Ernst and Peter Haas (1995) identify this problem of non-decomposability. Climate change is a non-decomposable problem, for example, because you cannot effectively address it without taking account of all linkages between the problem (global warming), action (all transport, industry, land use and agricultural practices) and place (the local, the national and the global). Others argue that establishing a WEO would merely replicate other IO structures not known for their effectiveness (von Moltke 2001).

UNEP was explicitly designed as a coordinating body to cut across the various functional issue areas of pre-existing UN bodies to achieve environmental gains, although it struggles to do so (Ivanova 2007). This brings us to examine why states created the IOs they did and whether they can address environmental problems.

Box 10.4 Should the UNSC Discuss Environmental Problems?

The UNSC has twice discussed whether climate change, as an overarching threat to humanity, falls within its remit. On 17 April 2007 the UNSC discussed the impacts of climate change on international peace and security. This was pushed by the UK, but rejected by China which argued that the best means of addressing climate change remained within the UN Framework Convention on Climate Change. The initiative was supported by small island developing states, which stand to lose their territory as a result of temperature increases. Climate change was raised again on 15 February 2013 in the Council, this time by Pakistan. Again debates ensued over whether this was the right forum to discuss the issue. There are concerns that the UNSC could have limited understanding to grapple with climate change, given its tools to prevent conflict, and the recommendations that could flow from it. Moreover, the Council remains a highly unequal body that is not representative of the 193 members of the UN. Should it address the single most global concern?

Yet the Council does have the power to have its resolutions enforced. Addressing climate change could better encompass the complex inter-relationship among environmental resource scarcity, conflict and human rights. The UNSC's efforts to address the implications of fuelling conflict through resources such as diamonds, minerals and timber are a start. For some, such as environmental expert Ken Conca (2015), the UN needs to grapple with environmental problems by going beyond its focus on law (environmental treaties) and (sustainable) development. The UN has four pillars, and the environment intersects with all of them: law, development, peace and human rights. Addressing all of them may lead to new avenues to solve environmental problems created by human activities, including an environmental responsibility to protect, a human right to a clean environment and environmental peace-building.

So why can't the UN take up new ideas? Conca argues that this is because the UN organisations have different degrees of autonomy and influence, which may limit how environmental ideas are shaped. Environmental advocates within the UN are constrained within interpretive frameworks that seek to modify the liberal international economic and political order rather than to establish new ways and means of addressing environmental problems (as a human right rather than development, for example). This fits within a constructivist organisational culture account of IOs' behaviour.

Explaining IOs' Behaviour in Addressing Environmental Problems

IR Theories

Can IR and IO-specific theories explain IOs' behaviour in relation to the environment? Traditional IR theories, neorealism and neoliberalism, are useful for assessing how and why states behave. They can assess who benefits from international environmental agreements in terms of relative versus absolute gains, and the strategies states use to achieve their preferences. As with other issue areas, states' power and influence do affect the outcomes of international negotiations. Yet grand IR theories do not dominate explanations of environmental politics. In part, this is the nature of environmental problems: they are cumulative over time and are not easily encompassed within state-centred analytical frameworks. Neorealism, for example, seeks only to explain a small number of big, important things, conceived of as traditional national security. Even though we can now recognise the planetary importance of global warming, neorealism is not an ideal lens through which to examine this threat, above all because responses do not necessarily include border protection and military preparedness. Neoliberal institutionalism is useful as a means of identifying states' interests and preferences for engaging in international environmental negotiations, but is less focused on whether cooperation actually works in terms of environmental outcomes. Broader **rationalist**, institutional approaches that focus on problems to do with collective action have been used to examine how **institutions** tackle environmental problems (Young *et al.* 2008).

The predominant approach for grappling with international environmental problems has been **regime** theory. This is because the concept can take into account the variety of actors and processes of cooperation and coordination required in order to achieve environmental outcomes. State and non-state actors at local, national, transnational and international levels engage to address specific environmental problems: air pollution, the Antarctic, biodiversity, climate, desertification, hazardous wastes, ocean pollution, ozone, regional seas and toxic chemicals. The climate regime is an example of how much non-state activity is taking place that is linked to, but beyond, intergovernmental UNFCCC negotiations (Widerberg and Pattberg 2017).

Scholars of regimes have sought to identify their effectiveness in terms of their output, outcome and impact (Andresen and Rosendal 2009). Output refers to the creation of rules and regulations for actors to abide by, while outcome speaks to a change in behaviour resulting from the outputs. Impact is whether or not this has led to environmental improvements. Recognisably there has been a plethora of rules and regulations on environmental issues as well as a changing of some behaviours. However, there has been far too little accomplished in terms of having an impact on environmental problems. To date the most successful regime is the ozone regime, because it has largely eliminated ozone-depleting substances. There are few other regimes where the conditions for effective outcomes and impacts are evident. IOs are important for setting the agenda, aggregating the interests of the members of the conference of the parties to agreements, and developing normative statements and rules.

IO-Specific Theories

Although UNEP was to be the anchor for environmental issues within the UN family, it was always recognised that environmental issues cross all sectors. This means that all IOs in some way have to engage with environmental issues. Yet mainstreaming environmental concerns or 'greening' non-environmentally specific IOs remains a challenge. This is because IOs have to identify how to integrate environmental concerns while taking into account organisational priorities, staffing and resources. Most crucially, this means thinking about how to incorporate new ideas and norms into existing organisational cultures. Much of the IO literature on greening has focused on the World Bank, owing to its predominant position in international development lending. It would also be the focus of large-scale environmental campaigns from the early 1980s as a range of environment problems hit international headlines (including ozone depletion, climate change and the burning of the Amazon rainforest). The P–A model, constructivist organisational culture arguments and a blend of the two have been used to explain the World Bank's incorporation of environmental concerns.

The P–A model identifies how member states demanded that the World Bank incorporate environmental concerns. This led management to outline an environmental strategy, create environmental units within the Bank, and increase funding and staff for environmental components of projects and for stand-alone environmental projects. Such top-down changes were not in the staff's interest (Nielson and Tierney 2003; Gutner 2005a).

The constructivist organisational culture and identity argument highlighted how efforts to incorporate environmental concerns ran against the Bank's pressure-to-lend culture, where staff were rewarded for the amount of money lent rather than for the loan's effectiveness and its impact on the local environment (Weaver 2008). ENGOs and transnational advocacy networks operated to socialise the World Bank (and the rest of the World Bank Group) to incorporate environmental ideas by making them part of the World Bank's project lending, policies and internal operations (Park 2010). According to blended rationalist–constructivist arguments member states and management could succeed in changing the IO if the norms they advocated were 'adjacent' to the IO's pre-existing culture (Nielson *et al.* 2006).

Beyond the World Bank, scholars have argued that incorporating green practices across IOs with different functions might not make sense. IOs like the WTO, IMF and OECD have specific organisational cultures where their professional economic expertise may not be the best means for integrating environmental concerns (Lehtonen 2007). While this may be true for broader environmental integration, some specific issues may fit. For example, recent scholarship examines how work on fossil-fuel subsidies fits within the dominant economic modelling of the IMF and the OECD, with these two IOs making different policy recommendations that fit their organisational cultures (Skovgaard 2017). IOs have difficulty retrofitting environmental concerns into their operations, but continued environmental deterioration and normative pressure demands that they do so.

Competition over Global Environmental Governance: ENGOs and Private and Hybrid Environmental Governance

ENGOs have been at the forefront of efforts to protect the environment, as advocates and implementers of environmental policy. For example, ECOSOC recognises over 3,500 NGOs working on sustainable development (ECOSOC 2011). ENGOs are increasing in size and resources, which gives them greater clout in international politics (Balboa 2017). ENGOs vary in size, structure and funding; in the level at which they operate (local, national, regional or international); in their ideology in terms of how they undertake their mandates; and in the specific environmental issues they prioritise.

The World Wide Fund for Nature (WWF, known as the World Wildlife Fund in the United States) is based in Switzerland, operates in over 100 countries and has five million supporters. Friends of the Earth International (FoEI) is a confederation of 76 independent national member groups comprised of over two million members. As with FoEI, Greenpeace International is headquartered in the Netherlands; Greenpeace operates in 41 countries and has nearly three million supporters (Park 2013).

ENGOs possess technical knowledge about the natural environment. They are dedicated to environmental concerns over and above national or personal interests, and they are able to mobilise the support of voters in domestic political arenas. ENGOs have been present at all of the mega-UN summits, pressing for change (Clark *et al.* 2005). ENGOs have been able to challenge the everyday practices of states, corporations and IOs like the World Bank to incorporate environmental issues.

They are also keen participants in MEA negotiations on transboundary air pollution, regional stocks, climate change, ozone depletion and biodiversity. Through participation ENGOs can frame the issue, set the agenda, and influence the positions of key states, with varying levels of influence over MEA outcomes. Environment experts Michelle Betsill and Elizabeth Correll (2008) have identified that ENGOs can have a high degree of influence over MEAs if they are able to shape the negotiation process and the outcome, as witnessed in the UN Convention to Combat Desertification (1993–1994). They had moderate influence over the Kyoto Protocol of the UNFCCC. ENGOs are therefore both a major collaborator and a competitor to IOs in attempting to solve environmental problems.

In the early 1990s states began to retreat from using regulation as a big stick to enforce environmental protection. This paved the way for increasing self-regulation of the private sector. Since then the number and diversity of private governance arrangements over environmental issues have proliferated. Corporations have established issue- or country-specific codes, indexes, projects and organisations to green their activities.

Private-sector initiatives are generally non-binding, voluntary, guidelines or recommendations of best practice such as the International Chamber of Commerce's (ICC's) Business Charter for Sustainable Development and the CERES Principles. Corporate governance tends to revolve around an industry or product, for example, the International Council of Chemical Associations' Responsible Care initiative, or certification standards for cocoa, coffee, flowers and forest and marine products.

Non-state market certification processes, such as those employed by the Marine Stewardship Council, attempt to use market mechanisms to eliminate environmental harms stemming from economic operations. NGOs and corporations are environmental rule-makers as a result of their delegated and entrepreneurial authority in international relations (Green 2014). What this chapter has shown is that the environment continues to degrade across nearly all indicators despite the number of environmental regimes, the efforts of the various UN agencies, pressure from ENGOs and the proliferation of efforts by the private sector to rein in its impact.

Chapter Summary

This chapter provided a brief history of the organisation of the environment internationally. States have periodically convened large-scale international environmental conferences to negotiate how to address environmental problems as they arose. This has resulted in a number of principles that have guided inter-state interactions, such as the precautionary principle. It has also led to the establishment of a number of IOs designed to promote sustainable development and the amelioration of environmental damage: UNEP, the CSD, the GEF and a range of MEA secretariats. UNEP was designed to be the UN flagship on addressing environmental problems. Despite being small and under-resourced given its broad mandate, it has nevertheless been a catalyst for environmental change, particularly through preparations for adopting more multilateral environmental agreements. States have adopted a range of MEAs to tackle environment problems. Of course, the issue remains whether states are complying with those agreements. ENGOs play an important role in monitoring state and non-state activities. Increasingly the private sector has taken up a role in governing how its actions affect the environment. Whether these efforts can mitigate adverse environmental impacts remains to be seen.

Guiding Questions

1. What inhibits international environmental cooperation?
2. What are UNEP's strengths?
3. Do we need a World Environment Organisation?

4. Do private and hybrid governing structures work for protecting the environment?

5. What role do ENGOs play in environmental governance?

Further References

Think Tank and NGO Reports

Bernstein, S., and J. Brunnée, 2011, Consultants' Report on Options for Broader Reform of the Institutional Framework for Sustainable Development (IFSD): Structural, Legal, and Financial Aspects. www.uncsd2012.org/index.php?page=view&type=400&nr=211&menu=45.

Internet Resources

Declaration of the United Nations Conference on the Human Environment: www.un-documents.net/unchedec.htm.

Declaration of the United National Conference on Environment and Development: www.un.org/documents/ga/conf151/aconf15126-1annex1.htm.

International Environmental Information: http://ieinfo.net/gep.html.

International Environmental Agreements Database: https://iea.uoregon.edu/.

Sustainable Development Goals Knowledge Hub, IISD: http://sdg.iisd.org/?utm_medium=email&utm_campaign=2017–05-02%20-%20SDG%20Update%20AE&utm_content=2017–05-02%20-%20SDG%20Update%20AE%20CID_162980346360dcb2ef24daded6649a70&utm_source=cm.

Further Reading

Andonova, L., 2018, *Governance Entrepreneurs: International Organizations and the Rise of Public-Private Partnerships*, Cambridge, Cambridge University Press.

Bayer, P., C. Marcoux and J. Urpelainen, 2015, 'When International Organizations Bargain: Evidence from the Global Environment Facility', *Journal of Conflict Resolution* 59 (6): 1074–1100.

Biermann, F., and B. Siebenhüner, 2009, *Managers of Global Change: The Influence of International Environmental Bureaucracies*, Cambridge, MA, MIT Press.

Cashore, B., G. Auld and D. Newsom, 2004, *Governing through Markets: Forest Certification and the Emergence of Non-state Authority*, New Haven, CT, Yale University Press.

Chasek, P., and L. Wagner (eds.), 2012, *The Roads from Rio: Lessons Learned from Twenty Years of Multilateral Environmental Negotiations*, London, RFF Press.

Chasek, P., D. L. Downie and J. Welsh Brown, 2017, *Global Environmental Politics*, seventh edition, Boulder, CO, Westview Press.

Conca, K., 2015, *An Unfinished Foundation: The United Nations and Global Environmental Governance*, Oxford, Oxford University Press.

Ivanova, M., 2007, 'Designing the United Nations Environment Programme: A Story of Compromise and Confrontation', *International Environmental Agreements*, 7 (4): 337–361.

Jinnah, S., 2014, *Post-Treaty Politics: Secretariat Influence in Global Environmental Governance*, Cambridge, MA, MIT Press.

Schrijver, N., 2010, *Development without Destruction: The UN and Global Resource Management*, Bloomington, IN, Indiana University Press.

11 Conclusion: If Global Governance Is the Answer, What Is the Question?

Introduction

This book examined how international cooperation between states has led to the proliferation of IOs to smooth relations between states and to address problems arising from inter-state interactions. States continue to create IOs to this day, yet IOs are heavily criticised for their actions. They are frequently accused of being both inefficient and ineffective. Does this mean that there is a crisis of multilateralism? Are the well-documented failures of IOs actually undermining how policy-makers and states address problems that require international cooperation? Or is this alarmism that overstates the problems inherent in inter-national cooperation, particularly when this is combined with bureaucracies that become entrenched in terms of their mandates, functions and structures? The trend is increasingly to analyse the range of actors working to address global concerns such as climate change, financial crises and pandemics through the concept of global governance. Here we examine the utility of the concept and whether it advances our understanding of actors in international relations and the organisation of the international system for global problem solving.

This chapter examines

- synthetically the main points arising from the theoretical and empirical analysis of IOs throughout the volume;
- whether the current structures of multilateralism are 'fit for the purpose' of tackling the problems of the twenty-first century;
- the major conceptual shift towards examining cooperation as constituting **global governance** rather than focusing on IOs specifically.

Evaluating IOs' Behaviour in International Relations

This book introduced students to the workings and theories of international organisations in order to help them understand why they operate the way they do, what **autonomy** and **authority** they have, and whether they help solve global problems. It provided the analytical tools to help identify whether IOs do what they are tasked to do, and to question whether alternatives other than IOs might be better for addressing international and global problems. To that end, the introductory chapter outlined the rise of **multilateralism** and defined what constitutes an IO. Although decision-making procedures within IOs vary, all IOs are comprised of member states, management and staff who field pressure with regard to how they address particular problems from state and non-state actors alike.

Four aims for the book were outlined at the beginning of the volume. These were to

1. identify the key IOs in the international system;
2. highlight the issues and problems dominant IOs are tasked with addressing;
3. use theory to examine the constraints and opportunities IOs face in meeting their mandates, including the tools at their disposal;
4. locate IOs within an increasingly crowded field of international and trans-national actors seeking to govern the globe.

The first aim, to identify the key IOs in the international system, was met in each of the thematic chapters (Chapters 3–11). Throughout the volume students were introduced to the main IOs operating in specific issue areas: the UNSC and regional organisations like the AU in minimising and halting conflict; the treaty bodies of the UN as well as Commissioners and the UN Human Rights Council for protecting human rights; the WHO, UNICEF, UNFPA and UNAIDS for tackling global health; the IMF, Bank for International Settlements and Financial Stability Board for financial governance, especially as compared with the efforts of the G7 and G20; the GATT/WTO and UNCTAD for international trade; the regional organisations including the EU, ASEAN and the OAS; the UN agencies and the MDBs such as the World Bank for furthering development; and the UNEP and multilateral environmental treaty bodies for protecting the environment.

The second aim, to use theory to examine the constraints and opportunities IOs face in meeting their mandates, including the tools at their disposal, was met by unpacking the main theoretical approaches in Chapter 2 as well as where identified in the literature for each of the IOs in the thematic chapters. The book provided the theoretical and conceptual tools for interrogating the capacity of IOs such as the UN for 'solving' international problems such as war by examining the structure and function of the IO alongside its power to act and its understanding of its mission.

Using IR and IO-specific theories, that take different **units of analysis** as their starting point, the book showed how the four main approaches shed light on IOs' efforts to tackle global problems. Chapter 2 documented the emergence of **liberal**, functionalist and **realist** approaches to assessing IOs, including the more contemporary **neorealist** and **neoliberal institutionalist** theories that have been used to identify the benefits of international cooperation through IOs. IO-specific approaches, such as the **principal–agent (P–A) model**, were then counterposed with the **constructivist organisational culture** approach that seeks to understand how the culture of an IO shapes its actions. Guiding questions were drawn from the four main theories for students to use to think through interrogating IOs' behaviour, particularly for independent research.

Each of these approaches seeks to identify the main basis for IOs' action in any of the given areas of international relations. Realist approaches view IOs as merely vehicles through which **sovereign states** achieve their interests. They may facilitate cooperation, but this remains the purview of states. In contrast, the different strands of liberal thinking argue that IOs can advance international cooperation to achieve peace and or prosperity for all within the international system. Current neorealist and neoliberal institutionalist arguments diverge as to whether states are able to cooperate over the long term and whether this reflects states' relative or absolute interests. Neorealists tend to focus their analysis on whether powerful states are able to achieve their interests and how weak states use IOs to gain a greater voice, or to strategically balance against the hegemon or bandwagon with it. In comparison, the neoliberal institutionalist approach tends to highlight the importance of IOs for overcoming problems associated with collective action between states and the functional benefits of having IOs for reducing transaction costs, providing information to states, and maximising states' utility.

IO-centric approaches zero in on the IO as an actor in international relations. Both the P–A model and the constructivist organisational culture approaches recognise that IOs have varying degrees of autonomy and authority to conduct their mandates. Where they differ is in how they explain the behaviour of these autonomous actors. The **P–A model** is a rationalist approach that sees the IO as behaving according to its interests and preferences as an agent of its member states (the principals). **Constructivist organisational culture**, on the other hand, examines how an IO's culture shapes the IO's decision-making even when it may work to the detriment of the organisation or when it prevents the IO from adequately responding to events and meeting its mission.

All of these approaches are used by scholars to better explain and understand IOs' behaviour and their capacity to change. Each of these approaches is invoked throughout the thematic chapters. This also met the third aim of the volume: to highlight the issues and problems dominant IOs are tasked with addressing. The changing nature of warfare; movements to minimise the use of weapons such as nuclear weapons and small and light weapons; and the banning of landmines are all major concerns that IOs have addressed.

Moreover, each of the thematic chapters incorporates cutting-edge theoretical research on IOs as we examine their ability to solve problems, including alternative theories (such as **critical theory**) when they have been used to analyse particular IOs. In the chapters on war and weapons, it is clear that IR theories have dominated our understanding of how security organisations operate, although this is changing. The chapter on trade is also dominated by neorealist and neoliberal explanations of trade decisions with implications for how the WTO can act. Significant work has been done by scholars employing the P–A model and by constructivists using organisational culture to explain finance, development, health, human rights and, increasingly, environment IOs' behaviour. Owing to the significance of the EU, several theories have been used to examine the variety of institutions constituting the supranational entity: functionalism, a variety of liberal approaches, the P–A model and the constructivist organisational culture approach.

The final aim of the volume was to locate IOs within an increasingly crowded field of international and transnational actors seeking to govern the globe. We should not only question the utility of the UN or the WTO and the EU but also ask whether alternatives to solving the problems they are tasked with addressing are any better. Each chapter highlighted the various forms of non-state actors that operate transnationally: NGOs; foundations; for-profit enterprises; corporations and industry associations; private security companies and mercenaries, are all acting ostensibly to solve international and global problems.

While many of them are legitimate actors with which IOs and states share the stage, they too must be analysed in terms of their autonomy and authority, including whether their interests, preferences and organisational cultures circumscribe their ability to meet their mandates and work with IOs. The final section of this concluding chapter discusses the plethora of actors working to solve international and global problems through the concept of global governance. First, however, we should assess recent arguments that there is a crisis of multilateralism.

The Problem: Multilateralism in Crisis?

Are we facing a crisis of multilateralism? Are the **institutions** and IOs established by states sufficient to withstand the pressures and limitations placed upon them? Are they able to provide the guidance and solutions required to address the myriad of issues at the international level? Many think not (Hale *et al.* 2013; Newman 2007). IOs continue to face charges that they are not solving problems within their purview: the WTO has been unable to break trade negotiation deadlock since 1999. The WHO faced worldwide ire for not responding as needed to the 2014 Ebola outbreak. The IMF was unable to predict or prevent the global financial crisis of 2008. The World Bank and the other MDBs have worked for decades, but it is difficult to identify how they have contributed to reducing global poverty.

The UN was sidelined in 2003 when the United States chose to establish a coalition of the willing for invading Iraq rather than seek consensus through the UN, which, critics contend, weakened the main vehicle for securing international peace. The UN has been unable to broker agreement on ending the Syrian War since it began in early 2011. It has faced widespread criticism for its peacekeeping efforts, including *introducing* a cholera epidemic to Haiti in 2010 during an earthquake emergency. The UN's oil-for-food scandal uncovered during the UN's post-invasion intervention in Iraq highlighted the organisation's lack of transparency and accountability (Grigorescu 2010).

Israel has remained on the UNSC's agenda for decades and is likely to remain so. Impasses are entrenched over a variety of issues within the UN as a result of North–South divisions, while turf battles constrain every attempt at restructuring the UN family to make it more streamlined and coherent (Weiss 2013). The ICC is increasingly under challenge from states choosing to withdraw. There are fears that compliance with, and the enforcement of, human rights treaties are under increasing threat. No IO has successfully grappled with the mass refugee crisis in Europe or elsewhere.

In June 2016 the UK voted in a national referendum to exit the EU, thus becoming the first state to invoke Article 50 of the Lisbon Treaty in order to leave. There has been a broader slowing of the creation of multilateral environmental treaties (Abbott *et al.* 2016), and on 1 June 2017 the United States decided to withdraw from the UNFCCC 2015 Paris Agreement that seeks to hold states accountable for reducing their carbon emissions to limit global warming to 2.5 degrees Celsius.

One could argue that the crisis of multilateralism is in the eye of the beholder. It is clear that many of these challenges are the result of state decision-making, particularly pertaining to creating, ratifying and complying with international conventions. Scholars recognise that a changing balance of power between states does affect the **international order**. There has been an increase in the economic power of China, Russia, Brazil and India, which are now challenging the dominance of the Western industrialised states which created and still dominate most of the universal IOs discussed within this volume. This has affected international trade politics through the WTO, and has led to revisions to the voting structures of the IMF and World Bank. It might also explain changes in voting in the UNSC over the last decade.

However, it cannot explain failures in the WHO and the IMF, and it does little to explain the UK's actions regarding the EU and those of the United States in relation to the UNFCCC. Changing power dynamics do affect multilateral efforts and states' calculations of their benefits, as realists and liberals recognise. But that is only part of the picture. States' relations with multilateralism are often strategic in relation to other states but also in relation to how this affects domestic dynamics. States often use IOs to tie their hands domestically, and IOs are frequently invoked as scapegoats for national-level problems (as the IMF is well aware). States may also *prefer* an IO that performs poorly (Lipson 2010). The crisis of multilateralism is much more complicated than blaming IOs for their (in)action. It speaks to the willingness of states to defend international institutions and organisations. Students of IOs need to be cognisant of these factors.

However, this is not to suggest that IOs do not have their own problems, including pathological and dysfunctional behaviour. Scholars identify IO performance as a key indicator of satisfaction with how IOs respond to problems (bearing in mind that states often allow and support **mission creep** and engage in **antinomic delegation**). Examining the performance of an IO requires an assessment as to whether the IO completed the task required of it, in addition to evaluating how it conducted its activities.

IR scholars Tamar Gutner and Alexander Thompson (2010) make clear that performance is distinct from effectiveness. The latter is based on whether or not an IO can solve problems irrespective of the constraints faced by the IO, such as its capacity. They argue that evaluating an IO's effectiveness for alleviating poverty or stopping war may be meaningless, and that it would be more meaningful to assess whether an IO has achieved specific, limited, well-defined goals. Of course, measurements for analysing IO performance may be manipulated by member states according to their interests and preferences, just as much as an IO can manipulate the evidence through its self-reporting. Nonetheless, Gutner and Thompson provide three tiers at which to evaluate an IO's performance: according to its narrow functions; its compliance with policy agendas; and its ability to resolve the macro-level problems identified at the beginning of this section.

The guiding questions at the end of Chapter 2 can help students identify whether it is even possible to argue that an IO is effective or whether analysis should be limited to evaluating an IO's performance. The next section reviews the trend, emerging in part over concerns about the limitations of IOs, towards tackling international and global problems through global governance.

Problem Solving through Global Governance

Although the focus of this book is on IOs, there is an overwhelmingly vast literature that goes beyond looking at IOs to examine global governance instead. This was popularly defined as 'the sum of the many ways individuals and institutions, public and private, manage their common affairs' by the Commission on Global Governance (1995). The Commission on Global Governance was established on behalf of the UN to identify the main problems confronting humanity and to examine how they might be tackled (Wilkinson 2005). The aim of the commission therefore was to document international cooperation and efforts to address international and global-level problems, and to propose actions for reinvigorating the UN as the main governing instrument globally.

Yet, as the definition demonstrates, there is more to global governance than the UN. The use and proliferation of the concept indicates that there is more to global governance than either the term **regimes** or the term **institutions** encapsulates, both of which go beyond the definition of IOs. Does global governance as a concept have analytical advantages or is it merely being used to encompass a wide range of activities that were already understood?

The Commission noted how the number of IOs has increased dramatically, in fact exponentially since the end of WWII, but they have been given in some cases increased autonomy and authority to act, and have expanded the range of issues they engage in. Issues such as nuclear proliferation, terrorism, global hunger and food security, poverty, development, health such as pandemics like Ebola, global environmental issues like climate change and the systemic nature of financial crises cannot be addressed at the level of the state alone, nor indeed, as this volume has shown, can they be the sole remit of any single IO.

Instead, these complex issues are being addressed by non-state actors, such as private banks; NGOs, such as Greenpeace; and private foundations like the Bill and Melinda Gates Foundation. Moreover, these actors are coordinating their activities in ways unaccounted for by the theoretical literature on IOs. For example, many traditional IOs are also engaged in hybrid activities such as GAVI and UNAIDS, and private influence is evident even in traditional IOs like the WHO. While we can attempt to explain this through rationalist or even liberal internationalist theories, much of the global governance literature seeks to map what these various actors are cooperating and coordinating for, and whether it contributes to addressing the specific issue.

Why not use the concept of regimes or institutions? The concept of **regimes** incorporates the role of states and IOs, and is a key concept in the literature for examining the governance of specific issue areas in international relations. Yet global governance goes beyond regimes to analyse the space between regimes and to examine the different ideas, norms and rules that come to dominate when regimes overlap or clash. For example, how does the trade regime conflict with the convention on the trade of endangered species? Moreover, global governance as a concept draws attention to two key factors that are implicit in the regime concept.

The first factor is that global governance, unlike regimes, is not state-centric. The definition of regimes does not refer to states, yet the concept was formulated by state-centric theorists, and often the actors whose expectations converge are states (Krasner 1983). NGOs are allowed into these mechanisms, usually as commentators or side-line actors to crucial inter-state negotiations of multilateral treaties, but they are not central; see, for example, Betsill and Corell (2008) on how NGOs try to insert themselves into inter-state negotiations.

The second factor is that both private actors and the various levels for action are incorporated into the concept of global governance. This is not evident in the regime literature. The regime definition tends to focus on principles (beliefs of fact, causation and rectitude), rules (specific prescriptions or proscriptions for action), norms (standards of behaviour defined in terms of rights and obligations) and decision-making procedures (prevailing practices for making and implementing collective choice) as the basis for international action (Krasner 1983). In contrast, global governance covers events and decisions at the local level, impacting at the global level, and all levels in between. Hence the Commission's definition that references the role of individuals.

Global governance also goes beyond **institutions** for two reasons. First, because global governance is more than just sets of rules that shape various actors' roles, activities and expectations. It is fundamentally about how different actors engage with each other to create these institutions or rules that then prescribe behavioural roles, constrain activity and shape expectations. Second, it goes beyond the definition of institutions because global governance comprises different forms of institutions themselves. For example, global climate change governance comprises the following: the various states engaged in climate change negotiations; the various oil, coal and gas multinationals and all private-sector actors dependent on their energy; environmental NGOs; and the various regulatory instruments established to govern climate change: the UNFCCC, the Kyoto Protocol, the Compliance Development Mechanism and the Joint Implementation process. The entities listed are all institutions or rules that prescribe behavioural roles, constrain activity and shape expectations. In sum, global governance as a concept goes beyond previous IR concepts that attempt to explain the nature of informal and formal interaction taking place at various levels of international politics. Global governance is not state-centric, and it is more encompassing than either regimes or institutions.

Wilkinson (2005) argues that there are four identifiable themes in global governance literature. First, there is work that extends the former focus on regimes and institutions, for example research on global health governance that retains states and the WHO at its centre. Second, there is work that seeks to enhance pre-existing IOs such as the UN in order to make them more operationally effective in conjunction with non-state actors. Third, there is scholarship that examines the transformative potential of global governance to shape international order (Murphy 2000). Finally, there is literature that focuses on refashioning global governance by interrogating how social movements and activism can reconfigure world politics.

Proponents of global governance view the concept as encompassing multi-actor, multi-level arrangements that seek to address transnationally and internationally a wealth of issues that cannot be addressed by states or IOs alone. The Commission readily engages in a discussion of the rise of non-state sources of governance. Recognising that there is no world government under anarchy, there is nonetheless a discernible difference in centres of decision-making. Compared with the post-WWII period when **sovereign** states were considered to be the source of decision-making, since the end of the Cold War there has been a proliferation of non-state actors that are recognised for their authority and legitimacy to act as global governors (Avant *et al.* 2010).

Let us take global financial governance as an example. Finance scholars Baker, Hudson and Woodward (2005) point out that there are in fact four different types of 'authority structures' that help govern finance. Authority structures refer to institutions that have the right to speak and be listened to in relation to governance arrangements. The first type consists of IOs like the IMF and OECD as well as informal multilateral institutions such as the G7, G30 and G20. The second component consists of transnational regulatory networks of a type identified in the 1970s by Keohane and Nye (1971); see also Slaughter (2004). These are networks of regulators that are comprised of national regulating agencies that work together in a network across a specific specialist area of financial governance, such as the Financial Action Task Force of the OECD (Sharman 2008). The third is regional regulatory cooperation such as the EU. Finally, private authority has emerged in the form of 'market ordering mechanisms' such as exchange-rate regimes, credit ratings, banking supervision standards and securities market regulations (Underhill and Zhang 2008). Market actors have acquired the authority to create rules and standards in industries where states lack information and knowledge, and have been willing to cede control (Cutler *et al.* 1999).

Therefore global governance as a concept seeks to recognise that there are more actors operating across borders that are working together to solve problems. Governance is therefore used to frame the act that various players engage in, where governance is a command mechanism of a social system that seeks to provide security and prosperity while creating order and continuity (Rosenau 1995). The idea that governance is a system of command, however, seems somewhat hierarchical when the aim is to demonstrate how various actors, both public and private, manage their common affairs.

Yet theorist James Rosenau argues that governance is a steering mechanism for society (Rosenau 1995). This means that governance mechanisms, and the technology and communications tools that they employ, can be used to steer multi-actor, multi-level responses to global and transnational issues. Global governance mechanisms can be understood as the total of millions of control mechanisms that have emerged as a result of different histories, goals, structures and processes. This, Rosenau suggests, is a form of disaggregated authority where there is no coherence and therefore comparison between governance mechanisms. It allows for innovation and experimentation in creating and implementing new control mechanisms (Rosenau 1995).

Recognisably, within global governance there is a great deal of duplicated effort, dispersed authority and fragmentation in terms of losing control over directing the agenda and meeting goals (Kramarz and Park 2016). Given its inclusivity, the concept may better reflect reality, but it may also be unwieldy as a means for identifying the loci for successful problem solving. More recent scholarship in the field returns the focus to IOs.

Current research on **orchestration** seeks to examine whether order can be established among the disparate actors within global governance (Abbott and Snidal 2013). This new wave of scholarship suggests that IOs can orchestrate the various actors in global governance in order to produce a sum which is greater than the parts (Hale and Roger 2014). In short, while the concept of global governance will remain, the heavy lifting is still being done by IOs in solving problems both empirically and analytically.

Chapter Summary

The chapter reviewed the key IOs in the international system examined throughout the book. It then highlighted how different IR and IO-specific theories have been used to examine the constraints and opportunities IOs face in meeting their mandates. It also took up the issue that IOs sit within an increasingly crowded field of international and transnational actors seeking to govern the globe. The chapter questioned whether global governance is a better concept for analysing the organisation of the international system than IOs, or even regimes or institutions. These are different concepts that have been employed to examine how and when states cooperate at the international level. While the chapter highlighted that global governance is indeed different from the pre-existing concepts, is it better to examine global governance instead of IOs? Each chapter included 'alternative' actors to IOs in their fields. Most of these non-state actors do not directly compete, although they do seek to frame problems in certain ways and not others, and they have different means to tackle those problems. Much of the literature focuses on global governance because of the intersections between these different actors. Yet IOs remain at the centre of global governance, and we need to know how and why they act the way they do.

Guiding Questions

1. Should the main unit of analysis be IOs or global governance for studying organisation in the international system?
2. What authority structures exist outside IOs?
3. Is multilateralism in crisis?
4. Given the increase in emanation IOs and hybrid structures like UNAIDS and GAVI, are we witnessing a decline of traditional IOs?

Further References

Think Tanks

The Global Governance Institute: www.globalgovernance.eu/about-us/.
The Centre for International Governance Innovation (University of Waterloo): www.cigionline.org.

Internet Resources

Center on Global Governance (Columbia University): www.law.columbia.edu/global-governance.
Global Economic Governance Programme (Oxford University): www.geg.ox.ac.uk.
Leuven Centre for Global Governance Studies (KU Leuven): https://ghum.kuleuven.be/ggs.

Further Reading

Abbott, K. W., J. F. Green and R. O. Keohane, 2016, 'Organizational Ecology and Institutional Change in Global Governance', *International Organization* 70 (2): 247–277.

Backstrand, K., and J. Kuyper, 2017, 'The Democratic Legitimacy of Orchestration: The UNFCCC, Non-State Actors, and Transnational Climate Governance', *Environmental Politics* 26 (4): 764–788.

Hale, T., D. Held and K. Young, *Gridlock: Why Global Cooperation Is Failing When We Need It Most*, Cambridge, Polity Press.

Murphy, C., 2000, 'Global Governance: Poorly Done and Poorly Understood', *International Affairs* 76 (4): 789–803.

Rosenau, J. N., 1995, 'Governance in the Twenty-First Century', *Global Governance* 1 (1): 13–43.

Glossary

Agency slack: Independent action by an agent that is undesired by the principal.

Agent: An actor contractually delegated to act on behalf of another (the principal).

Alliance: An agreement to cooperate between states regarding the use of force against other states.

Anarchy: The absence of a world government or central political authority in the international system.

Anthropocene: A new geological epoch, beginning in the 1950s, evidenced by the human alteration of atmospheric, geological, hydrological and biological Earth systems.

Anti-dumping duties: Article VI of the GATT makes it clear that contracting parties to the agreement should not 'dump' or sell a product to another country below its normal value. If an exporting state is found to be dumping, the importing state may impose an anti-dumping duty on the exporter.

Anti-globalisation movement: A protest movement comprised of individuals, groups and NGOs emerged to challenge the non-transparent decision-making of IOs on global trade, finance and investment that affects human rights, labour and the environment. Protests took place at major meetings of the World Economic Forum, G7, World Bank, IMF and WTO. The Occupy movement after the **Great Recession** was also fuelled by concerns over who benefits from national and global economic rules.

Antinomic delegation: When principals delegate to IOs conflicting or complex tasks that are difficult to institutionalise and implement.

Authority: Legitimate power to speak, create rules and lead.

Autonomy: The power to undertake action independently of others, including states.

Balance of payments: The equilibrium between a state's balance of trade in goods, services, profits and interest, as well as the inflows and outflows of money for investment, and grants and loans.

Balance of power: States have an unequal share of power but exist in equilibrium; the power of one or more states is countered by the power of other states.

Balancing: Allying with states against the threat from another state.

Bandwagon: Allying with a state that threatens international stability.

Beggar-thy-neighbour: Economic policies such as raising tariffs or devaluing one's currency that give a state economic advantage to the detriment of others.

Bilateralism: Formal or informal relations between two sovereign states.

Black box: The internal decision-making process of an IO that has not been examined.

Bubble: A non-sustainable pattern in the economy of price changes or cash flows.

Centralisation: When an organisation has a concrete and stable administrative apparatus to manage collective activities.

Classical economic liberalism: Economically liberal nineteenth-century theorists promoted ideas of free trade and comparative advantage as a means for increasing wealth. See also Comparative advantage, Free trade, Laissez-faire.

Classical realism: A theoretical approach where conflict between states is recurrent as a result of human imperfection and states struggle for power and national interest.

Cold War: Ideological conflict between the United States and the Soviet Union between 1947 and 1989 over the best economic system. They vied for dominance while avoiding war because of their nuclear capabilities.

Collaboration: Cooperation requiring actors to adjust their dominant strategy to achieve a better outcome than would be obtained had they not taken each other's strategies into account.

Collective action: Actors rationally choose to cooperate to maximise their interests, which maximises all participants' gains compared with individual action.

Collective defence: An agreement among three or more states to defend themselves against a potential aggressor.

Collective principals: Three or more member states (principals) that have a say in determining an IO's actions.

Collective security: An agreement among three or more states that views peace as indivisible such that the use of force against one member is considered an attack upon all, requiring a response.

Common market: An agreement allowing the free movement of factors of production (capital and labour) and finished products across borders that includes common external tariffs.

Comparative advantage: The concept that a state that is relatively more efficient at producing a product than its competitors should specialise in producing that good, compared with other products. If all states engaged in specialisation then there would be greater efficiency in production overall, which would increase all states' welfare.

Concert of Europe: An informal process of consultation to negotiate resolution of disputes among European powers during the nineteenth century.

Conditionality: The economic policy prescriptions attached as mandatory conditions to IMF agreements and World Bank loans to borrower member states. See also Washington Consensus.

Congress of Vienna: A diplomatic assembly held during 1814 and 1815 at which it was agreed that representatives of the Great Powers would meet to prevent conflict in times of peace at regular high-level political conferences.

Constructivism: A social theory that views the world as socially constructed. Social facts such as norms and rules shape how actors behave according to what is considered appropriate for their given identity.

Cooperation: The conformance of the policies of separate individuals or organisations that were not previously aligned.

Cooperative security: A multilateral approach to security that favours reassurance over deterrence, can coexist with alliances, and covers military and non-military conceptions of security.

Coordination: A form of cooperation where actors pursue a common strategy as opposed to divergent strategies to achieve an agreed-upon goal.

Critical theory: A theory that challenges the prevailing order through a critical reading of how power is maintained for the benefit of some over others, often by analysing discourse. A more specific Critical Theory (with capital letters) seeks to advance emancipation through social change.

Customs union: An agreement that gives preferential access to members' markets through eliminating internal trade barriers and imposes a common external tariff.

Debt crisis: When a state is unable to repay its international loans. Increasing debt may worsen a state's balance-of-payments problems, precipitating a crisis and requiring a bail-out.

Democratic deficit: Applying national-level democratic principles to international organisations including electoral and interest-group accountability in processes for deliberation and decision-making.

Dependency theory: A theory that articulates an unequal world based on a global capitalist system, whereby the core advanced economies exploit the periphery states through the extraction of their resources and labour.

Discretion: A characteristic of a contract where the principal specifies the agent's goals but not the means to achieve them.

Dysfunctional behaviour: Action that seeks to meet the stated goal of the IO but turns out to be counterproductive.

Economic and monetary union: An economic union is a single market that may be covered by common competition, structural, regional and macro-economic policies. A monetary union is comprised of a single currency, fixed exchange rates, a pooling of reserves, the free movement of capital and a central bank determining a common monetary policy.

Economic nationalism: A contemporary theory of international political economy that articulates the role of the state in pursuing wealth in order to maintain its power.

Emanation: When IOs are created by other IOs rather than through an international treaty composed, signed and ratified by states.

Embedded liberalism: An international economic order based on three components: an adherence to (Keynesian) economic liberalism; multilateralism; and the rule of law. See also Keynesian economic theory and Multilateralism.

Epidemic: The rapid spread of an infectious disease.

Epiphenomenal: When an agent's actions have no independent effect on others.

Epistemic communities: Experts with shared normative and causal beliefs who seek to affect policy.

Ethnic cleansing: Forcible expulsion of people of a particular ethnicity from a given territory, without seeking to exterminate the whole group.

Eurozone: Comprised of 19 of the European Union's member states that use the euro as their official currency: Austria, Belgium, Cyprus, Estonia, Finland, France, Germany, Greece, Ireland, Italy, Latvia, Lithuania, Luxembourg, Malta, the Netherlands, Portugal, Slovakia, Slovenia and Spain.

Fair trade: Trade that incorporates the true costs of producing a good such as environmental resources and labour, as opposed to current economic models that discount these inputs in determining price.

Feminism: A theoretical approach that takes women as the unit of analysis and seeks to examine the role of gender in the practice and theory of international relations.

Financial liberalisation: When states remove restrictions on the international flow of capital, the international activities of domestic banking institutions and the entry of foreign financial institutions.

Fire alarms: An oversight strategy of principals over agents that enables third parties such as NGOs to challenge agents that violate their mandates and to seek redress.

Forum IOs: IOs designed to provide an avenue for states to discuss, cooperate, coordinate and collaborate in international politics, for example the United Nations General Assembly.

Free-riding: When states or other actors do not contribute to the goods, services or agreements from which they benefit.

Free trade: The removal of political barriers and national and international regulations that restrict the free flow of goods and services across state borders.

Free-trade area: An agreement that gives preferential access to members' markets through eliminating internal trade barriers but does not impose a common external tariff.

Functionalism: A theory that argues that states can learn to cooperate at a bureaucratic and technical level to overcome barriers and improve welfare. Such cooperation can then extend to politically sensitive areas such as security, ultimately leading to peace.

Game theory: A way of analysing actors' interactions with each other (games) through formal mathematical modelling based on rational calculations of their interests and preferences.

Generalised System of Preferences: A waiver of the non-discrimination basis of the General Agreement on Tariffs and Trade for less-developed countries from 1971.

Genocide: Any act committed with intent to destroy, in whole or in part, a national, ethnic, racial or religious group.

Global commons: Natural resources and vital ecological systems that cannot be delineated into sovereign territories. Examples include Antarctica, the atmosphere, the global climate system, outer space, the high seas and deep-sea-bed minerals.

Global governance: The sum of the many ways individuals and institutions, public and private, manage their common affairs.

Global North: A term that geographically locates the majority of advanced industrialised states in the Northern Hemisphere.

Global South: A term that geographically identifies developing or less-developed states as predominately being in the Southern Hemisphere.

Globalisation: The increasing interconnection between states, non-state actors and individuals across borders owing to improvements in telecommunications and transport, facilitated by the removal of restrictions on the movement of capital, trade and people.

Good governance: The aim of ensuring public institutions adhere to high standards of participation, transparency, accountability and the rule of law, and are efficient and effective in establishing and implementing policies.

Great Depression: A depression is when states experience a 10 per cent drop in their GDP for two consecutive quarters. The Great Depression began in 1929: it was the longest, deepest and most widespread depression to date, with states not fully recovering until after WWII.

Great Powers: The most powerful states in the international system that are capable of successfully waging war.

Great Recession: The deepest economic downturn since the Great Depression. The United States and a number of European states experienced a decline in their GDP for two or more consecutive financial quarters between 2007 and 2009. The fallout was global, with a drastic decline in international credit and trade, a massive drop in capital flowing to developing countries and wild fluctuations in exchange rates.

Hague System: Two international peace conferences (1899 and 1907) that extended the European Concert system to all sovereign states and enacted new bureaucratic methods for conference diplomacy, including arbitration procedures for conflict resolution.

Hegemon: A state with preponderant power that occupies a central role in the international system and can influence other states' interests and preferences.

Hegemonic stability theory: A theory that argues that a liberal international economic order is dependent on a hegemon for international cooperation.

Human rights: Entitlements for all people on the basis of being human. These are considered to be universal, indivisible and inalienable.

Idealists: A term used to denote liberal scholars and practitioners in the inter-war period for advancing peace through extending democracy and the rule of law internationally.

Independence: The authority to act with a degree of autonomy in defined spheres.

Institutions: Persistent rules that stipulate the ways in which states should cooperate and compete, and shape expectations.

Integration: The creation of a new political community resulting from political actors in several distinct national settings shifting their loyalties, expectations and political activities to new institutions that are given jurisdiction over pre-existing states.

Interdependence: Where states are affected by the actions of other states. This may be symmetric, affecting both actors, or it may be asymmetric, affecting each actor to varying degrees.

Interests: The basis for actors' behaviour. International relations theories argue that states act according to their national interests, which may include survival, power and wealth maximisation or maintenance of their identity.

Intergovernmentalism: An approach to the study of integration that identifies how domestic interests determine states' national interests, and where the inter-state bargaining remains the primary process for decision-making.

International order: A stable pattern in the relationship among states normatively and institutionally.

International organisation: A permanent organisation designed to perform continuous tasks for a common purpose with three or more states represented.

International system: In Realist theory the international realm cannot be dissociated from the parts (states) and the over-riding principle of anarchy.

Intra-state conflict: A conflict occurring within a state's territory. This may be a civil war, a national liberation war or a war of secession. Internal conflicts within states may have international actors participating.

Jus ad bellum: A war is justified if the state has legitimate authority; has a just cause; has just intentions for using war to achieve its objectives; publicly declares its intentions; uses war as a last resort; acts proportionately in the use of war to achieve its aims; and engages in war only if there is a reasonable hope of achieving its objectives.

Jus in bello: The just conduct of war is based on discrimination or the immunity of non-combatants, and proportionality based on the amount and type of force used to achieve the objectives compared with the consequences of using that force.

Keynesian economic theory: A theory based on the work of twentieth-century economist John Maynard Keynes, who argued that states should engage in deficit spending to ensure full employment during economic downturns.

Laissez-faire: Translating as 'let it be, let it pass', it is used to describe liberal economic doctrines that advocate that governments should not interfere with the free flow of goods, services and capital (removing tariffs, subsidies and capital controls).

Liberal internationalism: A strand of liberal international relations theory that seeks to align states' conflicting interests in favour of peace, freedom and prosperity.

Liberalism: An international relations theory that advocates that the state should advance individual freedom, rights and equality.

Mercantilism: A power-based theory of international political economy that emerged in the fifteenth century. It argues that there is finite wealth in the world, and states must secure that wealth by blocking other states' efforts to accumulate it.

Mission creep: An expansion of an actor's operations beyond the original mandated scope of its activities.

Most-favoured nation: The first principle of the GATT (1947/1994) and WTO agreements (1994) of non-discrimination. All member states should give each other the most favourable treatment they offer to any other member.

Multilateralism: The coordination of national policies among groups of three or more states.

Multiple principals: Where an agent may have separate contracts that delegate authority, with more than one principal.

Mutually assured destruction: The capacity of the superpowers to use nuclear weapons to destroy each other even after being attacked first.

Neofunctionalism: An update on functionalist theory, that argues that states can achieve cooperation through technical experts working together who are aware of the political implications of their tasks. This gives IOs decision-making power to engage with transnational actors, thus shaping outcomes.

Neoliberal economic policies: Seeking to spur growth, these policies aim to control inflation through stabilisation and reduction of government spending; to reduce the money supply by raising interest rates; to liberalise all sectors of the economy; and to advance export-led growth. See also Washington Consensus.

Neoliberal institutionalism: An international relations theory that the international system is anarchic but that states can cooperate to achieve their interests, leading to absolute gains.

Neorealism: A structural, more scientific, realist theory that argues that the international system is anarchic, that states are the primary actors, and that they act to ensure their survival according to their military and economic capabilities.

New International Economic Order: Specific demands by less-developed states to significantly restructure international economic institutions, including to redress the international terms of trade and provide greater access to financial resources and technology.

Non-governmental organisation: An independent, non-profit organisation that is not beholden to government(s) or profit-making organisation(s).

Non-interference: States should not interfere with the domestic politics of other states as enshrined in the UN Charter.

Non-tariff barrier: Official and unofficial means for restricting imports into a state, including administrative regulations, quantitative restrictions and domestic subsidies.

Norms: Shared expectations about appropriate behaviour held by a community of actors.

Official development assistance: Financial assistance to states provided bilaterally and multilaterally for the promotion of recipient states' economic development that is concessional in character and conveys a grant element of at least 25 per cent.

Orchestration: Where IOs provide oversight and support for the efforts of state and non-state actors in global governance.

Organisational culture: Norms, rules and practices that govern staff expectations and behaviour.

Organised hypocrisy: Competing pressures may lead IOs to 'decouple' formal procedures used to comply with external expectations from incompatible internal organisational activities.

Pandemic: The simultaneous transmission of a new disease globally.

Pathological behaviour: When IO dysfunction can be traced to a bureaucratic culture.

Peace-enforcement: Intervention to gain agreement among parties to a conflict, where consent may not have been given.

Peacekeeping: Intervention led by the UN or by a regional IO into a hostile situation with the consent of the parties involved in the conflict.

Plurilateral agreements: Voluntary agreements accepted by sub-sets of the membership of the WTO, in contrast to the WTO's over-riding goals of non-discrimination and reciprocity.

Police patrols: An oversight strategy of principals over agents based on constant surveillance of the agent, including the imposition of monitoring, reporting and institutional checks.

Preferences: The primary outcome desired by an actor in order to achieve its interests.

Principal: An actor that can grant revokable authority to an agent to act on its behalf.

Principal–agent model: A contractual relationship between a 'principal' and its 'agent', where the former gives the latter authority to act on its behalf.

Protectionism: Erecting barriers to trade that prevent citizens from accessing foreign goods and services. This may be through tariff and non-tariff barriers.

Public goods: A good that is available to all to use and cannot be limited to use by a few (non-excludable). Making the good available to more users does not diminish the benefits of those already using it (non-rivalrous). Examples include the climate, international security and a stable international financial system.

Public international unions: International organisations created between 1850 and 1914 to regulate ostensibly non-political issue areas arising from increasing inter-state interactions and new technologies.

Rational–legal authority: The legitimate power to speak, create rules, and lead derived from an IO being a bureaucracy that operates according to impersonal legal rules and procedures and applies relevant knowledge rationally to determine a course of action.

Rationalism: Theories that seek to objectively analyse how actors seek the most efficient means to maximise their interests.

Realism: An international relations theory that posits that states are the central actors in the international system that are engaged in a battle for survival. States seek to maximise their own power and national interest primarily through self-help but may also engage in limited alliances.

Reflectivism: A range of theoretical approaches that reject the positivist basis for knowledge as objective and value-neutral. It seeks to understand how intangible power and social relations mediate actors' interactions with one another.

Regime: A set of implicit or explicit principles, norms, rules and decision-making procedures around which actors' expectations converge in a given area of international relations.

Regionalisation: Autonomous economic and social interactions that may lead to higher levels of interdependence and integration within a geographical area.

Regionalism: Institutions devised by a sub-set of states based upon a collective identity, purpose and geographical proximity. An example is the North American Free Trade Agreement (NAFTA).

Responsibility to protect: States have the responsibility to protect their people against ethnic cleansing, genocide, war crimes and crimes against humanity. Where they cannot, the UN Security Council has the responsibility to respond.

Security community: A shared understanding among states cooperating within an institution that conflict can be resolved peacefully.

Security dilemma: In an anarchical international system states secure their survival through a build-up of military capacity. This heightens the insecurity of other states, leading to a ratcheting up of suspicion and further military capacity, thus contributing to insecurity overall.

Service IOs: International organisations that have been given relative autonomy to undertake tasks mandated by their member states.

Shirking: The IO minimises the effort it exerts on its principal's behalf.

Singapore issues: From 1996, four issues advanced by developed states which developing states oppose within WTO negotiations: transparency in government procurement; trade facilitation (customs issues); trade and investment; and trade and competition.

Slack: The independent actions of the IO undesired by their principal(s).

Slippage: When an agent shifts policy away from its principal's preferred outcome and towards its own preferences.

Sovereign state: A political unit with territorial integrity and political autonomy that is recognised by other political units.

Spillover: A key concept of neofunctionalism, where increased integration between states in one area leads to increased pressure for integration in other areas.

Supranational: International organisations that have been invested with independent decision-making authority which enables them to impose decisions on member states, individuals and firms.

Sustainable development: Ensuring that development meets the needs of the present without compromising the ability of future generations to meet their own needs.

Tariff: A tax imposed by a state on imports.

Technical expertise: Actors may have specialised knowledge based on their work in a specific issue area as a result of their training or experience that is valued as authoritative because it is not readily available to other actors.

Terrorism: The illegitimate use of violence by a group against civilians for political ends.

Trade liberalisation: Removing regulations restricting the flow of goods and services across borders.

Underdevelopment: Popular from the 1940s, the idea that newly emergent states were not just not developed but were actively prevented from developing because their economies were tied into an international economic system that maintained their dependence on the former imperial powers.

Unit of analysis: The basic entity being studied. For realists this is the state; for many liberals it is the individual; for feminists it is women.

War: The organised use of violence by political entities for achieving their objectives.

Washington Consensus: Policy prescriptions attached to IMF agreements and World Bank loans to borrower member states, including establishing a competitive exchange rate; establishing and securing property rights; deregulation; fiscal discipline; liberalising interest rates; liberalisation of inward foreign direct investment; reordering public expenditure priorities; tax reform; trade liberalisation; and privatisation.

Weapons of mass destruction: This category includes atomic explosive weapons, radioactive-material weapons and lethal chemical and biological weapons. These have comparable destructive effect to the atomic bomb.

Bibliography

Abbott, K. W., and D. Snidal, 1998, 'Why States Act through Formal International Organizations', *Journal of Conflict Resolution* 42 (1): 3–33.

Abbott, K. W., and D. Snidal, 2010, 'International Regulation without International Government: Improving IO Performance through Orchestration', *Review of International Organizations* 5 (3): 315–344.

Abbott, K. W., and D. Snidal, 2013, 'Taking Responsive Regulation Transnational: Strategies for International Organizations', *Regulation & Governance* 7 (1): 95–113.

Abbott, K. W., J. F. Green and R. O. Keohane, 2016, 'Organizational Ecology and Institutional Change in Global Governance', *International Organization* 70 (2): 247–277.

Abdelal, R., 2006, 'Writing the Rules of Global Finance: France, Europe, and Capital Liberalization', *Review of International Political Economy* 13 (1): 1–27.

Abdelal, R., 2007, *Capital Rules: The Construction of Global Finance*, Cambridge, MA, Harvard University Press.

Acharya, A., 2001, *Constructing a Security Community in Southeast Asia: ASEAN and the Problem of Regional Order*, London, Routledge.

Acharya, A., 2007, 'ASEAN at 40 – Mid-life Rejuvenation?', *Foreign Affairs*, 15 August. www.foreignaffairs.com/articles/64249/amitav-acharya/asean-at-40-mid-life-rejuvenation#. Accessed 17 December 2012.

Adelman, H., and A. Suhrke, 2004, 'The Security Council and the Rwanda Genocide', in D. M. Malone (ed.), *The UN Security Council: From the Cold War to the 21st Century*, Boulder, CO, Lynne Rienner: 483–499.

African Union, 2000, *Constitutive Act of the African Union*, Addis Ababa, African Union.

AIIB, 2015, 'About AIIB'. www.aiib.org/en/about-aiib/index.html. Accessed 5 January 2018.

Allee, T., and J. Scalera, 2012, 'The Divergent Effects of Joining International Organizations: Trade Gains and the Rigors of WTO Accession', *International Organization* 66 (2): 243–276.

Alston, P., and J. Crawford (eds.), 2000, *The Future of Human Rights Treaty Monitoring*, Cambridge, Cambridge University Press.

Alston, P., and F. Mégret (eds.), 2012, *The United Nations and Human Rights: A Critical Appraisal*, second edition, Oxford, Oxford University Press.

Alter, K., 1998, 'Who are the "Masters of the Treaty?" European Governments and the European Court of Justice', *International Organization* 59 (1): 121–147.

Alter, K., 2008, 'Agents or Trustees? International Courts in Their Political Context', *European Journal of International Relations* 14 (1): 33–63.

Alter, K., 2014, *The New Terrain of International Law: Courts, Politics, Rights*, Princeton, NJ, Princeton University Press.

Amnesty International, 2005, 'Statute of Amnesty International, As Amended by the 27th International Council, Meeting in Morelos, Mexico, 14–20 August 2005'. www.amnesty.org/en/about-us/how-were-run/amnesty-internationals-statute/. Accessed 20 November 2017.

Andonova, L., 2018, *Governance Entrepreneurs: International Organizations and the Rise of Public-Private Partnerships*, Cambridge, Cambridge University Press.

Andresen, S., and K. Rosendal, 2009, 'The Role of the United Nations Environment Programme in the Coordination of Multilateral Environmental Agreements', in F. Biermann, B. Siebenhüner and A. Schreyögg (eds.), *International Organizations and Global Environmental Governance*, London and New York, Routledge: 133–150.

Anstee, M. J., 2012, 'Millennium Development Goals: Milestones on a Long Road', in R. Wilkinson and D. Hulme (eds.), *The Millennium Development Goals and Beyond*, London and New York, Routledge: 19–35.

ASEAN, 1967, 'The ASEAN Declaration (Bangkok Declaration), Bangkok, 8 August 1967'. http://asean.org/the-asean-declaration-bangkok-declaration-bangkok-8-august-1967/. Accessed 18 January 2018.

ASEAN, 2012, 'About the ASEAN Regional Forum'. http://aseanregionalforum.asean.org/about.html. Accessed 11 September 2012.

ASEAN, 2015, *The ASEAN Charter*, 15th edition. http://asean.org/asean/asean-charter/. Accessed 19 January 2018.

Auerswald, D. P., and S. M. Saideman, 2014, *NATO in Afghanistan: Fighting Together, Fighting Alone*, Princeton, NJ, Princeton University Press.

Autesserre, S., 2014, *Peaceland: Conflict Resolution and the Everyday Politics of International Intervention*, Cambridge, Cambridge University Press.

Avant, D. D., M. Finnemore and S. K. Sell, 2010, *Who Governs the Globe?*, Cambridge, Cambridge University Press.

Axelrod, R. S., 1985, *The Evolution of Cooperation*, New York, Basic Books.

Aykens, P., 2002, 'Conflicting Authorities: States, Currency Markets and the ERM Crisis of 1992–93', *Review of International Studies* 28 (2): 359–380.

Ba, A. D., 2009, *(Re)Negotiating East and Southeast Asia: Region, Regionalism, and the Association of Southeast Asian Nations*, Stanford, CT, Stanford University Press.

Babb, S., 2003, 'The IMF in Sociological Perspective: A Tale of Organizational Slippage', *Studies in Comparative International Development* 38 (2): 3–27.

Babb, S., 2009, *Behind the Development Banks*, Chicago, IL, Chicago University Press.

Backstrand, K., and J. Kuyper, 2017, 'The Democratic Legitimacy of Orchestration: The UNFCCC, Non-State Actors, and Transnational Climate Governance', *Environmental Politics* 26 (4): 764–788.

Baker, A., 2006, *The Group of Seven: Finance Ministries, Central Banks and Global Financial Governance*, London and New York, Routledge.

Baker, A., 2008, 'The Group of Seven', *New Political Economy* 13 (1): 103–115.

Baker, A., 2009, 'Deliberative Equality and the Transgovernmental Politics of the Global Financial Architecture', *Global Governance* 15 (2): 195–218.

Baker, A., 2014, 'The G20 and Monetary Policy Stasis', *International Organisations Research Journal* 9 (4): 19–31.

Baker, A., D. Hudson and R. Woodward (eds.), 2005, *Governing Financial Globalization: International Political Economy and Multi-level Governance*, London and New York, Routledge.

Balboa, C. M., 2015, 'The Accountability and Legitimacy of International NGOs', in W. E. DeMars and D. Dijkzeul (eds.), *The NGO Challenge to International Relations Theory*, New York, Routledge: 159–186.

Balboa, C., 2017, 'Mission Interference: How Competition Confounds Accountability for Environmental Nongovernmental Organizations', *Review of Policy Research* 34 (1): 110–131.

Baldwin, D. A. (ed.), 1993, *Neorealism and Neoliberalism: The Contemporary Debate*, New York, Columbia University Press.

Bank of International Settlements, 2016, 'Statutes of the Bank for International Settlements'. www.bis.org/about/statutes-en.pdf. Accessed 17 January 2016.

Barma, N., E. Ratner and S. Weber, 2014, 'Welcome to the World without the West', The National Interest, 12 November. http://nationalinterest.org/feature/welcome-the-world-without-the-west-11651. Accessed 17 November 2015.

Barnett, M., 2002, *Eyewitness to a Genocide: The United Nations and Rwanda*, Ithaca, NY, Cornell University Press.

Barnett, M., 2011, *Empire of Humanity: A History of Humanitarianism*, Ithaca, NY, Cornell University Press.

Barnett, M., and L. Coleman, 2005, 'Designing Police: Interpol and the Study of Change in International Organizations', *International Studies Quarterly* 49 (4): 593–620.

Barnett, M., and M. Finnemore, 1999, 'The Politics, Power and Pathologies of IOs', *International Organization* 53 (4): 699–732.

Barnett, M., and M. Finnemore, 2004, *Rules for the World: International Organizations in Global Politics*, Ithaca, NY and London, Cornell University Press.

Barnett, M., and M. Finnemore, 2005, 'The Power of Liberal International Organizations', in M. Barnett and R. Duvall (eds.), *Power in Global Governance*, Cambridge, Cambridge University Press: 161–184.

Barro, R. J., and J.-W. Lee, 2005, 'IMF Programs: Who Is Chosen and What Are the Effects?', *Journal of Monetary Economics* 52 (7): 1245–1269.

Bayer, P., C. Marcoux and J. Urpelainen, 2015, 'When International Organizations Bargain: Evidence from the Global Environment Facility', *Journal of Conflict Resolution* 59 (6): 1074–1100.

Bebbington, A., M. Woolcock, S. Guggenheim and E. O. Olson, 2006, *The Search for Empowerment: Social Capital As Idea and Practice at the World Bank*, Bloomfield, CT, Kumarian Press.

Beigbeder, Y., 2001, *New Challenges for UNICEF: Children, Women and Human Rights*, Basingstoke, Palgrave Macmillan.

Bellamy, A., and P. Williams, 2010, *Understanding Peacekeeping*, second edition, Cambridge, Polity Press.

Bergsten, C. F., 1988, *America in the World Economy: A Strategy for the 1990s*. Washington, D.C., Institute for International Economics.

Best, J., 2005, *The Limits of Transparency: Ambiguity and the History of International Finance*, Ithaca, NY and London, Cornell University Press.

Betsill, M., and E. Correll, 2008, *NGO Diplomacy: The Influence of Nongovernment Organizations in International Environmental Negotiations*, Cambridge, MA, MIT Press.

Betts, A., 2012, 'UNHCR, Autonomy and Mandate Change', in J. E. Oestreich (ed.), *International Organizations As Self-Directed Actors: A Framework for Analysis*, London and New York, Routledge: 118–140.

Beyers, J., 2005, 'Multiple Embeddedness and Socialization in Europe: The Case of the Council Officials', *International Organization* 59 (4): 899–936.

Bhagwati, J., 1991, *The World Trading System at Risk*, Princeton, NJ, Princeton University Press.

Biermann, F., and S. Bauer (eds.), 2005, *A World Environment Organization: Solution or Threat for Effective International Environmental Governance?*, Aldershot, Ashgate.

Biermann, F., and B. Siebenhüner (eds.), 2009, *Managers of Global Change: The Influence of International Environmental Bureaucracies*, Cambridge, MA, MIT Press.

Bill and Melinda Gates Foundation, 2015, 'Who We Are: Foundation Fact Sheet', www.gates foundation.org/Who-We-Are/General-Information/Foundation-Factsheet. Accessed 2 October 2015.

Bird, G., 1996, 'Borrowing from the IMF: The Policy Implications of Recent Empirical Research', *World Development* 24 (11): 1753–1760.

Bird, G., 1998, 'The Effectiveness of Conditionality and the Political Economy of Policy Reform: Is It Simply a Matter of Political Will?', *Journal of Policy Reform* 2 (1): 89–113.

Bird, G., 2001, 'IMF Programs: Do They Work? Can They Be Made to Work Better?', *World Development* 29 (11): 1849–1869.

Bird, G., and D. Rowland, 2001, 'IMF Lending: How Is It Affected by Economic, Political and Institutional Factors?', *Journal of Policy Reform* 4 (4): 243–270.

Black, M., 1987, *The Children and Nations: Growing Up Together in a Postwar World*, South Yarra, Macmillan.

Black, M., 1996, *Children First: The Story of UNICEF: Past and Present*, Oxford, Oxford University Press.

Blackhurst, R., 2014, 'The Role of the Director-General and the Secretariat', in A. Narlikar, M. Daunton and R. M. Stern (eds.), *The Oxford Handbook on the World Trade Organization*, Oxford, Oxford University Press.

Bloom, A., 2011, 'The Power of the Borrower: IMF Responsiveness to Emerging Market Economies', *New York University Journal of International Law and Politics* 43 (3): 767–810.

Boas, M., and D. McNeill, 2004, *Global Institutions and Development: Framing the World?*, London, Routledge.

Boström, M., and K. T. Hallström, 2010, 'NGO Power in Global Social and Environmental Standard-Setting', *Global Environmental Politics* 10 (4): 36–59.

Boughton, J., 2001, *Silent Revolution: The International Monetary Fund 1979–1989*, Washington, D.C., International Monetary Fund.

Bradley, M., 2016, *Protecting Civilians in War: The ICRC, UNHCR, and Their Limitations in Internal Armed Conflicts*, Cambridge, Cambridge University Press.

Broad, R., 2006, 'Research, Knowledge and the Art of Paradigm Maintenance: The World Bank's Development Economics Vice Presidency (DEC)', *Review of International Political Economy* 13 (3): 387–419.

Brown, G., 2010, 'Safeguarding Deliberative Global Governance: The Case of the Global Fund to Fight AIDS, Tuberculosis and Malaria', *Review of International Studies* 36 (2): 511–530.

Brown, R., 2015, *Nuclear Authority: The IAEA and the Absolute Weapon*, Washington, D.C., Georgetown University Press.

Brown, R., and J. Kaplow, 2014, 'Talking Peace, Making Weapons: IAEA Technical Cooperation and Nuclear Proliferation', *Journal of Conflict Resolution* 58 (3): 402–428.

Broz, J. L., and M. B. Hawes, 2006, 'US Domestic Politics and International Monetary Fund Policy', in D. G. Hawkins, D. A. Lake, D. L. Nielson and M. J. Tierney (eds.), *Delegation and Agency in International Organizations*, Cambridge, Cambridge University Press: 77–106.

Brummer, C., 2014, *Minilateralism: How Trade Alliances, Soft Law, and Financial Engineering Are Redefining Economic Statecraft*, Cambridge, Cambridge University Press.

Bruner, C. M., and R. Abdelal, 2005, 'To Judge Leviathan: Sovereign Credit Ratings, National Law, and the World Economy', *Journal of Public Policy* 25 (2): 191–217.

Brutger, R., and J. C. Morse, 2015, 'Balancing Law and Politics: Judicial Incentives in WTO Dispute Settlement', *Review of International Organizations* 10 (2): 179–205.

Busby, J., 2007, 'Bono Made Jesse Helms Cry: Jubilee 2000, Debt Relief, and Moral Action in International Politics', *International Studies Quarterly* 51 (2): 247–275.

Carnegie, A., 2015, *Power Plays: How International Institutions Reshape Coercive Diplomacy*, Cambridge, Cambridge University Press.

Carpenter, R. C., 2007, 'Studying Issue-(Non)Adoption in Transnational Advocacy Networks', *International Organization* 61 (3): 643–667.

Cashore, B., G. Auld and D. Newsom, 2004, *Governing through Markets: Forest Certification and the Emergence of Non-state Authority*, Cambridge, MA, MIT Press.

Chang, H.-J., 2013, 'Hamlet without the Prince of Denmark: How Development Has Disappeared from Today's "Development Discourse"', in D. Held and C. Roger (eds.), *Global Governance at Risk*, Cambridge, Polity Press.

Chasek, P., and L. Wagner (eds.), 2012, *The Roads from Rio: Lessons Learned from Twenty Years of Multilateral Environmental Negotiations*, London, RFF Press.

Chasek, P., D. L. Downie and J. Welsh Brown, 2017, *Global Environmental Politics*, seventh edition, Boulder, CO, Westview Press.

Chayes, A., and A. H. Chayes, 1993, 'On Compliance', *International Organization* 47 (2): 175–205.

Chesterman, S., 2007, *Secretary or General? The UN Secretary General in World Politics*, Cambridge, Cambridge University Press.

Chorev, N., 2005, 'The Institutional Project of Neo-liberal Globalism: The Case of the WTO', *Theory and Society* 34 (3): 317–355.

Chorev, N., 2012, *The World Health Organization between North and South*, Ithaca, NY, Cornell University Press.

Chwieroth, J. M., 2007, 'Testing and Measuring the Role of Ideas: The Case of Neoliberalism in the International Monetary Fund', *International Studies Quarterly* 51 (1): 5–30.

Chwieroth, J. M., 2008, 'Normative Change from Within: The International Monetary Fund's Approach to Capital Account Liberalization', *International Studies Quarterly* 52 (1): 129–158.

Chwieroth, J. M., 2010, *Capital Ideas: The IMF and the Rise of Financial Liberalization*, Princeton, NJ, Princeton University Press.

Chwieroth, J. M., 2015, 'Managing and Transforming Policy Stigmas in International Finance: Emerging Markets and Controlling Capital Inflows after the Crisis', *Review of International Political Economy* 22 (1): 44–76.

Cini, M., and N. Pérez-Solórzano Borragán, 2016, *European Union Politics*, fifth edition, Oxford, Oxford University Press.

Clapp, J., 1998, 'The Privatization of Global Environmental Governance: ISO 14000 and the Developing World', *Global Governance* 4 (3): 295–316.

Clapp, J., 2004, 'WTO Agricultural Trade Battles and Food Aid', *Third World Quarterly* 25 (8): 1439–1452.

Clark, A. M., 2001, *Diplomacy of Conscience: Amnesty International and Changing Human Rights Norms*, Princeton, NJ, Princeton University Press.

Clark, A. M., E. J. Friedman and K. Hochstetler, 2005, 'The Sovereign Limits of Global Civil Society: A Comparison of NGO Participation in UN World Conferences on the Environment, Human Rights and Women', in R. Wilkinson (ed.), *The Global Governance Reader*, London and New York, Routledge: 292–321.

Claude, I., 1971, *Swords into Ploughshares: The Problems and Progress of International Organization*, fourth edition, New York, Random House.

Cole, W. M., 2015, 'Mind the Gap: State Capacity and the Implementation of Human Rights Treaties', *International Organization* 69 (2): 405–441.

Coleman, K., 2007, *International Organisations and Peace Enforcement: The Politics of Inter-national Legitimacy*, Cambridge, Cambridge University Press.

Collier, P., 2007, *The Bottom Billion: Why the Poorest Countries Are Failing and What Can Be Done about It*, Oxford, Oxford University Press.

Commission on Global Governance, 1995, *Our Global Neighbourhood*, Oxford, Oxford University Press.

Conca, K., 1995, 'Greening the United Nations: Environmental Organisations and the UN System', *Third World Quarterly* 16 (3): 441–458.

Conca, K., 2015, *An Unfinished Foundation: The United Nations and Global Environmental Governance*, Oxford, Oxford University Press.

Conca, K., J. Thwaites and G. Lee, 2017, 'Climate Change and the UN Security Council: Bully Pulpit or Bull in a China Shop?', *Global Environmental Politics* 17 (2): 1–20.

Cooley, A., 2010, 'Outsourcing Authority: Project Contracts and Governance Networks', in D. D. Avant, M. Finnemore and S. K. Sell (eds.), *Who Governs the Globe?*, Cambridge, Cambridge University Press: 238–266.

Cooper, A., 2010, 'The G20 As an Improvised Crisis Committee and/or a Contested "Steering Committee" for the World', *International Affairs* 86 (3): 741–757.

Cooper, A., 2013, 'Squeezed or Revitalised? Middle Powers, the G20 and the Evolution of Global Governance', *Third World Quarterly* 34 (6): 963–984.

Copelovitch, M., 2010, *The International Monetary Fund in the Global Economy: Banks, Bonds and Bailouts*, Cambridge, Cambridge University Press.

Cortell, A. P., and S. Peterson, 2006, 'Dutiful Agents, Rogue Actors, or Both? Staffing, Voting Rules, and Slack in the WHO and WTO', in D. G. Hawkins, D. A. Lake, D. L. Nielson and M. J. Tierney (eds.), *Delegation and Agency in International Organizations*, Cambridge, Cambridge University Press: 255–280.

Cox, E., 2010, 'State Interests and the Creation and Functioning of the United Nations Human Rights Council', *Journal of International Law and International Relations* 6 (1): 87–120.

Cox, R. W., and H. K. Jacobson, 1973, *The Anatomy of Influence: Decision Making in International Organizations*, New Haven, CT, Yale University Press.

Crane, B. B., and J. L. Finkle, 1989, 'The United States, China, and the United Nations Population Fund: Dynamics of US Policymaking', *Population and Development Review* 15 (1): 23–59.

Crane, G. T., and A. Amawi, 1997 (eds.), *The Theoretical Evolution of International Political Economy: A Reader*, second edition, Oxford, Oxford University Press.

Croome, J., 1995, *Reshaping the World Trading System: A History of the Uruguay Round*, Geneva, WTO.

Cupitt, R., R. Witlock and L. W. Witlock, 2001, 'The (Im)mortality of International Governmental Organizations', in P. Diehl (ed.), *Politics of Global Governance*, second edition, Boulder, CO, Lynne Rienner: 44–60.

Cutler, C., V. Haufler and T. Porter (eds.), 1999, *Private Authority in International Affairs*, Albany, NY, SUNY Press.

Davies, S. E., 2010, *Global Politics of Health*, Cambridge, Cambridge University Press.

Deese, D., 2008, *World Trade Politics: Power, Principles and Leadership*, London and New York, Routledge.

Depledge, J., 2007, 'A Special Relationship: Chairpersons and the Secretariat in the Climate Change Negotiations', *Global Environmental Politics* 7 (1): 45–68.

DeSombre, E. R., 2006, *Global Environmental Institutions*, London and New York, Routledge.

Deutsch, K., 1957, *Political Community and the North Atlantic Area*, Princeton, NJ, Princeton University Press.

Dieter, H., 2006, 'The Decline of the IMF: Is It Reversible? Should It Be Reversed?', *Global Governance* 12 (4): 343–349.

Dimitrov, R., 2006, *Science and International Environmental Policy: Regimes and Nonregimes in Global Governance*, Lanham, MD, Rowman and Littlefield.

Dinan, D., 2014, *Origins and Evolution of the European Union*, second edition, Oxford, Oxford University Press.

Donnelly, J., 2002, *Universal Human Rights in Theory and Practice*, Ithaca, NY, Cornell University Press.

Downs, G. W., D. M. Rocke and P. N. Barsoom, 1998, 'Managing the Evolution of Muiltilateralism', *International Organization* 52 (2): 397–419.

Doyle, M., and N. Sambanis, 2006, *Making War and Building Peace: United Nations Peace Operations*, Princeton, NJ, Princeton University Press.

Dreher, A., 2006, 'IMF and Economic Growth: The Effects of Programs, Loans and Compliance with Conditionality', *World Development* 34 (5): 769–788.

Dreher, A., and N. Jensen, 2007, 'Independent Actor or Agent? An Empirical Analysis of the Impact of US interests on IMF Conditions', *The Journal of Law and Economics* 50 (1): 105–124.

Eagleton-Pierce, M., 2012, *Symbolic Power in the World Trade Organization*, Oxford, Oxford University Press.

Easterly, W., 2001, 'The Lost Decades: Developing Countries' Stagnation in Spite of Policy Reform 1980–1998', *Journal of Economic Growth* 6 (2): 135–157.

Easterly, W., 2006, *The White Man's Burden: Why the West's Efforts to Aid the Rest Have Done So Much Ill and So Little Good*, New York, Penguin Press.

Economist, The, 2001, 'Who Elected the WTO?' www.economist.com/node/796140. Accessed 27 February 2018.

ECOSOC, 1994, 'Resolution 1994/24: Joint and Co-sponsored United Nations Programme on Human Immunodeficiency Virus/Acquired Immunodeficiency Syndrome (HIV/AIDS)', 44th Plenary Meeting, 26 July 1994. www.un.org/documents/ecosoc/res/1994/eres1994-24.htm. Accessed 27 September 2017.

ECOSOC, 2011, 'Basic Facts about ECOSOC Status'. http://csonet.org/index.php?menu=17. Accessed 1 December 2011.

Eichengreen, B., 2008, *Globalizing Capital: A History of the International Monetary System*, second edition, Princeton, NJ and Oxford, Princeton University Press.

Elsig, M., 2010, 'Principal–Agent Theory and the World Trade Organization: Complex Agency and "Missing Delegation"' *European Journal of International Relations* 17 (3): 495–517.

Elsig, M., and M. A. Pollack, 2014, 'Agents, Trustees, and International Courts: The Politics of Judicial Appointment at the World Trade Organization', *European Journal of International Relations* 20 (2): 391–415.

Ervine, K., 2007, 'The Greying of Green Governance: Power Politics and the Global Environment Facility', *Capitalism Nature Socialism* 18 (4): 125–142.

Farley, L. T., 1982, *Change Processes in International Organizations*, Cambridge, MA, Schenkman Publishing.

Fawcett, L., and A. Hurrell (eds.), 1995, *Regionalism in World Politics*, Oxford, Oxford University Press.

Fearon, J., 1998, 'Bargaining, Enforcement, and International Cooperation', *International Organization* 52 (2): 269–305.

Fidler, D., 1999, *International Law and Infectious Diseases*, Oxford, Clarendon Press.

Fidler, D. P., 2004, *SARS, Governance and the Globalisation of Disease*, Basingstoke, Palgrave Macmillan.

Financial Stability Board, 2016, 'About the FSB'. www.fsb.org/about/. Accessed 17 January 2016.

Finnemore., M., 1996, *National Interests in International Society*, Ithaca, NY and London, Cornell University Press.

Føllesdal, A., J. Karlsson Schaffer and G. Ulfstein (eds.), 2014, *The Legitimacy of International Human Rights Regimes: Legal, Political and Philosophical Perspectives*, Cambridge, Cambridge University Press.

Foot, R., S. N. MacFarlane and M. Mastanduno, 2003, *US Hegemony and International Organizations*, Oxford, Oxford University Press.

Ford, J., 2003, *A Social Theory of the WTO*, Basingstoke, Palgrave Macmillan.

Ford Foundation, 2017, 'About Us'. www.fordfoundation.org/about-us. Accessed 29 September 2017.

Forsythe, D. P., 2000a, *Human Rights in International Relations*, Cambridge, Cambridge University Press.

Forsythe, D. P., 2000b, *Human Rights and Comparative Foreign Policy*, Tokyo, United Nations University Press.

Forsythe, D. P., 2005, *The Humanitarians: The International Committee of the Red Cross*, Cambridge, Cambridge University Press.

Forsythe, D. P., and B. A. Rieffer-Flanagan, 2007, *The International Committee of the Red Cross: A Neutral Humanitarian Actor*, London and New York, Routledge.

Franchino, F., 2007, *The Powers of the Union: Delegation in the EU*, Cambridge, Cambridge University Press.

Freedman, R., 2013, *The United Nations Human Rights Council: A Critique and Early Assessment*, New York, Routledge.

Fuhrmann, M., 2012, *Atomic Assistance: How 'Atoms for Peace' Cause Nuclear Insecurity*, Ithaca, NY, Cornell University Press.

Fukuda, Y., 2010, 'WTO Regime As a New Stage of Imperialism: Decaying Capitalism and Its Alternative', *The World Review of Political Economy* 1 (3): 485–499.

Gallagher, P., 2005, *The First Ten Years of the WTO: 1995–2005*, Geneva, WTO.

Gallagher, P., and A. Stoler, 2009, 'Critical Mass As an Alternative Framework for Multilateral Trade Negotiations', *Global Governance* 15: 375–392.

Gallarotti, G., 1991, 'The Limits of International Organization: The Systemic Failure in the Management of International Relations', *International Organization* 45 (2): 183–220.

Garrett, G., 1995, 'The Politics of Legal Integration in the European Union', *International Organization* 49 (1): 171–181.

GAVI, 2008, *GAVI Alliance Statutes*. www.gavi.org/library/gavi-documents/legal/. Accessed 2 November 2015.

GAVI, 2014, *The Vaccine Alliance Progress Report 2014*. www.gavi.org/progress-report-2014/. Accessed 2 November 2015.

Gehring, T., and S. Oberthür, 2008, 'Interplay: Exploring Institutional Interaction', in O. Young, L. King and H. Schroeder (eds.), *Institutions and Environmental Change*, Cambridge, MA, MIT Press: 187–223.

Germain, R., 2010, 'Financial Governance and Transnational Deliberative Democracy', *Review of International Studies* 36 (2): 493–509.

GFATM, 2012, *The Framework Document*. www.theglobalfund.org/media/6019/core_globalfund_ framework_en.pdf. Accessed 23 November 2015.

GFATM, 2015, 'Resource Mobilisation'. www.theglobalfund.org/en/replenishment/. Accessed 23 November 2015.

Gill, S., 2009, *American Hegemony and the Trilateral Commission*, Cambridge, Cambridge University Press.

Gilligan, M. J., 2004, 'Is There a Broader–Deeper Trade-off in International Multilateral Agreements?', *International Organization* 58 (3): 458–484.

Gilpin, R., 2001, *Global Political Economy*, Princeton, NJ, Princeton University Press.

Global Environment Facility, 2017, 'About the GEF'. www.thegef.org. Accessed 16 June 2017.

Godlee, F., 1995, 'WHO's Special Programmes: Undermining from Above', *British Medical Journal* 310 (6973): 178–182.

Goldbach, R., 2015, 'Asymmetric Influence in Global Banking Regulation', *Review of International Political Economy* 22 (6): 1087–1127.

Goldman, M., 2005, *Imperial Nature: The World Bank and Struggles for Social Justice in the Age of Globalization*, New Haven, CT and London, Yale University Press.

Goldstein, J., and L. L. Martin, 2000, 'Legalization, Trade Liberalization and Domestic Politics: A Cautionary Note', *International Organization* 54 (3): 603–632.

Goldstein, J. L., and R. H. Steinberg, 2008, 'Negotiate or Litigate? Effects of WTO Judicial Delegation on US Trade Politics', *Law and Contemporary Problems* 71: 257–282.

Goldstein, J. L., M. Kahler, R. O. Keohane and A.-M. Slaughter, 2001, *Legalization and World Politics*, Cambridge, MA, MIT Press.

Goldstone, R., 2007, 'International Criminal Court and Ad Hoc Tribunals', in T. G. Weiss and S. Daws (eds.), *The Oxford Handbook on the United Nations*, Oxford, Oxford University Press: 463–479.

Gould, E. R., 2003, 'Money Talks: Supplementary Financiers and International Monetary Fund Conditionality', *International Organization* 57 (3): 551–586.

Graham, E., 2014, 'International Organizations as Collective Agents: Fragmentation and the Limits of Principal Control at the World Health Organisation', *European Journal of International Relations* 20 (2): 366–390.

Grameen Bank, 2015, 'History'. www.grameen-info.org/history/. Accessed 30 November 2015.

Gray, M. A., 1990, 'The United Nations Environment Programme: An Assessment', *Environmental Law* 20 (2): 291–319.

Green, J., 2014, *Rethinking Private Authority: Agents and Entrepreneurs in Global Environmental Governance*, Princeton, NJ, Princeton University Press.

Grieco, J., 1990, *Cooperation Among Nations: Europe, America, and Non-Tariff Barriers to Trade*, Ithaca, NY, Cornell University Press.

Griffin, P., 2010, *Gendering the World Bank: Neoliberalism and the Gendered Foundations of Global Governance*, Basingstoke, Palgrave Macmillan.

Grigorescu, A., 2002, 'European Institutions and Unsuccessful Norm Transmission: The Case of Transparency', *International Politics* 39 (4): 467–489.

Grigorescu, A., 2010, 'The Spread of Bureaucratic Oversight Mechanisms across Intergovernmental Organizations', *International Studies Quarterly* 54 (3): 871–886.

Gruber, L., 2000, *Ruling the World: Power Politics and the Rise of Supranational Institutions*, Princeton, NJ, Princeton University Press.

Gruber, L., 2001, 'Power Politics and the Free Trade Bandwagon', *Comparative Political Studies* 34 (7): 703–741.

Gulli, H., and M. Berger, 1999, 'Microfinance and Poverty Reduction – Evidence from Latin America'. *Small Enterprise Development* 10(3): 16–28.

Gutner, T., 2005a, 'Explaining the Gaps between Mandate and Performance: Agency Theory and World Bank Environmental Reform', *Global Environmental Politics* 5 (2): 10–37.

Gutner, T., 2005b, 'World Bank Environmental Reform: Revisiting Lessons from Agency Theory', *International Organization* 59 (3): 773–783.

Gutner, T., 2010, 'When Doing Good Does Not: The IMF and the Millennium Development Goals', in D. D. Avant, M. Finnemore and S. K. Sell (eds.), *Who Governs the Globe?*, Cambridge, Cambridge University Press: 266–291.

Gutner, T., and A. Thompson, 2010, 'The Politics of IO Performance: A Framework', *Review of International Organizations* 5 (3): 227–248.

Haacke, J., 2003, *ASEAN's Diplomatic and Security Culture: Origins, Development and Prospects*, London, Routledge Curzon.

Haas, E. B., 1958, *The Uniting of Europe: Political, Social, and Economic Forces, 1950–1957*. Stanford, CA, Stanford University Press.

Haas, E. B., 1964, *Beyond the Nation-State: Functionalism and International Organization*, Stanford, CA, Stanford University Press.

Haas, E. B., 1990, *When Knowledge Is Power: Three Models of Change in International Organizations*, Berkeley, CA, University of California Press.

Haas, P. M., 2002, 'UN Conferences and Constructivist Governance of the Environment', *Global Governance* 8 (1): 73–91.

Haas, P. M., and E. B. Haas, 1995, 'Learning to Learn: Improving International Governance', *Global Governance* 1 (3): 255–284.

Hafner-Burton, E. M., 2013, *Making Human Rights a Reality*, Princeton, NJ and Oxford: Princeton University Press.

Haftel, Y., and A. Thompson, 2006, 'The Independence of International Organizations: Concept and Applications', *Journal of Conflict Resolution* 50 (2): 253–275.

Haggard, S., and S. Maxfield, 1996, 'The Political Economy of Financial Internationalization in the Developing World', *International Organization* 50 (1): 35–68.

Hale, T., and C. Roger, 2014, 'Orchestration and Transnational Governance', *Review of International Organizations* 9 (1): 59–82.

Hale, T., D. Held and K. Young, 2013, *Gridlock: Why Global Cooperation Is Failing When We Need It Most*, Cambridge, Polity Press.

Hall, R., and T. J. Biersteker (eds.), 2002, *The Emergence of Private Authority in Global Governance*, Cambridge, Cambridge University Press.

Hamieri, S., and L. Jones, 2015, *Governing Borderless Threats: Non-traditional Security and the Politics of State Transformation*, Cambridge, Cambridge University Press.

Hanrieder, T., 2015, *International Organization in Time: Fragmentation and Reform*, Oxford, Oxford University Press.

Harman, S., 2011, 'Searching for an Executive Head? Leadership and UNAIDS', *Global Governance* 17 (4): 429–446.

Harman, S., 2014, 'Global Health Governance', in T. G. Weiss and R. Wilkinson (eds.), *International Organizations and Global Governance*, London and New York, Routledge: 656–667.

Hawkins, D. G., D. A. Lake, D. L. Nielson and M J. Tierney, 2006, *Delegation and Agency in International Organizations*, Cambridge, Cambridge University Press.

Held, D., 2006, 'Reframing Global Governance: Apocalypse Soon or Reform!', *New Political Economy* 11 (2): 157–176.

Held, D., and C. Roger, 2013, *Global Governance at Risk*, Cambridge, Polity Press.

Helleiner, E., 2010, 'A Bretton Woods Moment? The 2007–2008 Crisis and the Future of Global Finance', *International Affairs* 86 (3): 619–636.

Helleiner, E., S. Pagliari and H. Zimmerman (eds.), 2010, *Global Finance in Crisis: The Politics of International Regulatory Change*, London, Routledge.

Herz, M., 2011, *The Organization of American States (OAS): Global Governance Away from the Media*, London and New York, Routledge.

Hettne, B., 2005, 'Beyond the "New" Regionalism', *New Political Economy* 10 (4): 543–571.

Hoekman, B., and M. Kostecki, 2001, *The Political Economy of the World Trading System: The WTO and Beyond*, second edition, Oxford, Oxford University Press.

Holroyd, C., and B. Momani, 2012, 'Japan's Rescue of the IMF', *Social Science Japan Journal* 15 (2): 201–218.

Hooghe, L., 2005, 'Several Roads Lead to International Norms, but Few Via International Socialization: A Case Study of the European Commission', *International Organization* 59 (4): 861–898.

Hopewell, K., 2016, *Breaking the WTO: How Emerging Powers Disrupted the Neoliberal Project*, Stanford, CA, Stanford University Press.

Hopgood, S., 2006, *Keepers of the Flame: Understanding Amnesty International*, Ithaca, NY, Cornell University Press.

Hug, S., and R. Lukács, 2014, 'Preferences or Blocs? Voting in the United Nations Human Rights Council', *Review of International Organizations* 9 (1): 83–106.

Hulme, D., and J. Scott, 2010, 'The Political Economy of the MDGs: Retrospect and Prospect for the World's Biggest Promise', *New Political Economy* 15 (2): 293–306.

Human Rights Watch, 2017, 'About'. www.hrw.org/about. Accessed 20 November 2017.

Hurd, I., 2005, 'The Strategic Use of Liberal Internationalism: Libya and the UN Sanctions 1992–2003', *International Organization* 59 (3): 495–526.

Hurd, I., 2011, *International Organizations: Politics, Law, Practice*, Cambridge, Cambridge University Press.

Hurrell, A., 1995, 'Regionalism in Theoretical Perspective', in L. Fawcett and A. Hurrell (eds.), *Regionalism in World Politics: Regional Organization and International Order*, Oxford, Oxford University Press: 37–73.

International Atomic Energy Agency, 2017, 'About Us'. www.iaea.org/about/overview/budget. Accessed 15 January 2018.

International Commission on Intervention and State Sovereignty, 2001, *The Responsibility to Protect: Report of the International Commission on Intervention and State Sovereignty*, Ottawa, International Development Research Centre. www.idrc.ca/en/book/responsibility-protect-report-international-commission-intervention-and-state-sovereignty. Accessed 18 March 2018.

International Criminal Court, 2017, 'About'. www.icc-cpi.int/about. Accessed 8 November 2017.

International Monetary Fund, 2003, *Evaluation Report: Fiscal Adjustment in IMF Supported Programs*, Washington, D.C., International Monetary Fund.

International Monetary Fund, 2008, 'IMF Survey: Directors Back Reforms to Overhaul IMF Quotas and Voice', 28 March. www.imf.org/external/pubs/ft/survey/so/2008/NEW032808A.htm. Accessed 22 January 2016.

International Monetary Fund, 2010, 'Press Release: IMF Executive Board Approves Major Overhaul of Quotas and Governance', 5 November. www.imf.org/external/np/sec/pr/2010/pr10418.htm. Accessed 22 January 2016.

International Monetary Fund, 2011a, 'Articles of Agreement for the International Monetary Fund, Amended 3 March 2011'. www.imf.org/external/pubs/ft/aa/pdf/aa.pdf. Accessed 4 December 2012.

International Monetary Fund, 2011b, 'Press Release: The IMF's 2008 Quota and Voice Reforms Take Effect', 3 March. www.imf.org/external/np/sec/pr/2011/pr1164.htm. Accessed 22 January 2016.

International Monetary Fund, 2013, 'Quota and Voting Shares Before and After Implementation of Reforms Agreed in 2008 and 2010'. www.imf.org/external/np/sec/pr/2011/pdfs/quota_tbl.pdf. Accessed 22 January 2016.

International Monetary Fund, 2015a, 'IMF Members' Quotas and Voting Power, and IMF Board of Governors'. www.imf.org/external/np/sec/memdir/members.aspx. Accessed 17 September 2015.

International Monetary Fund, 2015b, 'Press Release: IMF Managing Director Christine Lagarde Welcomes U.S. Congressional Approval of the 2010 Quota and Governance Reforms', December 18. www.imf.org/external/np/sec/pr/2015/pr15573.htm. Accessed 22 January 2016.

International Monetary Fund, 2016, 'IMF Executive Directors and Voting Power'. www.imf.org/external/np/sec/memdir/eds.aspx. Accessed 22 January 2016.

Isenberg, D., 2007, 'A Government in Search of Cover: Private Military Companies in Iraq', in S. Chesterman and C. Lehnardt (eds.), *From Mercenaries to Market: The Rise and Regulation of Private Military Companies*, Oxford, Oxford University Press: 82–93.

Ivanova, M., 2007, 'Designing the United Nations Environment Programme: A Story of Compromise and Confrontation', *International Environmental Agreements* 7 (4): 337–361.

Ivanova, M., 2010, 'UNEP in Global Environmental Governance: Design, Leadership, Location', *Global Environmental Politics* 10 (1): 30–59.

Ivanova, M., 2011, 'Brief 1: Financing International Environmental Governance: Lessons from the United Nations Environment Programme', Center for Governance and Sustainability, University of Massachusetts Boston. https://scholarworks.umb.edu/cgi/viewcontent.cgi?article=1000&context=cgs_issue_brief_series.

Ivanova, M., 2013, 'The Contested Legacy of Rio+20', *Global Environmental Politics* 13 (4): 1–11.

Jacobson, H. K., 1984, *Networks of Independence: International Organizations and the Global Political System*, second edition, New York, Alfred A. Knopf.

Jacobson, H. K., W. M. Reisinger and T. Mathers, 1986, 'National Entanglements in International Governmental Organizations', *American Political Science Review* 80 (1): 141–159.

Jaspers, N., and R. Falkner, 2013, 'International Trade, the Environment, and Climate Change', in R. Falkner (ed.), *The Handbook of Global Climate and Environment Policy*, Chichester, Wiley-Blackwell: 412–427.

Jervis, R., 1999, 'Realism, Neoliberalism, and Cooperation', *International Security* 24 (1): 42–63.

Jinnah, S., 2014, *Post-Treaty Politics: Secretariat Influence in Global Environmental Governance*, Cambridge, MA, MIT Press.

Johnston, A., 2001, 'Treating International Institutions As Social Environments', *International Studies Quarterly* 45 (4): 487–515.

Johnston, A., 2008, *Social States: China in International Institutions, 1980–2000*, Princeton, NJ, Princeton University Press.

Jolly, R., 2014, *UNICEF (United Nations Children's Fund): Global Governance that Works*, Basingstoke, Palgrave Macmillan.

Jolly, R., L. Emmerij, D. Ghai and F. Lapeyre, 2004, *UN Contributions to Development Thinking and Practice*, Bloomington, IN, Indiana University Press.

Joyce, J. P., 2013, *The IMF and the Global Financial Crisis: Phoenix Rising?*, Cambridge, Cambridge University Press.

Kaldor, M., 1999, *New and Old Wars: Organized Violence in a Global Era*, Stanford, CA, Stanford University Press.

Kamradt-Scott, A., 2015, *Managing Global Health Security: The World Health Organization and Disease Outbreak Control*, Basingstoke, Palgrave Macmillan.

Kamradt-Scott, A., 2016, 'WHO's to Blame? The World Health Organization and the 2014 Ebola Outbreak in West Africa', *Third World Quarterly* 37 (3): 401–418.

Kamradt-Scott, A., and K. Lee, 2011, 'The 2011 Pandemic Influenza Preparedness Framework: Global Health Secured or a Missed Opportunity?', *Political Studies* 59 (4): 831–847.

Kant, I., 1796, *Project for a Perpetual Peace: A Philosophical Essay*, London, Vernor and Hood.

Kanter, J., and A. Kanter, 2006, *The Struggle for International Consensus on Population and Development*, Basingstoke, Palgrave Macmillan.

Kapur, D., and R. Webb, 2000, 'Governance-Related Conditionalities of the International Financial Institutions', G-24 Discussion Paper Series. http://213.154.74.164/invenio/record/16107/files/kupur.pdf.

Kay, A., and O. Williams, 2009, *Global Health Governance: Crisis, Institutions and Political Economy*, Basingstoke, Palgrave Macmillan.

Kaya, A., 2015, *Power and Global Economic Institutions*, Cambridge, Cambridge University Press.

Keck, M., and K. Sikkink, 1998, *Activists beyond Borders: Advocacy Networks in International Politics*, Ithaca, NY and London, Cornell University Press.

Keller, H., and G. Ulfstein (eds.), 2012, *UN Human Rights Treaty Bodies: Law and Legitimacy*, Cambridge, Cambridge University Press.

Kenealy, D., J. Peterson and R. Corbett, 2015, *The European Union: How Does It Work?*, fourth edition, Oxford, Oxford University Press.

Keohane, R. O., 1984, *After Hegemony: Cooperation and Discord in the World Political Economy*, Princeton, NJ, Princeton University Press.

Keohane, R. O., 1986, 'Reciprocity in International Relations', *International Organization* 40 (1): 1–27.

Keohane, R. O., 1988, 'International Institutions: Two Approaches', *International Studies Quarterly* 32 (4): 379–396.

Keohane, R. O., 1990, 'Multilateralism: An Agenda for Research', *International Journal* 45 (4): 731–764.

Keohane, R. O., 1993, 'Institutional Theory and the Realist Challenge after the Cold War', in D. A. Baldwin (ed.), *Neorealism and Neoliberalism: The Contemporary Debate*, New York, Columbia University Press: 269–300.

Keohane, R. O., 2012, 'Twenty Years of Liberal Institutionalism', *International Relations* 26 (2): 125–138.

Keohane, R. O., and J. Nye, 1971, 'Transnational Relations and World Politics: An Introduction', *International Organization* 25 (3): 329–349.

Kiewiet, D. R., and M. D. McCubbins, 1991, *The Logic of Delegation: Congressional Parties and the Appropriations Process*, Chicago, IL and London, University of Chicago Press.

Killick, T., 1995, *IMF Programs in Developing Countries: Design and Impact*, London, Routledge.

Kirsch, P., J. T. Holmes and M. Johnson, 2004, 'International Tribunals and Courts', in D. M. Malone (ed.), *The UN Security Council: From the Cold War to the 21st Century*, Boulder, CO, Lynne Rienner: 281–295.

Knight, L., 2008, *UNAIDS: The First Ten Years, 1996–2006*, Geneva, Joint United Nations Programme on HIV/AIDS.

Korey, W., 2001, *NGOs and the Universal Declaration of Human Rights*, Basingstoke, Palgrave.

Kramarz, T., and S. Park, 2016, 'Accountability in Global Environmental Governance: A Meaningful Tool for Action?', *Global Environmental Politics* 16 (2): 1–21.

Krasner, S. (ed.), 1983, *International Regimes*, Ithaca, NY, Cornell University Press.

Kratochwil, F., and J. G. Ruggie, 1986, 'International Organizations: A State of the Art on the Art of the State', *International Organization* 40 (4): 753–776.

Krommendijk, J., 2015, 'The Domestic Effectiveness of International Human Rights Monitoring in Established Democracies. The Case of the UN Human Rights Treaty Bodies', *Review of International Organizations* 10 (4): 489–512.

Kütting, G., 2001, 'Back to the Future: Time, the Environment and IR Theory', *Global Society* 15 (4): 345–360.

Kütting, G., and R. Lipschutz (eds.), 2009, *Environmental Governance: Power and Knowledge in a Local-Global World*, London and New York, Routledge.

Lacy, M., 2005, *Security and Climate Change: International Relations and the Limits of Climate Change*, New York, Routledge.

Lall, R., 2012, 'From Failure to Failure: The Politics of International Banking Regulation', *Review of International Political Economy* 19 (4): 609–638.

Lang, A., 2011, *World Trade Law after Neoliberalism: Reimagining the Global Economic Order*, Oxford, Oxford University Press.

Lavelle, K., 2011, *Legislating International Organization: The US Congress, the IMF and the World Bank*, Oxford, Oxford University Press.

Leach, F., and S. Sitaram, 2002, 'Microfinance and Women's Empowerment: A Lesson from India', *Development in Practice* 12 (5): 575–588.

League of Nations, 1924, 'The Covenant of the League of Nations', including amendments adopted to December 1924. http://avalon.law.yale.edu/20th_century/leagcov.asp. Accessed 14 September 2017.

Lebovic, J. H., and E. Voeten, 2006, 'The Politics of Shame: The Condemnation of Country Human Rights Practices in the UNCHR', *International Studies Quarterly* 50 (4): 861–888.

Lebovic, J. H., and E. Voeten, 2009, 'The Cost of Shame: International Organizations and Foreign Aid in the Punishing of Human Rights Violators', *Journal of Peace Research* 46 (1): 79–97.

Lebow, R. N., 2007, 'Classical Realism', in T. Dunne, M. Kurki and S. Smith (eds.), *International Relations Theories: Discipline and Diversity*, Oxford, Oxford University Press: 52–70.

Lee, K., 1994, 'The UNFPA: Twenty-Five Years and Beyond', *Health, Policy and Planning* 9 (2): 223–228.

Lee, K., 2009, *The World Health Organization*, London and New York, Routledge.

Lehtonen, M., 2007, 'Environmental Policy Integration through OECD Peer Reviews: Integrating the Economy with the Environment or the Environment with the Economy?', *Environmental Politics* 16 (1): 15–35.

Leiteritz, R., 2005, 'Explaining Organizational Outcomes: The International Monetary Fund and Capital Account Liberalization', *Journal of International Relations and Development* 8 (1): 1–26.

Leiteritz, R., and M. Moschella, 2010, 'The IMF and Capital Account Liberalization: A Case of Failed Norm Institutionalisation', in S. Park and A. Vetterlein (eds.), *Owning Development: Creating Global Policy Norms in the IMF and the World Bank*, Cambridge, Cambridge University Press: 163–180.

Lewis, J., 2005, 'The Janus Face of Brussels: Socialization and Everyday Decision Making in the European Union', *International Organization* 59 (4): 937–971.

Lie, H. S., 2015, *Developmentality: An Ethnography of the World Bank–Uganda Partnership*, New York and Oxford, Berghahn Books.

Lipson, C., 1991, 'Why Are Some International Agreements Informal?', *International Organization* 45 (4): 495–538.

Lipson, C., 1993, 'International Cooperation in Economic and Security Affairs,' in D. A. Baldwin (ed.), *Neorealism and Neoliberalism: The Contemporary Debate*, New York, Columbia University Press: 60–84.

Lipson, M., 2010, 'Performance under Ambiguity: International Organization Performance in UN Peacekeeping', *Review of International Organizations*, 5 (3): 249–284.

Lisk, F., 2009, *Global Institutions and the HIV/AIDS Epidemic: Responding to an International Crisis*, London, Routledge.

Litfin, K., 1994, *Ozone Discourses: Science and Politics in International Environmental Cooperation*, New York, Columbia University Press.

Loescher, G., 2001, 'The UNHCR and World Politics: State Interests vs. Institutional Autonomy', *The International Migration Review* 35 (1): 33–56.

Love, R., 2007, 'Corporate Wealth or Public Health? WTO/TRIPS Flexibilities and Access to HIV/AIDS Antiretroviral Drugs by Developing Countries', *Development in Practice* 17 (2): 208–219.

Low, P., 2010, 'Potential Future Functions of the World Trade Organization', *Global Governance* 15 (3): 327–334.

Luck, E., 2006, *UN Security Council: Practice and Promise*, London and New York, Routledge.

Luken, R., 2009, 'Greening an International Organization: UNIDO's Strategic Responses', *Review of International Organizations* 4 (2): 159–184.

Lupia, A., and M. D. McCubbins, 1994, 'Learning from Oversight: Fire Alarms and Police Patrols Reconstructed', *Journal of Law, Economics and Organization* 10 (1): 96–125.

Makinda, S., F. W. Okumu and D. Mickler, 2016, *The African Union: Addressing the Challenges of Peace, Security and Governance*, second edition, London and New York, Routledge.

Malik, M., 1995, 'Do We Need a New Theory of International Organizations?', in R. V. Bartlett, P. A. Kurian and M. Malik (eds.), *International Organizations and Environmental Policy*, Westport, CT, Greenwood Press: 223–239.

Malone, D. M., 2004a, 'Security Council', in T. G. Weiss and S. Daws (eds.), *The Oxford Handbook on the United Nations*, Oxford, Oxford University Press: 117–136.

Malone, D. M. (ed.), 2004b, *The UN Security Council: From the Cold War to the 21st Century*, Boulder, CO, Lynne Rienner.

Mansfield, E., and H. Milner, 1999, 'The New Wave of Regionalism', *International Organization* 53 (3): 589–627.

Mansfield, E., and H. Milner, 2012, *Votes, Vetoes, and the Political Economy of International Trade Agreements*, Princeton, NJ, Princeton University Press.

Martens, K., 2006, 'Institutionalizing Societal Activism within Global Governance Structures: Amnesty International and the United Nations System', *Journal of International Relations and Development* 9 (4): 371–395.

Martin, L. L., 1992, 'Interests, Power, and Multilateralism', *International Organization* 46 (4): 765–792.

Martin, L. L., and B. Simmons, 1998, 'Theories and Empirical Studies of International Institutions', *International Organization* 52 (4): 729–757.

Mayerfeld, 2003, 'Who Shall Be Judge? The United States, the International Criminal Court and the Enforcement of Human Rights', *Human Rights Quarterly* 25 (1): 93–129.

McCormick, J., 1995, 'Environmental Policy and the European Union', in R. V. Bartlett, P. A. Kurian and M. Malik (eds.), *International Organizations and Environmental Policy*, Westport, CT, Greenwood Press: 37–49.

McCormick, J., 2001, *Understanding the European Union*, Basingstoke, Palgrave Macmillan.

McCormick, J., 2011, 'The Role of Environmental NGOs in International Regimes', in R. S. Axelrod, S. D. VanDeveer and D. L. Downie, *The Global Environment: Institutions, Law and Policy*, Washington, D.C., CQ Press: 92–109.

McCubbins, M. D., and T. Schwartz, 1984, 'Congressional Oversight Overlooked: Police Patrols versus Fire Alarms', *American Journal of Political Science* 28 (1): 165–179.

McCubbins, M. D., R. G. Noll and B. R. Weingast, 1987, 'Administrative Procedures as Instruments of Political Control', *Journal of Law, Economics and Organization* 3 (2): 243–277.

McCubbins, M. D., R. G. Noll and B. R. Weingast, 1989, 'Structure and Process, Politics and Policy: Administrative Arrangements and the Political Control of Agencies', *Virginia Law Review* 75 (2): 431–482.

McGoldrick, D., P. Rowe and E. Donnelly (eds.), 2004, *The Permanent International Criminal Court: Legal and Policy Issues*, Oxford, Hart Publishing.

McMahon, E., and M. Aschiero, 2012, 'A Step Ahead in Promoting Human Rights? The Universal Periodic Review of the UN Human Rights Council', *Global Governance* 18 (2): 231–248.

McNamara, K., 1998, *The Currency of Ideas: Monetary Politics in the European Union*, Ithaca, NY, Cornell University Press.

McNamara, K., 2015, *The Politics of Everyday Europe: Constructing Authority in the European Union*, Oxford, Oxford University Press.

McNeill, D., and K. I. Sandberg, 2014, 'Trust in Global Health Governance: The GAVI Experience', *Global Governance* 20 (2): 325–343.

Mearsheimer, J. J., 1990, 'Back to the Future: Instability in Europe after the Cold War', *International Security* 15 (1): 5–56.

Mearsheimer, J. J., 1994–1995, 'The False Promise of International Institutions', *International Security* 19 (3): 5–49.

Médecins Sans Frontières, 2014, 'Financial Report 2014: Key Figures'. www.msf.org/sites/msf.org/files/msf_finance_summary_2014.pdf. Accessed 19 November 2015.

Médecins Sans Frontières, 2017, 'MSF Charter and Principles'. www.msf.org/en/msf-charter-and-principles. Accessed 30 September 2017.

Meernik, J., R. Aloisi, M. Sowell and A. Nichols, 2012, 'The Impact of Human Rights Organizations on Naming and Shaming Campaigns', *Journal of Conflict Resolution*, 56 (2): 233–256.

Mercer, J., 1995, 'Anarchy and Identity', *International Organization* 49 (2): 229–252.

Mertus, J. A., 2004, *Bait and Switch: Human Rights and U.S. Foreign Policy*. New York, Routledge.

Mertus, J. A., 2009, *The United Nations and Human Rights: A Guide for a New Era*, second edition, London and New York, Routledge.

Mertus, J., 2014, 'Human Rights and Global Governance', in T. G. Weiss and R. Wilkinson (eds.), *International Organization and Global Governance*, London and New York, Routledge: 466–477.

Miller, G. J., 2005, 'The Political Evolution of Principal–Agent Models', *Annual Review of Political Science* 8: 203–225.

Miller, L., 2001, 'The Idea and Reality of Collective Security', in P. Diehl (ed.), *The Politics of Global Governance*, second edition, Boulder, CO, Lynne Rienner: 171–201.

Mills, K., 2012, 'Bashir Is Dividing Us: Africa and the International Criminal Court', *Human Rights Quarterly* 34 (2): 404–447.

Milner, H. V., and D. Tingley, 2013, 'The Choice for Multilateralism: Foreign Aid and American Foreign Policy', *Review of International Organizations* 8 (3): 313–341.

Mingst, K., 1990, *Politics and the African Development Bank*, Lexington, KY, University of Kentucky Press.

Mitchell, R. B., 2002–2016. *International Environmental Agreements (IEA) Database Project* (Version 2014.3). http://iea.uoregon.edu/. Accessed 24 May 2015.

Mitrany, D., 1975, 'A Working Peace System' [1943], in D. Mitrany, *The Functional Theory of Politics*, London, London School of Economics and Political Science: 123–135.

Momani, B., 2004, 'American Politicization of the International Monetary Fund', *Review of International Political Economy* 11 (5): 880–904.

Momani, B., 2005, 'Limits on Streamlining Fund Conditionality: The International Monetary Fund's Organizational Culture', *Journal of International Relations and Development* 8 (2): 142–163.

Momani, B., 2010, 'Internal and External Norm Champions: The IMF and Multilateral Debt Relief', in S. Park and A. Vetterlein (eds.), *Owning Development: Creating Policy Norms in the IMF and the World Bank*. Cambridge, Cambridge University Press: 29–47.

Momani, B., 2014, 'Global Financial Governance', in T. G. Weiss and R. Wilkinson (eds.), *International Organizations and Global Governance*, London and New York, Routledge: 539–552.

Moravcsik, A., 1993, 'Preferences and Power in the European Community: A Liberal Intergovern-mentalist Approach', *Journal of Common Market Studies* 31 (4): 473–524.

Moravcsik, A., 1997, 'Taking Preferences Seriously: A Liberal Theory of International Politics', *International Organization* 51 (4): 513–553.

Moravcsik, A., 2004, 'Is There a "Democratic Deficit" in World Politics? A Framework for Analysis', *Government and Opposition* 39 (2): 336–363.

Morgenthau, H. J., 1940, 'Positivism, Functionalism and International Law', *American Journal of International Law* 34 (2): 260–284.

Morgenthau, H. J., 1966, *Politics among Nations: The Struggle for Power and Peace*, New York, Alfred A. Knopf.

Morris, J., 2015, *The Origins of UNICEF 1946–53*, Lanham, MD, Lexington Books.

Mortensen, J., 2012, 'Seeing Like the WTO: Numbers, Frames and Trade Law', *New Political Economy* 17 (1): 77–95.

Moschella, M., 2010, *Governing Risk: The IMF and Global Financial Crises*, Basingstoke, Palgrave Macmillan.

Moschella, M., and C. Weaver (eds.), 2013, *Handbook of Global Economic Governance*, London and New York, Routledge.

Mosley, P., J. Harrigan and J. Toye, 1991, *Aid and Power: The World Bank and Policy-Based Lending*, Vols. I and II, London, Routledge.

Mueller, J., 2011, 'The IMF, Neoliberalism and Hegemony', *Global Society* 25 (3): 377–402.

Mühlen-Schulte, A., 2012, 'Full Faith in Credit? The Power of Numbers in Rating Frontier Sovereigns and the Global Governance of Development by the UNDP', *Journal of International Relations and Development* 15 (4): 466–485.

Murphy, C., 1994, *International Organization and Industrial Change: Global Governance since 1850*, London, Polity Press and Oxford University Press.

Murphy, C., 2000, 'Global Governance: Poorly Done and Poorly Understood', *International Affairs* 76 (4): 789–803.

Murphy, C., 2004, *The United Nations Development Programme: A Better Way?*, Cambridge, Cambridge University Press.

Narlikar, A., 2005, *The World Trade Organization: A Very Short Introduction*, Oxford, Oxford University Press.

Narlikar, A., and P. Van Houten, 2010, 'Know the Enemy: Uncertainty and Deadlock in the WTO', in A. Narlikar (ed.), *Deadlocks in Multilateral Negotiations*, Cambridge, Cambridge University Press: 142–163.

NATO, 2017, 'A Short History of NATO'. www.nato.int/cps/en/natohq/declassified_139339.htm. Accessed 22 December 2017.

Nelson, S. C., 2014, 'Playing Favorites: How Shared Beliefs Shape the IMF's Lending Decisions', *International Organization* 68 (2): 297–328.

Nesadurai, H. E. S., 2008, 'The Association of Southeast Asian Nations', *New Political Economy*, 13 (2): 225–239.

Neuman, G., 2008, 'Import, Export and Regional Consent in the Inter-American Court of Human Rights', *The European Journal of International Law* 19 (1): 101–123.

Neumann, I., and O. J. Sending, 2010, *Governing the Global Polity: Practice, Mentality, Rationality*, Ann Arbor, MI, University of Michigan Press.

Neumayer, E., 2005, 'Do International Human Rights Treaties Improve Respect for Human Rights?', *Journal of Conflict Resolution* 49 (6): 925–953.

Newman, E., 2007, *A Crisis of Global Institutions? Multilateralism and Global Security*, London and New York, Routledge.

Nielson, D. L., and M. J. Tierney, 2003, 'Delegation to International Organizations: Agency Theory and World Bank Environmental Reform', *International Organization* 57 (2): 241–276.

Nielson, D. L., and M. J. Tierney, 2005, 'Theory, Data, and Hypothesis Testing: World Bank Environmental Reform Redux', *International Organization* 59 (3): 785–800.

Nielson, D. L., M. J. Tierney and C. E. Weaver, 2006, 'Bridging the Rationalist–Constructivist Divide: Re-engineering the Culture of the World Bank', *Journal of International Relations and Development* 9 (2): 107–139.

Niskanen, W. A., 1971, *Bureaucracy and Representative Government*, Chicago, IL and New York; Aldine-Atherton.

Norchi, C., 2004, 'Human Rights: A Global Common Interest', in J. Krasno (ed.), *The United Nations: Confronting the Challenges of a Global Society*, Boulder, CO, Lynne Rienner.

Oatley, T., and J. Yackee, 2004, 'American Interests in IMF Lending', *International Politics* 41 (3): 415–429.

Oberthür, S., and O. S. Stokke, 2011, *Managing Institutional Complexity: Regime Interplay and Global Environmental Change*, Cambridge, MA, MIT Press.

O'Brien, R., and M. Williams, 2007, *Global Political Economy: Evolution and Dynamics*, second edition, Basingstoke, Palgrave Macmillan.

Odell, J. S., 2009, 'Breaking Deadlocks in International Institutional Negotiations: The WTO, Seattle, and Doha', *International Studies Quarterly* 53 (2): 273–299.

Odinkalu, A. C., 2001, 'Analysis of Paralysis or Paralysis by Analysis? Implementing Economic, Social, and Cultural Rights under the African Charter on Human and Peoples' Rights', *Human Rights Quarterly* 23 (2): 327–369.

OECD, 2011, 'Measuring Aid: 50 Years of DAC Statistics – 1961–2011'. www.oecd.org/dac/stats/documentupload/MeasuringAid50yearsDACStats.pdf. Accessed 26 November 2015.

OECD, 2015, 'About the OECD: Our Mission'. www.oecd.org/about/. Accessed 17 November 2015.

OECD DAC, 2015, 'Official Development Assistance – Definition and Coverage'. www.oecd.org/dac/stats/officialdevelopmentassistancedefinitionandcoverage.htm#Definition. Accessed 17 November 2015.

Oestreich, J. E., 2007, *Power and Principle: Human Rights Programming in International Organizations*, Washington, D.C., Georgetown University Press.

Oestreich, J. E. (ed.), 2012, *International Organizations as Self-Directed Actors: A Framework for Analysis*, London and New York, Routledge.

OHCHR, 2017, 'The Core International Human Rights Instruments and Their Monitoring Bodies'. www.ohchr.org/EN/ProfessionalInterest/Pages/CoreInstruments.aspx. Accessed 26 October 2017.

Orchard, P., 2014, *A Right to Flee: Refugees, States, and the Construction of International Cooperation*, Cambridge, Cambridge University Press.

Organization of American States, 1993, 'Charter of the Organization of American States'. www.oas.org/en/sla/dil/docs/inter_american_treaties_A-41_charter_OAS.pdf. Accessed 19 January 2016.

Oye, K. A. (ed.), 1986, *Cooperation under Anarchy*, Princeton, NJ, Princeton University Press.

Ozgercin, K., 2012, 'Seeing Like the BIS on Capital Rules: Institutionalising Self-Regulation in Global Finance', *New Political Economy* 17 (1): 97–116.

Pagliari, S., 2012, 'Who Governs Finance? The Shifting Public–Private Divide in the Regulation of Derivatives, Rating Agencies and Hedge Funds', *European Law Journal* 18 (1): 44–61.

Paraskeva, C., 2007, 'Reforming the European Court of Human Rights: An Ongoing Challenge', *Nordic Journal of International Law* 76 (2): 185–216.

Park, S., 2010, *The World Bank Group and Environmentalists: Changing International Organization Identities*, London, Manchester University Press.

Park, S., 2013, 'Transnational Environmental Activism', in R. Falkner (ed.), *The Handbook of Global Climate and Environment Policy*, Oxford, Wiley-Blackwell: 268–285.

Park, S., and J. Strand, 2015, *Global Economic Governance and the Development Practices of the Multilateral Development Banks*, London and New York, Routledge.

Park, S., and A. Vetterlein, 2010, *Owning Development: Creating Global Policy Norms in the IMF and the World Bank*, Cambridge, Cambridge University Press.

Pastor, M., 1987, *The International Monetary Fund and Latin America: Economic Stabilization and Class Conflict*, Boulder, CO, Westview Press.

Pauly, L., 1995, 'Capital Mobility, State Autonomy and Political Legitimacy', *Journal of International Affairs* 48 (2): 369–388.

Pauly, L., 2002, 'Global Finance, Political Authority and the Problem of Legitimation', in R. Hall and T. J. Biersteker (eds.), *The Emergence of Private Authority in Global Governance*, Cambridge, Cambridge University Press: 76–90.

Payne, R., and N. H. Samhat, 2004, *Democratizing Global Politics*, Albany, NY, SUNY Press.

Peabody, J. W., 1995, 'An Organizational Analysis of the World Health Organization: Narrowing the Gap between Promise and Performance', *Social Science and Medicine* 40 (6): 731–742.

Peet, R., 2003, *Unholy Trinity: The IMF, World Bank and WTO*, London and New York, Zed Books.

Pegram, T., 2010, 'Diffusion across Political Systems: The Global Spread of National Human Rights Institutions', *Human Rights Quarterly* 32 (3): 729–760.

Pelc, K. J., 2011, 'Why Do Some Countries Get Better WTO Accession Terms Than Others?', *International Organization* 65 (4): 639–672.

Percy, S., 2007, *Mercenaries: The History of a Norm in International Relations*, Oxford, Oxford University Press.

Pettersson, T., and P. Wallensteen, 2015, 'Armed Conflicts 1946–2014', *Journal of Peace Research* 52 (4): 536–550.

Piiparinen, T., 2008, 'The Rise and Fall of Bureaucratic Rationalization: Exploring the Possibilities and Limits of the UN Secretariat in Conflict Prevention', *European Journal of International Relations* 14 (4): 697–724.

Pollack, M. A., 1997, 'Delegation, Agency and Agenda Setting in the European Community', *International Organization* 51 (1): 99–134.

Pollack, M. A., 2003, *The Engines of European Integration*, Cambridge, Cambridge University Press.

Powers, J., 1981, *Amnesty International: The Human Rights Story*, New York, McGraw-Hill.

Prantl, J., 2005, 'Informal Groups of States and the UN Security Council', *International Organization* 59 (3): 559–592.

Prantl, J., 2006, *The UN Security Council and Informal Groups of States: Complementing or Competing for Governance?*, Oxford, Oxford University Press.

Przeworski, A., and J. R. Vreeland, 2000, 'The Effect of IMF Programs on Economic Growth', *Journal of Development Economics* 62 (2): 385–421.

Putnam, R. D., 1988, 'Diplomacy and Domestic Politics: The Logic of Two-Level Games', *International Organization* 42 (3): 427–460.

Putnam, R. D., and N. Bayne, 1987, *Hanging Together: Cooperation and Conflict in the Seven-Power Summits*, London, Sage.

Rahmani-Ocora, L., 2006, 'Giving the Emperor Real Clothes: The UN Human Rights Council', *Global Governance* 12 (1): 15–20.

Ramcharan, B., 2008, 'Norms and Machinery', in T. G. Weiss and S. Daws (eds.), *The Oxford Handbook on the United Nations*, Oxford, Oxford University Press: 439–463.

Ravenhill, J., 2005a, *Global Political Economy*, Oxford, Oxford University Press.

Ravenhill, J., 2005b, 'The Study of Global Political Economy', in J. Ravenhill (ed.), *Global Political Economy*, Oxford, Oxford University Press: 4–15.

Ravenhill, J., 2009, 'East Asian Regionalism: Much Ado about Nothing?', *Review of International Studies* 35 (unnumbered February special issue): 215–235.

Razeq, R., 2014, *UNDP's Engagement with the Private Sector, 1994–2011*, Basingstoke, Palgrave Macmillan.

Reinalda, B., and Verbeek, B. (eds.), 1998, *Autonomous Policy Making by International Organizations*, London and New York, Routledge.

Review of International Political Economy, 2015, special issue 'The Political Economy of the Euro Area's Sovereign Debt Crisis', *Review of International Political Economy*, 22 (3).

Richardson, L., 2015, 'Economic, Social and Cultural Rights (and Beyond) in the Human Rights Council', *Human Rights Law Review* 15 (3): 409–440.

Rittberger, V., and B. Zangl, 2006, *International Organization: Polity, Politics and Policies*, Basingstoke, Palgrave Macmillan.

Roberts, A., 2004, 'The Use of Force', in D. M. Malone (ed.), *The UN Security Council: From the Cold War to the 21st Century*, Boulder, CO, Lynne Rienner.

Rochester, J., 1986, 'The Rise and Fall of International Organization as a Field of Study', *International Organization* 40 (4): 777–813.

Rockefeller Foundation, 2016, *The Rockefeller 2015 Annual Report*. www.rockefellerfoundation .org/about-us/governance-reports/annual-reports/annual-report-2015/. Accessed 29 September 2017.

Rockefeller Foundation, 2017, 'Our Work'. www.rockefellerfoundation.org/our-work/. Accessed 29 September 2017.

Rodriquez, L. J., 2003, 'Banking Stability and the Basel Capital Standards', *Cato Journal* 23 (1): 115–126.

Ron, J., H. Ramos and K. Rodgers, 2005, 'Transnational Information Politics: NGO Human Rights Reporting, 1986–2000', *International Studies Quarterly* 49 (3): 557–587.

Rosecrance, R., 2001, 'Has Realism Become Cost–Benefit Analysis? A Review Essay', *International Security* 26 (2): 132–154.

Rosenau, J. N., 1995, 'Governance in the Twenty-First Century', *Global Governance* 1 (1): 13–43.

Rosenau, J. N., and E. Czempiel, 1992, *Governance without Government: Order and Change in World Politics*, Cambridge, Cambridge University Press.

Rosenthal, G., 2007, 'Economic and Social Council', in T. G. Weiss and S. Daws (eds.), *The Oxford Handbook on the United Nations*, Oxford, Oxford University Press: 136–148.

Ross, S., 2011, *The World Food Programme in Global Politics*, Boulder, CO, Lynne Rienner.

Roth, K., 2004, 'Defending Economic, Social and Cultural Rights: Practical Issues Faced by an International Human Rights Organization', *Human Rights Quarterly* 26 (1): 63–73.

Ruggie, J. G., 1982, 'International Regimes, Transactions, and Change: Embedded Liberalism in the Postwar Economic Order', *International Organization* 36 (2): 379–415.

Ruggie, J. G., 1992, 'Multilateralism: The Anatomy of an Institution', *International Organization* 46 (3): 561–598.

Ruggie, J. G., 1993, 'The Anatomy of an Institution', in H. Milner and J. G. Ruggie (eds.), *Multilateralism Matters: The Theory and Praxis of an Institutional Form*, New York, Columbia University Press: 3–50.

Rughaven, C., 1990, *Recolonization: GATT, the Uruguay Round and the Third World*, London and New York, Zed Books.

Russett, B., and J. O'Neal, 2001, *Triangulating Peace: Democracy, Interdependence and International Organizations*, New York and London, W. W. Norton and Co.

Ryan, J., 2012, 'Infrastructures for Peace as a Path to Resilient Societies: An Institutional Perspective', *Journal of Peacebuilding and Development* 7 (3): 14–24.

Sadik, N. (ed.), 2002, *An Agenda for People: The UNFPA through Three Decades*, New York and London, UNFPA and New York University Press.

Salas, R., 1976, *People: An International Choice: The Multilateral Approach to Population*, Oxford, Pergamon Press,

Sandholtz, W., and A. Stone Sweet, 1998, *European Integration and Supranational Governance*, Oxford, Oxford University Press.

Santiso, C., 2002, 'Promoting Democratic Governance and Preventing the Recurrence of Conflict: The Role of the United Nations Development Programme in Post-conflict Peace-Building', *Journal of Latin American Studies* 34 (3): 555–586.

Save the Children International, 2017a, 'About Us'. www.savethechildren.net/about-us/. Accessed 30 September 2017.

Save the Children International, 2017b, *Trustees' Report, Strategic Report and Financial Statement for 2016*. www.savethechildren.net/sites/default/files/libraries/Save%20the%20Children%20 International%20Trustees%20Report.pdf. Accessed 30 September 2017.

Schimmelfennig, F., 2003, *The EU, NATO and the Integration of Europe*, Cambridge, Cambridge University Press.

Schirm, S. A., 2013, 'Global Politics Are Domestic Politics: A Societal Approach to Divergence in the G20', *Review of International Studies* 39 (3): 685–706.

Schrijver, N., 2010, *Development without Destruction: The UN and Global Resource Management*, Bloomington, IN, Indiana University Press.

Schweller, R. L., and D. Priess, 1997, 'A Tale of Two Realisms: Expanding the Institutions Debate', *Mershon International Studies Review* 41 (1): 1–32.

Scott, S. V., 2004, *International Law in World Politics: An Introduction*, Boulder, CO, Lynne Rienner.

Seabrooke, L., 2006, 'Global Monitor: The Bank for International Settlements', *New Political Economy*, 11 (1): 141–149.

Seabrooke, L., 2007, 'Legitimacy Gaps in the World Economy: Explaining the Sources of the IMF's Legitimacy Crisis', *International Politics* 44 (2–3): 250–268.

Sebedi, S., 2011, 'Protection of Human Rights through the Mechanism of UN Special Rapporteurs', *Human Rights Quarterly* 33 (1): 201–228.

Selin, H., 2010, *Global Governance of Hazardous Chemicals: Challenges of Multi-level Governance*, Cambridge, MA: MIT Press.

Sen, A., 1999, *Development As Freedom*, Oxford, Oxford University Press.

Shaffer, G. C., and R. Meléndez-Ortiz, 2013, *Dispute Settlement at the WTO: The Developing Country Experience*, Cambridge, Cambridge University Press.

Shanks, C., H. Jacobson and J. Kaplan, 1996, 'Inertia and Change in the Constellation of International Governmental Organizations, 1981–1992', *International Organization* 50 (4): 593–627.

Sharma, P., 2013, 'Bureaucratic Imperatives and Policy Outcomes: The Origins of World Bank Structural Adjustment Lending', *Review of International Political Economy* 20 (4): 667–686.

Sharma, S., 2014, *Global Financial Contagion: Building a Resilient World Economy after the Subprime Crisis*, Cambridge, Cambridge University Press.

Sharman, J. C., 2008, 'Power and Discourse in Policy Diffusion: Anti-Money Laundering in Developing States', *International Studies Quarterly* 52 (3): 635–656.

Sharman, J. C., 2012, 'Seeing Like the OECD on Tax', *New Political Economy* 17 (1): 17–33.

Shaw, D., 2011, *The World's Largest Humanitarian Agency: The Transformation of the UN World Food Programme and of Food Aid*, Basingstoke, Palgrave Macmillan.

Siddiqi, J., 1995, *World Health and World Politics: The World Health Organization and the UN System*, London, Hurst.

Simmons, B. A., and L. A. Martin, 2002, 'International Organizations and Institutions', in W. Carlsnaes, T. Risse and B. A. Simmons (eds.), *Handbook of International Relations*, London, Sage: 192–211.

Simpson, A., and S. Park, 2013, 'The Asian Development Bank as a Global Risk Regulator in Myanmar', *Third World Quarterly* 34 (10): 1858–1871.

Sinclair, T., 2005, *The New Masters of Capitalism: American Bond Rating Agencies and the Politics of Creditworthiness*, Ithaca, NY, Cornell University Press.

Singh, J., 1998, *Creating a New Consensus on Population*, second edition, Abingdon, Earthscan.

Skovgaard, J., 2017, 'The Devil Lies in the Definition: Competing Approaches to Fossil Fuel Subsidies at the IMF and the OECD', *International Environmental Agreement* 17 (3): 341–353.

Slaughter, A., 2004, *A New World Order*, Princeton, NJ, Princeton University Press.

Slaughter, S., 2013, 'The Prospects of Deliberative Global Governance in the G20: Legitimacy, Accountability, and Public Contestation', *Review of International Studies* 39 (1): 71–90.

Smith, F., 2009, 'WHO Governs? Limited Global Governance by the World Health Organization during the SARS Outbreak', *Social Alternatives* 28 (2): 9–12.

Smith, J., R. Pagnucco and G. A. Lopez, 1998, 'Globalizing Human Rights: The Work of Transnational Human Rights NGOs in the 1990s', *Human Rights Quarterly* 20 (2): 379–412.

Smith, R., 2013, '"To See Themselves As Others See Them": The Five Permanent Members of the Security Council and the Human Rights Council's Universal Periodic Review', *Human Rights Quarterly* 35 (1): 1–32.

Soederberg, S., 2010, 'The Politics of Representation and Financial Fetishism: The Case of the G20 Summits', *Third World Quarterly* 31 (4): 523–540.

Solingen, E., 2008, 'The Genesis, Design and Effects of Regional Institutions: Lessons from East Asia and the Middle East', *International Studies Quarterly* 52 (2): 261–294.

Stein, M., 1996, 'Conflict Prevention in Transition Economies: A Role for the European Bank for Reconstruction and Development?', in A. Chayes and A. H. Chayes (eds.), *Preventing Conflict in the Post-Communist World: Mobilizing International and Regional Organizations*, Washington, D.C., Brookings Institution: 339–378.

Steinberg, R., 2002, 'In the Shadow of Law or Power? Consensus-Based Bargaining and Outcomes in the GATT/WTO', *International Organization* 56 (2): 339–374.

Stiglitz, J., 2002, *Globalization and Its Discontents*, London and New York, W. W. Norton and Co.

Stiles, K., 1991, *Negotiating Debt: The IMF Lending Process*, Boulder, CO, Westview Press.

Stokke, O., 2009, *The UN and Development: From Aid to Cooperation*, Bloomington, IN, Indiana University Press.

Stone, R. W., 2002, *Lending Credibility: The International Monetary Fund and the Post-Communist Transition*, Princeton, NJ and Oxford, Princeton University Press.

Stone, R. W., 2004, 'Lending Credibility in Africa', *American Political Science Review* 98 (4): 577–591.

Stone, R. W., 2011, *Controlling Institutions: International Organizations and the Global Economy*, Cambridge, Cambridge University Press.

Strand, J., and M. Trevathan, 2016, 'Implications of Accommodating Rising Powers for the Regional Development Banks', in S. Park and J. R. Strand (eds.), *Global Economic Governance and the Development Practices of the Multilateral Development Banks*, London and New York, Routledge: 121–142.

Strand, J. R., and T. M. Zappile, 2015, 'Always Vote for Principle, Though You May Vote Alone: Explaining United States Political Support for Multilateral Development Loans', *World Development* 72 (C): 224–39.

Strange, S., 1996, *The Retreat of the State: The Diffusion of Power in the World Economy*, Cambridge, Cambridge University Press.

Streck, C., 2001, 'The Global Environment Facility – A Role Model for International Governance?', *Global Environmental Politics* 1 (2): 71–94.

Tallberg, J., 2000, 'The Anatomy of Autonomy: An Institutional Account of Variation in Supranational Influence', *Journal of Common Market Studies* 38 (5): 843–864.

Tardy, T., 2007, 'The UN and the Use of Force: A Marriage against Nature', *Security Dialogue* 38 (1): 49–70.

Taylor, I., and K. Smith, 2007, *United Nations Conference on Trade and Development*, Routledge, London and New York.

Terlingen, Y., 2007, 'The Human Rights Council: A New Era in UN Human Rights Work?', *Ethics and International Affairs* 21 (2): 167–178.

Terry, F., 2002, *Condemned to Repeat? The Paradox of Humanitarian Action*, Ithaca, NY, Cornell University Press.

Thacker, S. C., 1999, 'The High Politics of IMF Lending', *World Politics* 52 (1): 38–75.

The Nature Conservancy, 2015, *Our World: 2015 Annual Report*, Arlington, VA, The Nature Conservancy.

Thirkell-White, B., 2006, 'Private Authority and Legitimacy in the International System', *International Relations* 20 (3): 335–342.

Thomas, C., 2001, 'Globalisation and Development in the South', in J. Ravenhill (ed.), *Global Political Economy*, Oxford, Oxford University Press.

Thomas, C., and M. Weber, 2004, 'The Politics of Global Health Governance: Whatever Happened to "Health for All by the Year 2000"?', *Global Governance* 10 (2): 187–205.

Thompson, A. S., 2006, 'Coercion through IOs: The Security Council and the Logic of Information Transmission', *International Organization* 60 (1): 1–34.

Thompson, A. S., 2008, 'Beyond Expression: Amnesty International's Decision to Oppose Capital Punishment, 1973', *Journal of Human Rights*, 7 (4): 327–340.

Tomuschat, C., 2014, *Human Rights: Between Idealism and Realism*, third edition, Oxford, Oxford University Press.

Toye, J., and R. Toye, 2004, *The UN and the Global Political Economy: Trade, Finance and Development*, Bloomington, IN and Indianapolis, IN, Indiana University Press.

True, J., and M. Mintrom, 2001, 'Transnational Networks and Policy Diffusion: The Case of Gender Mainstreaming', *International Studies Quarterly* 45 (1): 27–57.

Tsingou, E., 2010, 'Global Financial Governance and the Developing Anti-Money Laundering Regime: What Lessons for International Political Economy?', *International Politics* 47 (6): 617–637.

UNAIDS, 2017a, 'Programme Coordinating Board Membership 2017'. www.unaids.org/en/resources/documents/2016/PCB_composition_current-year. Accessed 27 September 2017.

UNAIDS, 2017b, *UNAIDS Budget: 2018–2019*. www.unaids.org/sites/default/files/media_asset/20170609_PCB40_2018-2019-Budget_17.9_EN.pdf. Accessed 27 September 2017.

Underhill, G. R. D., 1997, *The New World Order in International Finance*, Basingstoke, Macmillan.

Underhill, G. R. D., and X. Zhang, 2008, 'Setting the Rules: Private Power, Political Underpinnings, and Legitimacy in Global Monetary and Financial Governance', *International Affairs* 84 (3): 535–554.

UNICEF, 2017, 'UNICEF Executive Board'. www.unicef.org/about/execboard/. Accessed 25 September 2017.

Union of International Associations, 2015, *Yearbook of International Organizations 2015*, Brussels, UAI. [Data collected for 2014.]

United Nations, 1948a, *Charter of the United Nations*. www.un.org/en/charter-united-nations/index.html. Accessed 19 December 2012.

United Nations, 1948b, 'Preamble', *Universal Declaration of Human Rights*. www.un.org/en/universal-declaration-human-rights/. Accessed 19 November 2015.

United Nations, 1948c, 'Convention on the Prevention and Punishment of the Crime of Genocide, Approved and Proposed for Signature and Ratification or Accession by General Assembly Resolution 260 A (III) of 9 December 1948'. www.ohchr.org/EN/ProfessionalInterest/Pages/CrimeOfGenocide.aspx. Accessed 8 November 2017.

United Nations, 1948d, 'Commission for Conventional Armaments'. http://undocs.org/S/C.3/32/Rev.1. Accessed 6 March 2018.

United Nations, 1998, *Rome Statute of the International Criminal Court*. www.icc-cpi.int/nr/rdonlyres/ea9aeff7-5752-4f84-be94-0a655eb30e16/0/rome_statute_english.pdf. Accessed 8 November 2017.

United Nations, 2010, 'Amendments to the Rome Statute of the International Criminal Court, Kampala 11 June 2010'. https://asp.icc-cpi.int/iccdocs/asp_docs/RC2010/AMENDMENTS/CN.651.2010-ENG-CoA.pdf. Accessed 8 November 2017.

United Nations, 2015a, 'Financing for Development. Third International Conference, 13–16 July 2015, Addis Ababa, Ethiopia: Time for Global Action'. www.un.org/esa/ffd/ffd3/conference/history.html. Accessed 18 November 2015.

United Nations, 2015b, 'Financing for Development'. www.un.org/esa/ffd/ffd-follow-up/ecosoc.html. Accessed 18 November 2015.

United Nations, 2015c, *The Millennium Development Goals Report 2015*. www.un.org/millenniumgoals/2015_MDG_Report/pdf/MDG%202015%20rev%20(July%201).pdf. Accessed 23 November 2015.

United Nations, 2017, 'Funds and Programmes'. www.unsceb.org/members/funds-and-programmes. Accessed 21 September 2017.

United Nations, 2018, 'Syria Conflict: 2017 Deadliest Year for Children, UN Aid Official Reports', *UN News*, 13 March. https://news.un.org/en/story/2018/03/1004802. Accessed 18 March 2018.

United Nations Development Programme, 1990, *Human Development Report*, Oxford: Oxford University Press.

United Nations Development Programme, 2013, *Working with Civil Society in Foreign Aid: Possibilities for South–South Cooperation*. www.undp.org/content/dam/undp/documents/partners/civil_society/publications/2013_UNDP-CH-Working-With-Civil-Society-in-Foreign-Aid_EN.pdf. Accessed 1 December 2015.

United Nations Development Programme, 2015a, 'Human Development Index (HDI)'. http://hdr.undp.org/en/content/human-development-index-hdi. Accessed 23 November 2015.

United Nations Development Programme, 2015b, 'Human Development Index Table 2: Human Development Index Trends, 1980–2013'. http://hdr.undp.org/en/content/table-2-human-development-index-trends-1980-2013. Accessed 23 November 2015.

United Nations Development Programme, 2015c, 'Information Note about the Executive Board of UNDP, UNFPA and UNOPS'. www.undp.org/content/undp/en/home/operations/executive_board/information_noteontheexecutiveboard/. Accessed 1 October 2015.

United Nations Development Programme, 2017, 'About Us'. www.undp.org/content/undp/en/home/about-us.html. Accessed 8 September 2017.

United Nations Environment Programme, 1997, 'Nairobi Declaration on the Role and Mandate of the United Nations Environment Programme'. www.un-documents.net/nair-dec.htm. Accessed 12 March 2018.

United Nations Environment Programme, 2012, *Global Environmental Outlook 5*, Nairobi, UNEP.

United Nations Environment Programme, 2017, 'UNEP 2016 Annual Report'. http://web.unep.org/annualreport/2016/index.php. Accessed 15 June 2017.

United Nations General Assembly, 1992, 'Report of the United Nations Conference on Environment and Development (Rio de Janeiro 3–14 June 1992), Annex 1 Rio Declaration on Environment and Development'. www.un.org/documents/ga/conf151/aconf15126-1annex1.htm. Accessed 21 June 2017.

United Nations General Assembly, 1993a, 'Vienna Declaration and Programme of Action'. www.ohchr.org/EN/ProfessionalInterest/Pages/Vienna.aspx. Accessed 30 September 2017.

United Nations General Assembly, 1993b, 'United Nations General Assembly Resolution 48/141: High Commissioner for the Promotion and Protection of All Human Rights, UNGA A/RES/48/141, 85th Plenary Meeting, 20 December 1993'. www.un.org/documents/ga/res/48/a48r141.htm. Accessed 30 October 2017.

United Nations General Assembly, 2006, 'Resolution Adopted by the General Assembly on 15 March 2006'. www.un.org/en/ga/search/view_doc.asp?symbol=A/RES/60/251. Accessed 12 March 2018.

United Nations High Commissioner for Refugees, 2017, 'History of UNHCR'. www.unhcr.org/en-au/history-of-unhcr.html. Accessed 16 November 2017.

United Nations Office of the High Commissioner for Human Rights, 2017a, 'Who We Are'. www.ohchr.org/EN/AboutUs/Pages/WhoWeAre.aspx. Accessed 1 November 2017.

United Nations Office of the High Commissioner for Human Rights, 2017b, 'OHCHR's Funding and Budget'. www.ohchr.org/EN/AboutUs/Pages/FundingBudget.aspx. Accessed 2 November 2017.

United Nations Population Fund, 2017, 'Funds and Funding'. www.unfpa.org/funds-and-funding. Accessed 28 September 2017.

United Nations Population Information Network (UNPOPIN), UN Population Division, Department of Economic and Social Affairs, with support from the UN Population Fund (UNFPA), 1994, 'Background Document on the Population Programme of the UN'. www.un.org/popin/icpd/conference/bkg/unpop.html. Accessed 28 September 2017.

United Nations Security Council, 2017, 'The Veto'. www.securitycouncilreport.org/un-security-council-working-methods/the-veto.php. Accessed 15 December 2017.

United States Centers for Disease Control and Prevention, 2016, '2014 Ebola Outbreak in West Africa – Case Counts'. www.cdc.gov/vhf/ebola/outbreaks/2014-west-africa/case-counts.html. Accessed 12 September 2017.

Vaky, V. P., and H. Muñoz, 1993, *The Future of the Organization of American States*, New York, Twentieth Century Fund Press.

Varin, C., 2015, *Mercenaries, Hybrid Armies and National Security: Private Soldiers and the State in the 21st Century*, London and New York, Routledge.

Vaubel, R., 1986, 'A Public Choice Approach to International Organizations', *Public Choice* 51 (1): 39–57.

Vaubel, R., A. Dreher and U. Soylu, 2007, 'Staff Growth in International Organizations: A Principal–Agent Problem? An Empirical Analysis', *Public Choice* 133 (3–4): 275–295.

Vaughan, J. P., S. Mogedal, S. Kruse, K. Lee, G. Walt and K. de Wilde, 1996, 'Financing the World Health Organisation: Global Importance of Extrabudgetary Funds', *Health Policy* 35 (3): 229–245.

Vennesson, P., 2014, 'War under Transnational Surveillance: Framing Ambiguity and the Politics of Shame', *Review of International Studies* 40 (1): 25–51.

Verbeek, B., 1998, 'International Organizations: The Ugly Duckling of International Relations Theory?', in B. Reinalda and B. Verbeek (eds.), *Autonomous Policy Making in International Organizations*, London, Routledge: 11–26.

Vestergaard, J., and R. Wade, 2012, 'The Governance Response to the Great Recession: The "Success" of the G20', *Journal of Economic Issues* 46 (2): 481–490.

Vetterlein, A., 2007, 'Change in International Organisations: Innovation or Adaptation? A Comparison of the World Bank and the International Monetary Fund', in D. Stone and C. Wright (eds.), *The World Bank and Governance: A Decade of Reform and Reaction*, New York, Routledge: 144–63.

Vetterlein, A., 2010, 'Lacking Ownership: The IMF and its Engagement with Social Development As a Policy Norm', in S. Park and A. Vetterlein (eds.), *Owning Development: Creating Policy Norms for the IMF and World Bank*, Cambridge, Cambridge University Press: 93–112.

Viljoen, F., 2012, *International Human Rights Law in Africa*, second edition, Oxford, Oxford University Press.

Vines, D., and C. Gilbert (eds.), 2004, *The IMF and its Critics: Reform of Global Financial Architecture*, Cambridge, Cambridge University Press.

Voeten, E., 2007, 'The Politics of International Judicial Appointments: Evidence from the European Court of Human Rights', *International Organization* 61 (4): 669–701.

Voeten, E., 2014, 'A World without the West: Not So Fast', Monkey Cage, *The Washington Post*, 14 November. www.washingtonpost.com/news/monkey-cage/wp/2014/11/14/a-world-with out-the-west-not-so-fast/?utm_term=.3daa96d48ca6. Accessed 17 November 2015.

Vogel, D., 2008, 'Private Global Business Regulation', *Annual Review of Political Science* 11: 261–282.

von Moltke, K., 2001, 'The Organization of the Impossible', *Global Environmental Politics* 1 (1): 23–28.

Vreeland, J., 2002, 'The Effect of IMF Programs on Labor', *World Development* 30 (1): 121–139.

Vreeland, J., 2007, *The International Monetary Fund: Politics of Conditional Lending*, Abingdon, Routledge.

Vreeland, J., and A. Dreher, 2014, *The Political Economy of the United Nations Security Council*, Cambridge, Cambridge University Press.

Wade, R., 1996, 'Japan, the World Bank, and the Art of Paradigm Maintenance: The East Asian Miracle in Political Perspective', *New Left Review* (217): 1–36.

Wade, R., 2003, 'What Strategies Are Viable for Developing Countries Today? The World Trade Organization and the Shrinking of "Development Space"', *Review of International Political Economy* 10 (4): 621–644.

Wade, R., and F. Veneroso, 1998, 'The Asian Crisis: The High Debt Model Versus the Wall Street–Treasury–IMF Complex', *New Left Review* (228): 3–20.

Wade, R. H., and J. Vestergaard, 2013, 'Protecting Power: How Western States Retain the Dominant Voice in the World Bank's Governance', *World Development*, 46: 153–164.

Wallensteen, P., and P. Johansson, 2004, 'Security Council Decisions in Perspective', in D. M. Malone (ed.), *The UN Security Council: From the Cold War to the 21st Century*, Boulder, CO, Lynne Rienner: 17–36.

Waltz, K., 1979, *Theory of International Politics*, Reading, MA, Addison-Wesley.

Waltz, K., 2000, 'Structural Realism after the Cold War', *International Security* 25 (1): 5–41.

Wang, M., 2008, *Global Health Partnerships: The Pharmaceutical Industry and BRICA*, Basingstoke, Palgrave Macmillan.

Wapenhans, W., on behalf of the Portfolio Management Task Force, 1992, *Effective Implementation: Key to Development Impact*, Washington, D.C., World Bank.

Wapner, P., 1995, 'Politics beyond the State: Environmental Activism and World Civic Politics', *World Politics* 47 (3): 311–340.

Watson, A., 2004, 'Human Rights Watch', *New Political Economy* 9 (3): 441–453.

Watson, M., 2017, 'Global Trade and Global Finance', in J. Baylis, S. Smith and P. Owens, *The Globalisation of World Politics*, seventh edition, Oxford, Oxford University Press: 450–462.

Weaver, C., 2008, *The Hypocrisy Trap: The World Bank and the Poverty of Reform*, Princeton, NJ, Princeton University Press.

Weaver, C., and R. J. Leiteritz, 2005, '"Our Poverty Is a World Full of Dreams": Reforming the World Bank', *Global Governance* 11 (3): 369–388.

Weber, H., 2004, 'The "New Economy" and Social Risk: Banking on the Poor?', *Review of International Political Economy* 11(2): 356–386.

Weindling, P., 1995, *International Health Organisations and Movements, 1918–1939*, Cambridge, Cambridge University Press.

Weisburd, A., 2016, *The Failings of the International Court of Justice*, Oxford, Oxford University Press.

Weiss, E., and H. K. Jacobson, 2000, *Engaging Countries: Strengthening Compliance with International Environmental Accords*, Cambridge, MA, MIT Press.

Weiss, L., 1998, *The Myth of the Powerless State: Governing the Economy in a Global Era*, Cambridge, Polity Press.

Weiss, T., 2012, 'ECOSOC and the MDGs: What Can Be Done?', in R. Wilkinson and D. Hulme, *The Millennium Development Goals and Beyond*, London and New York, Routledge: 117–128.

Weiss, T., 2013, *What's Wrong with the United Nations and How to Fix It*, Cambridge, Polity Press.

Weiss, T., and L. Gordenker (eds.), 1996, *NGOs, the UN and Global Governance*, Boulder, CO, Lynne Rienner.

Weiss, T., D. Forsythe, R. Coate and K. Pease, 2010, *The United Nations and Changing World Politics*, sixth edition, Boulder, CO, Westview Press.

Welch, C., 2001, *NGOs and Human Rights: Promise and Performance*, Philadelphia, PA, University of Pennsylvania Press.

Wendt, A., 1999, *Social Theory of International Politics*, Cambridge, Cambridge University Press.

Weschler, J., 2004, 'Human Rights', in D. M. Malone (ed.), *The UN Security Council: From the Cold War to the 21st Century*, Boulder, CO, Lynne Rienner: 55–69.

Wheeler, N., 2002, *Saving Strangers: Humanitarian Intervention in International Society*, Oxford, Oxford University Press.

Widerberg, O., and P. Pattberg, 2017, 'Accountability Challenges in the Transnational Regime Complex for Climate Change', *Review of Policy Research* 34 (1): 68–87.

Widerberg, O. E., and F. van Laerhoven, 2014, 'Measuring the Autonomous Influence of an International Bureaucracy: The Division for Sustainable Development', *International Environmental Agreement* 14 (4): 303–327.

Wiener, A., and T. Dietz, 2004, *EU Integration Theory*, Oxford, Oxford University Press.

Wilkinson, R. (ed.), 2005, *The Global Governance Reader*, London and New York, Routledge.

Wilkinson, R., 2014, *What's Wrong with the WTO and How to Fix It*, Cambridge, Polity Press.

Wilkinson, R., and J. Scott, 2013, *Trade, Poverty, Development: Getting Beyond the WTO's Doha Deadlock*, London and New York, Routledge.

Willetts, P., 1996, *The Conscience of the World: The Influence of Non-Governmental Organisations in the UN System*, Washington, D.C., The Brookings Institution.

Willetts, P., 2011, 'What Is a Non-Governmental Organization? Section 1: Institutional and Infrastructure Resource Issues'. www.staff.city.ac.uk/p.willetts/CS-NTWKS/NGO-ART.HTM#Part10. Accessed 1 December 2011.

Williams, M., 2005, 'Globalization and Civil Society', in J. Ravenhill (ed.), *Global Political Economy*, Oxford, Oxford University Press: 344–370.

Williamson, J., 1990, 'What Washington Means by Policy Reform', in J. Williamson (ed.), *Latin American Adjustment: How Much Has Happened*, Washington, D.C., Institute for International Economics.

Winham, G., 2005, 'The Evolution of the Global Trade Regime', in J. Ravenhill (ed.), *Global Political Economy*, Oxford, Oxford University Press: 87–116.

Wong, W., 2012, *Internal Affairs: How the Structure of NGOs Transforms Human Rights*, Ithaca, NY, Cornell University Press.

Woods, N., 2000, 'The Challenge of Good Governance for the IMF and the World Bank Themselves', *World Development* 28 (5): 823–841.

Woods, N., 2006a, *The Globalizers: The IMF, the World Bank and their Borrowers*, Ithaca, NY, Cornell University Press.

Woods, N., 2006b, 'Understanding Pathways through Financial Crises and the Impact of the IMF: An Introduction', *Global Governance* 12 (4): 373–393.

Woods, N., and D., Lombardi, 2006, 'Uneven Patterns of Governance: How Developing Countries Are Represented in the IMF', *Review of International Political Economy* 13 (3): 480–515.

Woodward, R., 2004, 'The Organisation for Economic Cooperation and Development', *New Political Economy* 9 (1): 113–127.

World Bank, 1993, *The East Asian Miracle: Economic Growth and Public Policy*, Oxford, Oxford University Press.

World Bank, 2010, 'Global Preferential Trade Agreements Database'. http://wits.worldbank.org/gptad/database_landing.aspx. Accessed 6 April 2017.

World Bank, 2012a, Homepage of the World Bank. www.worldbank.org/. Accessed 19 December 2012.

World Bank, 2012b, *IBRD Articles of Agreement*. http://go.worldbank.org/WAUZA5KF90. Accessed 7 March 2018.

World Bank, 2015, 'GDP Ranking'. http://data.worldbank.org/data-catalog/GDP-ranking-table. Accessed 22 January 2016.

World Commission on Environment and Development, 1987, *Our Common Future*, Oxford, Oxford University Press.

World Health Organization, 1958, 'The First Ten Years of the World Health Organization'. http://apps.who.int/iris/handle/10665/37089. Accessed 13 September 2017.

World Health Organization, 2006, 'Constitution of the World Health Organization, Basic Documents, Forty-Fifth Edition, Supplement'. www.who.int/governance/eb/who_constitution_en.pdf. Accessed 13 September 2017.

World Health Organization, 2012, 'The Ottawa Charter for Health Promotion'. www.who.int/healthpromotion/conferences/previous/ottawa/en/. Accessed 19 December 2012.

World Health Organization, 2015, 'One Year into the Ebola Epidemic: A Deadly, Tenacious and Unforgiving Virus'. www.who.int/csr/disease/ebola/one-year-report/introduction/en/. Accessed 12 September 2017.

World Health Organization, 2016, 'Zika Situation Report: Neurological Syndrome and Congenitial Anomalies'. http://apps.who.int/iris/bitstream/10665/204348/1/zikasitrep_5Feb2016_eng.pdf. Accessed 12 September 2017.

World Health Organization, 2017a, 'Zika Virus and Complications: Questions and Answers'. www.who.int/features/qa/zika/en/. Accessed 13 September 2017.

World Health Organization, 2017b, 'Seventieth World Health Assembly Update, 24 May'. www.who.int/mediacentre/news/releases/2017/programme-budget/en/. Accessed 19 September 2017.

World Trade Organization, 1994a, 'General Agreement on Tariffs and Trade', www.wto.org/english/res_e/booksp_e/analytic_index_e/gatt1994_01_e.htm. Accessed 20 March 2018.

World Trade Organization, 1994b, 'Agreement Establishing the World Trade Organization'. www.wto.org/english/docs_e/legal_e/final_e.htm. Accessed 24 March 2017.

World Trade Organization, 2017, 'What Is the WTO?'. www.wto.org/english/thewto_e/thewto_e.htm. Accessed 24 March 2017.

World Trade Organization, 2018, 'Welcome to the Regional Trade Agreements Information System (RTA-IS)'. http://rtais.wto.org/UI/PublicMaintainRTAHome.aspx. Accessed 18 January 2018.

Xu, Y.-C., and P. Weller, 2004, *The Governance of World Trade*, Cheltenham, Edward Elgar.

Young, K., 2012, 'Transnational Regulatory Capture? An Empirical Examination of the Transnational Lobbying of the Basel Committee on Banking Supervision', *Review of International Political Economy* 19 (4): 663–688.

Young, O. (ed.), 1997, *Global Governance: Drawing Insights from the Environmental Experience*, Cambridge, MA, MIT Press.

Young, O. R., L. A. King and H. Schroeder, 2008, *Institutions and Environmental Change*, Cambridge, MA, MIT Press.

Young, Z., 2002, *A New Green Order? The World Bank and the Politics of the Global Environment Facility*, London, Pluto Press.

Zacher, M., and T. Keefe, 2008, *The Politics of Global Health Governance: United by Contagion*, Basingstoke, Palgrave Macmillan.

Zappile, T., 2016, 'Sub-Regional Development Banks: Development as Usual?', in S. Park and J. Strand (eds.), *Global Economic Governance and the Development Practices of the Multilateral Development Banks*, Abingdon, Routledge: 187–212.

Index